"My Clan Against the World"

US and Coalition Forces in Somalia
1992-1994

Robert F. Baumann and Lawrence A. Yates
with Versalle F. Washington

Published by Books Express Publishing
Copyright © Books Express, 2012
ISBN 978-1-78039-675-0

Books Express publications are available from all good retail and online booksellers. For
publishing proposals and direct ordering please contact us at: info@books-express.com

Foreword

"My Clan Against the World": US and Coalition Operations in Somalia, 1992-94 represents another in a series of military case studies published by the Combat Studies Institute (CSI) at Fort Leavenworth, Kansas. The impetus for this project came from the commanding general, US Army Training and Doctrine Command, Fort Monroe, Virginia, who directed CSI to examine the American military's experience with urban operations in Somalia, particularly in the capital city of Mogadishu. That original focus can be found in the following pages, but the authors address other, broader issues as well, to include planning for a multinational intervention; workable and unworkable command and control arrangements; the advantages and problems inherent in coalition operations; the need for cultural awareness in a clan-based society whose status as a nation-state is problematic; the continuous adjustments required by a dynamic, often unpredictable situation; the political dimension of military activities at the operational and tactical levels; and the ability to match military power and capabilities to the mission at hand.

This case study also cautions against the misuse and overuse of "lessons" learned from any given military undertaking. As with the lessons of Vietnam, one of which dictated that conventional units should not engage in unconventional warfare, the US experience in Somalia left many military analysts and policymakers convinced that the United States should eschew any undertaking that smacked of nation building. Yet, as this book is published, just ten years after the US exit from Somalia, American forces are engaged in several locations against an unconventional foe and are involved in nation building in both Afghanistan and Iraq. Perhaps the first lesson to be learned about extracting lessons is, in the words of a once-popular motion picture, "Never Say Never Again."

Another principal aim of the authors was to provide an analytical narrative of each phase of the US military involvement in Somalia. For many Americans, the mention of that African country conjures up one memory, that of the fierce firefight between US troops and Somali militia on 3-4 October 1993. As this overview seeks to remind the reader, the United States had a military presence in Somalia from December 1992 to the end of March 1994. During that period, much was accomplished of a positive nature. Starving and mistreated Somalis were provided food and a modicum of security, while some progress was made toward peace in the country. That the broader goals of political reconciliation and stability ultimately were not achieved was in part a consequence of the intractability of the contending factions and the complexities of a country that defies Western definitions of "modern." Yet, US involvement in countries that have much in common with Somalia is a current reality and a future likelihood. For the professional officer, then, as well as the American public at large, it would be instructive to revisit the US experience in Somalia.

LAWYN C. EDWARDS
COL, AV
Director, Combat Studies

Preface

From the outset of this project, our goals have been modest. In keeping with a tasking from the commanding general of the US Army's Training and Doctrine Command, we set out to examine military operations in an urban environment, specifically in this case, Mogadishu. A broader goal was to write something that was peculiarly lacking several years after the United States ended its military presence in Somalia: a one-volume, monograph-sized overview of the American involvement in that country from 1992 to 1994.

Any work of history constitutes a journey of sorts for its author or authors. The effort necessarily begins with some vision of the scope, depth, and substance of the study upon completion. Guided by this intent, the authors embark on a quest of discovery familiar to researchers in any field. Their goal is to gather and amass information in the hope that upon careful reflection it will yield understanding. Along the way, as one becomes fully versed on the subject, the work begins to assume a life of its own and the product is at once more fascinating and more frustrating that at first imagined. In other words, as the authors master their topic and uncover unforeseen nuances, they simultaneously gain a painful appreciation of what they still do not know. The conscientious historian remains vexed by a disturbing awareness that the work is never complete and that many conclusions contained therein are provisional and in some cases incorrect.

The challenge of writing the history of relatively recent events is a uniquely interesting one. The lack of perspective afforded by distance in time poses many risks, the foremost of which is that the consequences of events painstakingly examined have yet to manifest themselves and may well do so in entirely unexpected ways. This is the "butterfly effect" that gives rise to subsequent histories that can sharply alter the perceptions of the past.

The great virtue of recent history, however, is proximity to the subject matter. This study, to the extent that it has merit, benefited enormously from extensive opportunities for the authors to discuss events with those who participated in them. Perhaps the most obvious revelation that arises from this process is the awareness that no two people truly share the same experience. Moreover, memories often diverge over time. As a class of professionals, historians are trained to rely above all on documents, immutable writings that seem to form a solid database for investigation.

Yet, those who engage extensively in the conduct of so-called oral histories often find out that the record on paper is incomplete, misleading, or occasionally false. Only the participants can put flesh on those bones. Thus, the task at hand for the authors has been to integrate these two categories of sources to achieve as rounded an account as possible.

The authors owe an enormous debt of gratitude to those individuals who gave generously of their time or from their personal records. Their contributions are all the more valued because they were made voluntarily. These individuals are too numerous to list here, but they range in rank from general officer to specialist, some still on active duty and some retired, and their names are liberally sprinkled throughout the endnotes for each chapter. To be sure, there were also individuals who elected not to speak with the authors and we respect their decisions.

Our intent in this military history has been to capture the story of the mission in Somalia in such a way as to bring to light not only successes, but failures, disagreements, and more broadly the complex dynamic that constitutes real life in current military operations. In addition, it is our hope to impart insights and occasional lessons, especially for those whose professions, whether civilian or military, would involve them in missions such as the one in Somalia. Although we attempted to deal broadly with joint and multinational issues, time and resource constraints dictated that we focus first and foremost on the experience of the US Army. With that in mind, we fully expect that other historians will take those roads we were unable to follow.

In the main, this study flows chronologically, beginning with review of historical context. The following chapters deal in turn with the successive stages of operations in Somalia, each including a mixture of narrative, analysis, and carefully considered observations. The final chapter offers a brief summation of our findings.

Robert F. Baumann, CSI
Lawrence Yates, CSI
Versalle Washington, University of Dayton

Table of Contents

Foreword i

Preface iii

Table of Contents v

Illustrations vii

Introduction.   The Meaning of Somalia 1

Chapter 1.   Setting the Stage 9

Chapter 2.   Operation RESTORE HOPE: Phases I and II,
                December 1992 23

Chapter 3.   Operation RESTORE HOPE: Phases III and IV,
                December 1992 - May 1993 61

Chapter 4.   UNOSOM II 99

Chapter 5.   UNOSOM II: PART II - The Battle of Mogadishu 139

Chapter 6.   Buildup and Withdrawal, October 1993 –
                March 1994 165

Conclusion 201

Index 213

About the authors 219

Illustrations

Maps

Map 1. Map of Africa..viii

Map 2. Map of Somalia ix

Map 3. Somali Clan Map... 11

Map 4. HRS Map 27

Map 5. Mogadishu – UNITAF.. 28

Map 6. Mogadishu – UNOSOM II 101

Map 7 UNOSOM II – Force Structure, 4 May 1993 105

Map 8. Contact Under Fire 128

Map 9. Mogadishu – Black Hawk Down... 141

Map 10. Battle at Mogadishu, 3-4 October 1993................................. 149

Map 11. Mogadishu Map... 160-161

Map 12. Mogadishu – JTF Somalia... 175

Figures

Figure 1. Somali Clan Structure.. 10

Figure 2. US Forces in UNITAF... 31

Figure 3. UNITAF Somalia – Command and Control......................... 31

Figure 4. UNOSOM II Command Structure.. 102

Figure 5. USFORSOM – Command and Control................................ 106

Figure 6. QRF Attack on ABDI House – 12 July 1993 117

Figure 7. USFORSOM/JTF Somalia – Command and Control 180

Figure 8. JTF Somalia Forces 182

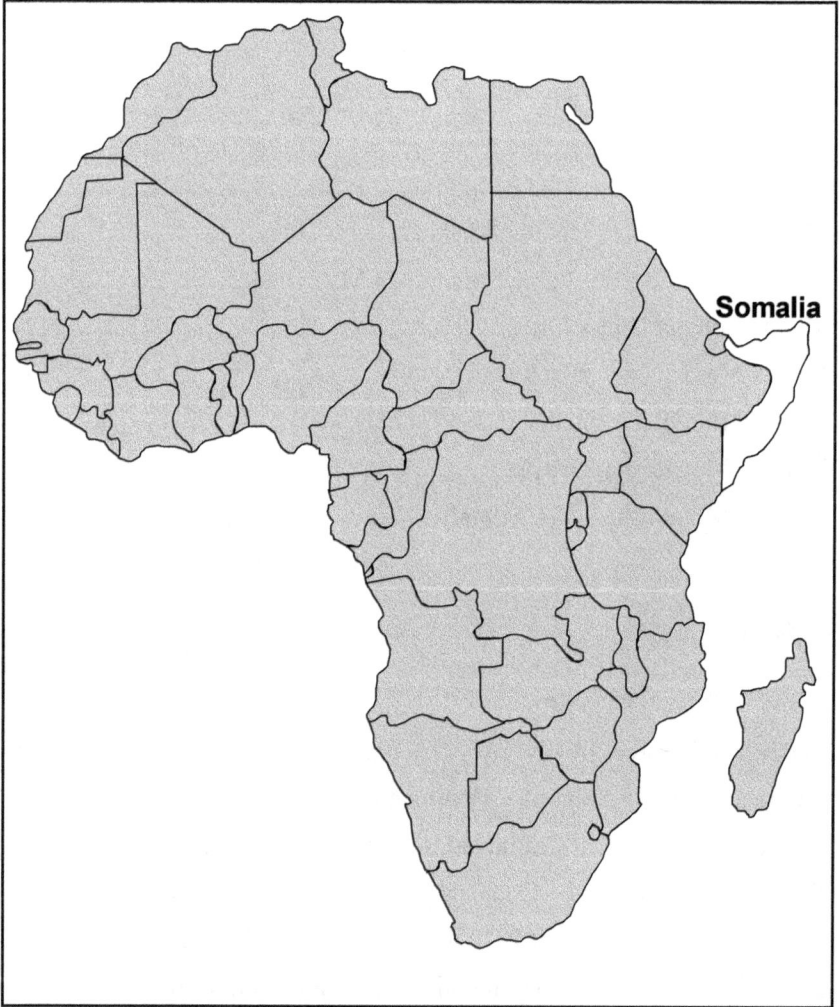

Map 1. Map of Africa

Map 2. Map of Somalia

Introduction

The Meaning of Somalia

Robert F. Baumann

American participation in the international humanitarian mission to Somalia is best remembered today as a well-intentioned venture that somehow went terribly wrong. To most Americans, this endeavor reflected both the nobility and naivety of US foreign policy impulses and was a poignant reminder of how little we understand distant cultures and the motives that animate people whose societal values are removed from our own. Prompted first of all by compelling video images of emaciated mothers and children in a country ravaged by unbridled civil war, the mission to Somalia took US military personnel on a completely unforeseen and bewildering ascent along the spectrum of violence.

What started as an apparently straightforward quest to assist humanitarian relief organizations in disseminating emergency food supplies devolved almost imperceptibly into a politico-military operation to marginalize rogue warlords and climaxed, finally, in an escalating series of tactical military operations. Remarkably, over a progression of months, operations in Somalia lost public visibility, thereby maximizing the shock effect of the desperate gun battle that marked 3-4 October 1993. Jarred suddenly out of a state of complacency by news images of jubilant Somalis dragging the corpses of American soldiers through the streets of Mogadishu, US public opinion grew critical and questioning. In turn, congressional critics of the mission demanded explanations and a focal point for blame.

Confronting a crisis it had not anticipated, President Bill Clinton's administration responded in a way that epitomized its conflicted view of using military force. On one hand, it moved quickly to strengthen the US military presence in the region as if to warn recalcitrant Somali warlord Mohamed Farah Aideed that it was prepared to crush any further opposition. On the other hand, it proclaimed within days that US military personnel would be pulling out of Somalia after a decent interval of a few months.

The latter action proved to be the true harbinger of events to follow. Within weeks, Secretary of Defense Les Aspin submitted his resignation to the president. Though no explicit official link was made to events in Somalia, most observers inferred just such a connection.[1] The lesson was clear: the administration regarded the military mission as a failure. A perception took hold that the public would not accept military casualties, especially in the course of what were described as peacekeeping missions with dubious relevance to national interests. Some observers, such as retired Chairman of the Joint Chiefs of Staff General Colin Powell, pondered with incredulity the drift in Washington thinking since the high-water mark of the undeclared Vietnam War. As Powell noted, a solitary firefight resulting in 18 deaths over a 24-hour period would not have merited a press conference, never mind intense media scrutiny, during the period of his service in Southeast Asia.[2]

Powell's thinking focused on what some would later refer to as "Somalia syndrome" or, in the words of Clinton administration envoy Richard Holbrooke, "Vietmalia syndrome."[3] By this, the veteran foreign policy adviser meant that the experience of Somalia had reinforced the habits of thinking born of the national trauma associated with the Vietnam War. This apparent phenomenon manifested itself as a reluctance to employ military forces, particularly in situations in which hostilities were possible or likely. Of course, the irony in this situation was painfully obvious, given that these are not only the very circumstances in which professional soldiers are normally used but, in fact, are also among the very ones for which they exist. Strikingly, an intensified concern over potential casualties became a preoccupation not only of Washington politicians but also of many military leaders.

One clear consequence was the rise of "force protection" in all military planning. Based on a sound initial premise that commanders must secure their troops, this admirable notion ballooned in practice to exceed the bounds of common sense. The problem was that the force-protection mind-set could find no logical limits. Under pressure to avoid casualties, commanders could always justify additional precautions. Somalia, as a case in which an ostensible humanitarian mission gradually turned into a combat operation, cemented the reasoning that commanders could never err by seeking too much security. In other words, concern over possible casualties in subtle ways came to rival mission objectives as a matter of command focus. This tendency was particularly pronounced in a military culture that widely regarded peacekeeping or nation-building operations as distractions from the primary mission of "warfighting."

To be sure, steps to secure the force in Somalia were measured and in proportion to the threat the faction militias posed. Unfortunately, a climate of apprehension that any subsequent mission might turn out to be a Somalia or Vietnam gripped many political and military leaders alike. A mere week after the infamous Mogadishu firefight, the US vessel *Harlan*

County withdrew from the Haitian harbor at Port-au-Prince in the face of a small crowd of hostile, lightly armed demonstrators. Pointedly, some protesting at the docks held up signs announcing that Haiti would be another Somalia for the United States. Thus, what was widely perceived to be another public humiliation for US policy helped create a boomerang effect in popular opinion. A cornered administration did not feel it could back down and secretly began planning for an invasion of Haitian. When US forces deployed to Haiti in September 1994, they arrived in massive strength. Indeed, the specter of American military might led to a last-minute compromise in which Haiti's military dictator agreed to relinquish power in exchange for a respectable life in exile.

Then, remarkably, most US conventional forces in Haiti gave a demonstration of force protection in practice. Fearing that Port-au-Prince might in fact be another Mogadishu, the Army's conventional forces maintained a posture of maximum vigilance while assuming minimum risk to its personnel. The anomalous result was that, in what proved to be a relatively benign environment, displays of force were constant. A populace that was disposed to view US soldiers as liberators encountered conventional forces that behaved almost like an occupation force. The unfortunate irony was that an occupation was the last thing the Americans wanted. From the moment of arrival, the goal was to leave. The memory of Somalia hung over the Haiti mission like a dark cloud. Selecting the 10th Mountain Division, including many personnel fresh from the Somali ordeal, as the lead force in Haiti all but ensured comparisons in the minds of both participants and observers.

Most 10th Mountain Division personnel in Port-au-Prince remained permanently locked down in well-bunkered compounds. Direct engagement of the populace was minimal, at least within the limits of the Haitian capital. In fairness, US forces effectively guaranteed the personal security of restored Haitian President Jean Bertrand Aristide and provided conscientious overwatch as Haiti's civilian government slowly returned. Strictly speaking, the Americans accomplished the short-term military objective, and responsibility for preserving stability in Haiti passed within six months to a UN peacekeeping force. Still, the Haitian intervention signaled a renewed caution in US military behavior.

Such a psychology, although perhaps to a lesser extent, prevailed again with the advent of a peace-enforcement mission in Bosnia in 1995. Although increasingly sensing a need and perhaps even a US responsibility to become involved, Clinton and most of his key advisers were deeply reluctant to put American soldiers on the ground. Despite limited diplomatic efforts by the Clinton administration and its European allies, the unrelenting brutality of civil war in the Balkans raged on, and the immediacy of televised reporting ever more reduced the president's options. As retired Admiral Jonathan T. Howe, an experienced warrior-diplomat, subsequently wrote, "Ignoring circumstances such as genocide, ethnic cleansing, or mass starvation is not consistent with US values as a society or with the founding principles of the UN."[4]

Finally, in November 1995, an American-brokered peace agreement signed in Dayton, Ohio, established acceptable conditions for deploying US troops to stabilize Bosnia. Meanwhile, there was ample reason for concern that rogue elements might try to sabotage the peace process by launching attacks on the US-led Implementation Force. In this context, it was striking that for the first time force protection, historically an implicit consideration in any deployment within the framework of overall military objectives, appeared explicitly in an Army mission statement.[5] At the same time, to preclude any possible recurrence of conditions in Mogadishu, the Americans arrived in overwhelming force, including the full panoply of armor, aerial, and reconnaissance assets. As a result, compliance among the warring factions was far better than many feared.

Several years later, a reluctance to put soldiers in harm's way was once again evident during NATO's brief war in Kosovo. In contrast to the situation in Bosnia, in this instance no peace agreement was in place before entry. Consequently, the Clinton administration decided to stick with what some would judge to be the future solution to America's battles—air power. The idea was that by operating from extended ranges without putting troops on the ground, the United States would wield military force, minimally risking casualties. To some critics, this approach was disturbingly reminiscent of the gradualist, limited bombing campaigns of the Vietnam War. In point of fact, air power eventually succeeded in forcing Yugoslav armed forces to withdraw from Kosovo. However, this occurred only after months of bombing, backed up by hints of the arrival of ground forces and a bit of friendly Russian diplomatic advice to Yugoslav President Slobodan Milosevic. Many observers suspected in the aftermath that perhaps air power would not be able to provide a comprehensive solution to future conflicts.

Then, stunningly, on 11 September 2001, devastating terrorist attacks on the World Trade Center in New York and on the Pentagon in Washington, DC, precipitated a drastic change in the politico-military climate. Bloodied at home, Americans seemed to cast their hesitancy aside. Within weeks, US special forces personnel, to be followed by elements of the 10th Mountain Division and the 101st Airborne Division, deployed to Afghanistan to wage a war against terror. Few blanched at the assumption of significant risk. Public support for conducting military operations swelled. Ironically, even as the new war on terror seemed to mark a departure from the Somalia experience in terms of showing a clear resolve to press the fight, it vaguely suggested a return to Somalia in another sense. Wracked by civil war, Afghanistan was a chaotic, xenophobic, heavily armed, clan-based society that scarcely resembled a modern state. Military analysts quickly recognized something familiar about the Afghan social landscape. A sense of urgency grew concerning the need to understand the experience of Somalia as the United States sent its armed forces into another austere, rugged, and confusing Third World environment.

Born, in part, out of an appreciation that such conflicts might occur more than once in the future, this study will address the experience of Somalia. Surprisingly, perhaps, to some, it will show that while serious errors occurred, US and UN soldiers and marines in many instances performed with great effectiveness. That fact is often lost in the public dialog about Somalia because the mission there ended in policy reversal and political failure. Still, that the international coalition achieved as much as it did is particularly noteworthy in light of the extraordinarily complex environment in which it operated. Yet, as then Marine Brigadier General Anthony Zinni would later observe, what above all made Somalia a tough place to do business was the United States' lack of comprehension of its intricate and unfamiliar social and cultural fabric.[6] All too often, peacekeepers experienced great difficulty in interpreting the signs around them or the dynamic of politically and culturally conditioned violence that made them targets. Wary Somalis and their leaders would not keep the welcome mat out for long to outside intruders, whatever their ostensible intentions. The aggressively xenophobic strain in the local culture meant that the surface calm of life could easily mislead the uninitiated.[7] Somalia's social fabric of interwoven clans, tribes, and military leaders—widely referred to as warlords—posed a formidable intelligence challenge. So, too, did this sad country's widely varying social and topographical landscape.

Hardly less difficult was the complexity of conducting multinational military operations in such a context. Mogadishu, especially, tested the mettle of the foreign peacekeeping contingents. Consisting of a mosaic of distinct neighborhoods, its nuances were barely perceptible to outside observers. Plain enough, however, were the dangers it presented as a tactical environment. Densely built-up areas and narrow, constricting streets offered perils at every turn among the heavily armed militias and citizenry. Even with their extraordinary technological assets, US forces had to tread with great care.

This study will focus on the major aspects of the Somalia mission. It will discuss the Somalis, their history, their collective experiences, and their outlook. It will also review the mission's logic and evolution at each successive stage. These mark not only a chronological division of the mission but also discrete periods entailing varying strategic approaches and entirely different sets of leaders and units. The initial UN-sponsored humanitarian mission, the UN Operation in Somalia (UNOSOM) I, gave way in late 1992 to a potent US-led peacekeeping force referred to as the Unified Task Force. Then, in May 1993, another UN force, UNOSOM II, took over with an expanded nation-building mandate but with a less robust capability with which to implement it. Through each phase of the Somali adventure, this study will consider the roles of joint and multinational commands as well as individual military units conducting tactical operations on the ground. In addition, it will identify and examine critical insights gained from the mission to Somalia, especially as they pertain to a range of military issues from command and control to military operations in an urban environment to coping with clan-based factions in collapsed states.

Notes

1.   Mark Bowden, *Black Hawk Down: A Story of Modern War* (New York: Atlantic Monthly Press, 1999), 335; Colin Powell with Joseph Persico, *My American Journey* (New York: Ballantine Books, 1996), 573; and David Halberstam, *War in a Time of Peace: Bush, Clinton, and the Generals* (New York: Scribner, 2001), 263-64.

2.   Bowden, 341.

3.   Halberstam, 265. For a detailed account of the Haitian mission and the question of force protection, see Walter E. Kretchik, Robert F. Baumann, and John T. Fishel, *Invasion, Intervention, "Intervasion": A Concise History of the U.S. Army in Operation Uphold Democracy* (Fort Leavenworth, KS: US Army Command and General Staff College Press, 1998).

4.   Jonathan T. Howe, "Relations Between the United States and United Nations in Dealing With Somalia," *Learning From Somalia: The Lessons of Armed Humanitarian Intervention*, Walter Clarke and Jeffrey Herbst, eds. (Boulder, CO: Westview Press, 1996), 187.

5.   Robert F. Baumann, George W. Gawrych, and Walter E. Kretchik, unpublished monograph provisionally titled *Armed Peacekeepers in Bosnia: The U.S. and Multinational Experience*.

6.   Norman Cooling, "Operation Restore Hope in Somalia: A Tactical Action Turned Strategic Defeat," *Marine Corps Gazette* (September 2001), 102-106.

7.   Ambassador Robert Oakley, Public Broadcasting Service FRONTLINE Interview, "Ambush in Mogadishu," at <www.pbs.org/wgbh/pages/frontline/shows/ambush/interviews/oakley.html>.

Chapter 1

Setting the Stage

Versalle F. Washington

Before people talk about the future, it is necessary to understand what brought this situation about. It is not only a question of what the solution is, but firstly understanding how and why all this happened. A part of the solution must lie in the answer to that question.

—Khadra Muhumed Abdi[1]

When US troops embarked on Operation RESTORE HOPE, they set off on what many believed to be a relatively simple mission. Their task was to assist the UN in its efforts to deliver food to the Somali people. The US role would be both logistic and tactical in that it would provide assistance through transport and, more important, by protecting the workers and means of distribution. The troops would find a country different from any they had seen, with rules and customs they did not understand, a climate that made even routine operations difficult, and a people who, while needing their assistance, did not necessarily appreciate the requirement. This combination of circumstances was not what the American forces anticipated and would cause a chain of events that would see President Bill Clinton withdraw from the American commitment.

Somalis are a people divided by their sameness. Unlike much of the rest of Africa, Somalia's postcolonial borders enclose only a single ethnic group, the Samaal. The Samaal have occupied this region since biblical times. Nearly all Somalis are Muslim. These people have been followers of Islam since as early as the 18th century, but their first contact with Islam is believed to have been in the eighth century.[2] Somalis speak Somali as their official language. Somali, however, is a language that has only had a written component since the early 1970s. It has several dialects, of which three predominate, with common Somali being the most widely used. Some 10 percent of Somalis speak either English or Italian, and they use some Arabic, primarily in connection with religious observances. Until the Somali government's collapse in 1991, literacy was on the upswing, and in 1990, the UN estimated that Somali literacy was at 24 percent.[3]

The Somalis' constant presence in the Horn of Africa as a homogenous people did not lead to a harmonious history. While much of the conflict can be attributed to incursions by outsiders, much is also a product of

9

the Somalis' reliance on clans as the primary social and governmental organization. Although Somalis descend from a single ethnicity, present-day Somalis still show their primary allegiance to the clans and subclans. There are six primary clans and perhaps as many as 20 subclans. The Samaal clans are the Isaaq, Hawiye, Dir, and Darood. These clans share a primarily nomadic heritage. The Saab clans, which have an agricultural heritage, are the Digil and the Rahanwein. The clans provide structure to the daily lives of the Somali people. In *Collapse of the Somali State*, Abdisalam Issa-Salwe that the clan is the most important political unit.[4] Issa-Salwe argues that the Somalis pay allegiance to their "descent group unit."[5]

The clan structure is a primary factor in Somalia's continued fragmentation. Because the people do not perceive a function to a national or state allegiance, getting the various clans to cooperate has largely been a fruitless endeavor. Despite this, colonizing the Somali lands created a nationalist movement in the 20th century, mainly as a reaction to the imposition of colonial governance.

Somalia's colonial period, from 1891 until 1960, saw Somalia divided among Great Britain (British Somaliland), Italy (Italian Somaliland), France (French Somaliland/Djibouti), Ethiopia (Ogaden), and Kenya (Northern Frontier District). This five-part division of the Somali people had only a partial end when the former Italian Somaliland and the former British Somaliland merged to form the Republic of Somalia. The new Somalia's borders did not reflect the extent of the Somali people, as large Somali minorities remained in Ethiopia and Kenya, and Djibouti remained

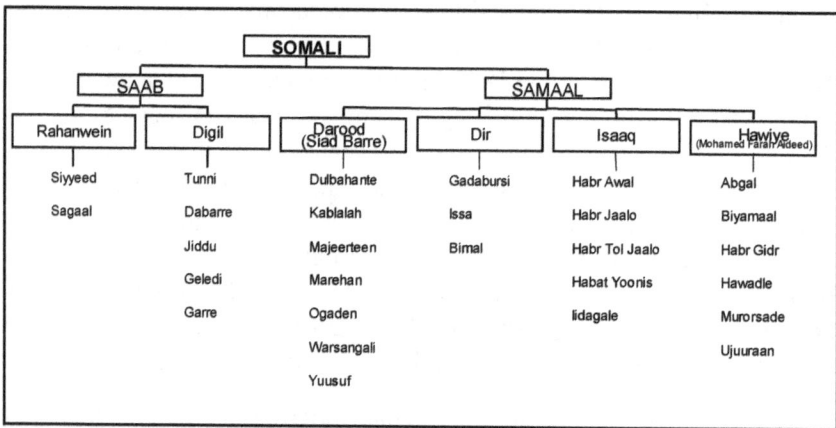

SAAB		SAMAAL			
Rahanwein	Digil	Darood (Siad Barre)	Dir	Isaaq	Hawiye (Mohamed Farah Aideed)
Siyyeed	Tunni	Dulbahante	Gadabursi	Habr Awal	Abgal
Sagaal	Dabarre	Kablalah	Issa	Habr Jaalo	Biyamaal
	Jiddu	Majeerteen	Bimal	Habr Tol Jaalo	Habr Gidr
	Geledi	Marehan		Habat Yoonis	Hawadle
	Garre	Ogaden		Iidagale	Murorsade
		Warsangali			Ujuuraan
		Yuusuf			

Figure 1. Somali Clan Structure

10

under French control until 1977. The map of the Horn of Africa shows the difficulty this posed for the Somalis in terms of gaining their national identity (see the map). The further effects of this period on the Somali people are a source of some disagreement among scholars, but when the Italian and British colonial powers pulled out in 1960, Somalia had a relatively successful postcolonial period for nine years.

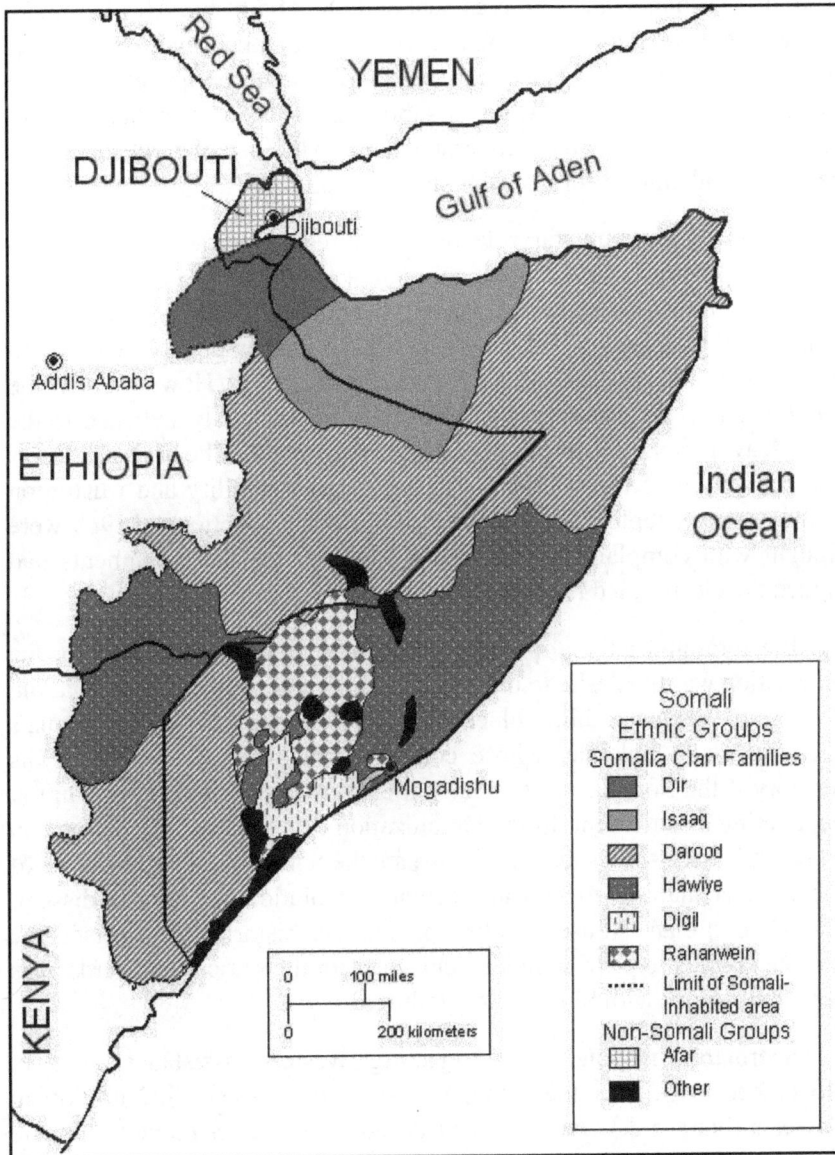

Map 3. Somali Clan Map

The new Somalia had major difficulties to overcome because the Italian and British colonial systems had left it with two distinct sets of laws, customs, economies, and languages. The nation merged on 1 July 1960, the same day the Italians ceded control to the Somalis in their former colony and only 5 days after the British left their former colony. The country opted for a democratic form of government and elected Aden Abdullah Osman as the first president and Dr. Abdirashid Ali Shermarke as the first prime minister. Osman came from the Italian south, Shermarke from the British north. The country elected a single parliament, allowed freedom of press, and was remarkably free of human rights abuses.[6] However, the parliamentary government led to the rise of parties intent on gaining an advantage for clan and subclan groupings.

The 1964 parliamentary elections featured 18 parties vying for 123 seats, and by the 1969 elections, more than 1,000 candidates represented 60 parties, all in a population of about 5 million. The primary party, the Somali Youth League (SYL), dominated the parliament following both elections, holding 90 seats after 1964 and 74 after 1969. However, after the 1969 election, opposition politicians nearly unanimously switched to the SYL, leaving Somalia essentially a single-party state.[7] The basic weakness and corruption of the political system created instability and frustration in the Somali people. Like the 1964 elections, the elections in 1969 were fraught with complaints of fraud and a belief that the incumbents had rigged the election led to widespread dissatisfaction.

Electoral and internal politics aside, the major political issue for the new nation was the desire to unite all of the Somali people into one nation. This issue was a stumbling block for the government because Ethiopia's Emperor Haile Selassie, whose country stood to lose one-fifth of its territory if the Somalis were to have their way, blocked every attempt at negotiating a settlement. In the Organization of African Unity Summit in May 1963, Selassie maneuvered to isolate the Somali position.[8] A result of the Somalis' inability to gain an acceptable resolution was internal dissent. The Darood clan, whose Ogadeni people had historically traversed the disputed border to provide fodder and water for their flocks and herds, was especially angry with Shermarke's failures.

Shermarke responded by rejecting Western assistance and, in November 1963, announced that Somalia would accept $22 million in Soviet military aid.[9] Over the next decade, the Soviet money built the Somali army into a regional power, but the focus on the army ensured that the infrastructure, education, and other social programs remained unfunded. To all appearances, Somalia was preparing to go to war over three regions: the Ethiopian-controlled Ogaden, the northern province of Kenya, and Djibouti. Shermarke's election as president changed this perception; his premier, Mahamed Haji Ibrahim Igal, opted for a more conciliatory strategy. This strategy, however, brought the Somalis no closer to their aims and also alienated Igal's administration from the Somali people on the eve of the 1969 parliamentary elections.[10]

While outwardly democratic, the Somali government officials remained focused on the personal benefits of public office rather than on their duties to further their state's development. Political power was seen as a path to personal fortune or, at best, as a method of gaining perquisites for individual subclans. As a result, the government was ineffectual in the eyes of its citizens. This all came to an abrupt end when Major General Mohammed Siad Barre took power in a bloodless coup in late 1969, following Shermarke's assassination.[11]

Barre's government would lead to the destruction of the Somali state. When his Supreme Revolutionary Council (SRC) first took power, the Somali people welcomed the change. The SRC's 25 military and police officers had the advantage of unity, so the SRC did not have the endless debates that had characterized the Somali parliament. Barre instituted a number of reforms, including selecting the official orthography for written Somali, emplacing adult literacy programs, and creating settlements for people displaced by drought.[12] In 1970, Barre announced his selection of "scientific socialism" as the official SRC ideology and outlawed clan affiliations and political parties other than his Somali Revolutionary Socialist Party (SRSP).

The socialist Somalia was significantly different from its democratic predecessor. A primary goal of the Barre regime was to remove the clan as the primary Somali allegiance. Barre took several measures to fulfill this goal, all of which took functions that had been reserved for clan leaders and made them state functions. No longer were marriages a clan matter. Somalis wishing to be married had to go to an orientation center, where they were wed in a civil ceremony. Clan elders became simply minor government functionaries. Barre's purpose was to turn a "nation of nomads" into a modern state, with the state rather than the clans handling the daily necessities of administration and governance.[13] Among the more notorious of the many changes was establishing the National Security Service (NSS). The NSS, headed by Barre's son-in-law, General Ahmed S. Abdulle, was an organ of repression. Chief among its characteristics were

13

torture and abusive interrogation. Its decisions were not subject to appeal, and it frequently jailed dissidents.[14]

Another chilling facet of socialist Somalia was the Victory Pioneers, led by another Barre son-in-law, Abdirahman Gulwade. This group's function was to instill the "revolutionary spirit" into the Somali people by demanding their compulsory attendance at classes given in the indoctrination centers and at political rallies. The Victory Pioneers also had detention authority, and like that of the NSS, its authority was not subject to appeal. This organization recruited Somali youth for its cadres and inspired a sense of fear by keeping a close watch on people's activities.[15] Despite his stated intention of removing clans from the Somalis' minds, the years of Barre's dictatorship taught the Somalis not to trust people outside their clans.

Because Barre needed a way to maintain power, he leaned heavily on his own Darood clan, even while officially banning them. Most of his ministers and advisers came from the Mareehaan (his father's), Ogaden (his mother's), and Dulbahante (his son-in-law's) subclans, which led to his regime being unofficially labeled the MOD.[16] The MOD considered one of its chief aims to be to restore a pan-Somali nation. The 1974 overthrow of Selassie, coupled with the impetus of the Somali drought that same year, convinced Barre that his Soviet-equipped and -trained army would be able to win a war for the Ogaden. However, he failed to consider the Soviets' aspirations. The Soviets also saw opportunity in Selassie's overthrow. In 1976, they sought to encourage socialist harmony in the region by bringing Ethiopia, Somalia, and Yemen together. Somalia, however, refused the Soviet overtures until there was a solution to the border dispute over the Ogaden. The Ethiopian political situation remained unsettled, though, and in late 1976, Ethiopia experienced its third coup in as many years, and Lieutenant Colonel (LTC) Mengistu Haile Meriam took power.[17]

Seeking to take advantage of the turmoil, Barre struck. In 1977, he launched his forces across the Ethiopian border and, in coordination with the Western Somali Liberation Front (WSLF), captured a number of Ethiopian towns, apparently moving toward his goal. However, the Soviets were interested in having a larger hold over the Horn of Africa than just Somalia. When Ethiopia declared itself a Marxist-Leninist state and called for Soviet assistance, the Somalia-based Soviet advisers flew from Mogadishu to Addis Ababa. There they joined with some 18,000 Cuban soldiers and Yemeni and East German technical advisers and, in 1978, drove the Somalis back across the disputed border.

14

This dramatic shift in fortunes was too much for the Somali nation to bear. It turned to the West for assistance and found the United States willing to provide assistance in exchange for access to the former Soviet naval facilities at Berbera. The United States gave Barre $100 million per year in development and direct military aid. This aid continued until the Barre government's collapse and was supplemented with aid from Saudi Arabia, China, South Africa, and other nations. All of this military aid would find its way into the hands of the various warlords, providing them with the means for waging their civil wars.

The Somali loss in the Ogaden war left Barre in a vulnerable position. He had lost the single unifying factor in his government, and shortly after the loss, army officers from the Majeerteen clan staged a coup against him. Although the coup was unsuccessful, it spawned the Somali Salvation Democratic Front (SSDF). The SSDF took up arms and from sanctuary in Ethiopia raided central Somalia. Barre's response to the SSDF activities was to strike against the Majeerteen clan. In a brutal campaign during May and June 1979, Barre's Red Berets (the presidential guard) killed more than 2,000 Majeerteen clan members in the Mudug region.[18]

This was only the beginning. Each time the SSDF acted within Somalia, the government would then retaliate against the Majeerteen. The retaliations went beyond attacks against individuals or even villages—the Barre regime put the Mudug region under special laws; closed schools, hospitals, and other essential services; and banned trade with the region. Thousands more Majeerteen died when government forces destroyed wells and reservoirs and slaughtered Majeerteen flocks and herds.[19] These actions hardened the Majeerteen against the Barre regime, and thousands of Majeerteen fled Somalia and became politically active, in many cases joining guerilla forces intent on ousting Barre.

After his actions against the Majeerteen, Barre moved against the Isaaq clan, but the Isaaqs proved to be a much more formidable opponent. In 1981, expatriate Isaaqs formed the Somali National Movement (SNM). The SNM's chief grievances were that approximately 500,000 refugees of the Ogaden war encroached on their grazing lands, and it objected to the systematic elimination of Isaaq clansmen from government service.[20] The Isaaqs, who lived in the northern regions of Somalia, participated in limited antigovernment activities and gave their support to the SNM.

This low level of unrest boiled over in 1988 when Barre and Ethiopia's LTC Meriam signed an agreement banning support to their respective antigovernment forces. As a sign of good faith, Meriam moved against

15

the SSDF, closing its Ethiopian bases and confiscating many of its heavy weapons. Rather than wait for a similar fate, the SNM entered Somalia in force. In open combat, it defeated Somali army forces, capturing large portions of Hargeisa. Barre moved additional forces north, but again the army was unable to defeat the SNM forces. The army then turned its weapons on the Isaaq populace and on the Darood refugees, killing an estimated 50,000 civilians; an additional 350,000 refugees streamed across the Ethiopian border.[21]

Although Barre had counted on the MOD's support for his regime, that support also crumbled after the Ogaden war. The primary factor for this change was the deluge of Ogadeni refugees, many of whom enlisted in the army and all of whom upset the traditional MOD balance of power. Previously, the favored clans had priority on available resources. Now, the massive influx of Ogaden refugees strained all resources, leading to competition between the Ogaden and Marehan clans. In an attempt to reduce the Ogadenis' growing influence, Barre fired his minister of defense, Ogadeni Aden Gabiyo, in May 1989 and purged Ogadeni officers from all sensitive posts. This led to a revolt among the Ogadeni soldiers in the Kismayo base, and Ogaden clansman formed another armed resistance group, the Somali Patriotic Movement (SPM). In June, Colonel Omar Jess defected to the SPM with the Ogadeni garrison in Hargeisa.[22] This defection completed the rupture of the MOD.

Barre's collapse followed shortly after the rise of the SPM, but it was more directly linked to the emergence of the Hawiye-based United Somali Congress (USC). In October 1989, Hawiye soldiers stationed in Galcayo mutinied, and in retaliation, Barre cracked down on the Hawiye clan. The formerly political USC became an armed militant organization with General Mohamed Farah Aideed's rise as its leader. Unlike his predecessors, Aideed favored a military solution to the problems the Barre regime had brought about. The resultant conflict spread throughout central Somalia, and in coordination with the SNM and SPM, the rebels drove the tottering Barre forces back into Mogadishu.

In May 1990, a new political entity spoke out against Barre. The Manifesto Group—former government officials, intellectuals, and clan leaders—brought their grievances to Barre. This multiclan organization called for an end to the human rights abuses and for an interim government to allow free elections. Barre's response was predictable, and most of the Manifesto Group wound up on trial for treason. Forty-six of the 114 members received death sentences, but a massive throng of demonstrators surrounded the court building, causing Barre to back away from the sentences.[23]

Compounding Barre's difficulties was the US reaction to his strife with the Hawiye. Frustrated by his inability to defeat the USC forces, Barre ordered his Red Berets to attack Hawiye civilians. This act had the unfortunate consequences of turning his stronghold (Mogadishu sits squarely in Hawiye region) into a hostile camp and causing the United States to withdraw its support after news of the atrocities being committed in Mogadishu became well known in America.[24]

By the end of July 1990, Barre had essentially run out of options in Mogadishu. He remained in a virtual state of siege as Aideed's forces drew the net more tightly around Mogadishu. By December, USC forces were prepared for the final drive into Mogadishu. Italy and Egypt offered to host a peace conference in Cairo, but the USC, SNM, and SPM all rejected the overture. On 3 December 1990, USC forces entered Mogadishu and attacked the strongholds of Barre and his Red Berets. The battle for Mogadishu raged for the next two months; on 4 and 5 January 1991, the United States airlifted US and UN personnel to a waiting aircraft carrier.[25] On 26 January, Barre fled Mogadishu for Gedo in southwest Somalia. There he attempted to rally his broken army under the banner of the Somali National Front (SNF), but he finally gave up, going into exile the following April.

The fall of the Barre regime did not bring the hoped-for relief to the people of Somalia. There were far too many weapons in the hands of far too many groups with far too different agendas. USC leader Ali Mahdi Mohamed was named interim president, with Omar Arteh Ghalib as his prime minister; without the support of Aideed and the military faction of the USC, the pair had little chance. Rid of their common opponent, the clans turned on each other, and the USC, SPM, SNF, and other forces repeatedly invaded the towns of southern Somalia. The USC split along clan lines—the Abgal clan supported their kinsman, Ali Mahdi Mohamed, while the Habr Gidr supported Aideed. Fighting between these clans raged over Mogadishu and its environs until a UN-brokered cease-fire took effect in April 1992.

Human rights abuses, long a charge leveled against the Barre regime, became even more prevalent. A descending spiral of rape, murder, torture, destruction of crops and water supplies, and wholesale slaughter led to mass starvation and forced literally hundreds of thousands of Somalis to flee to neighboring countries.[26] This exodus began to capture the attention of human rights and humanitarian relief organizations as the Somali problem suddenly acquired international ramifications. The refugees exhausted the capabilities of Ethiopia, Djibouti, and Kenya to absorb them and provide their basic necessities. The crisis called for international intervention, but the UN was still not ready to act.

Unfortunately for Somalia, the flood of foreign military assistance during the Barre years meant an abundance of military hardware, weapons, vehicles, and ammunition for the warring clans to employ. While the United States supplied $403 million to Somalia during this period, it merely headed a long list of suppliers that included the USSR, China, Italy, Germany, South Africa, and Libya. As soldiers deserted the army and as the various factions captured stocks and equipment, the major clans became increasingly well armed. Maintenance proved to be a problem for most of the armor and aircraft, but the clans devised "technicals"—truck-mounted heavy weapons. These vehicles were highly mobile and added the firepower of heavy machine guns, light cannon, and mortars.

The primary tactic of all the clans was to deny food to their opposition. This brought the fighters into conflict with the humanitarian relief organizations that were desperately trying to stem the tide of starvation. In April 1992, the UN passed Resolution 751, allocating more than $20 million in food aid and sending a 550-man Pakistani peacekeeping force to Somalia.[27] This effort, which was called the UN Operation in Somalia (UNOSOM), was to fall woefully short of what was needed. Although it was clear that the effort could only succeed with the warring clans' compliance, it soon became apparent that the clans were unwilling to surrender any advantage for fear that an opposing clan also might not give up their arms. Without clan disarmament, UNOSOM's mission was in jeopardy. As the UN report emphasized, "the lawlessness, insecurity, and violence prevented the delivery of much of the food aid in the pipeline."[28] Looters stole food intended for the refugees, and armed gangs would stop the aid workers and take their supplies. Without the consent of all the warring parties, security for all workers and for the relief distribution system was impossible. Despite the growing scale of the operation, Somalis continued to die in dramatic numbers.[29]

The Pakistani battalion lacked any heavy weapons, air support, or artillery. Consequently, the local gangs with their technicals outgunned the peacekeepers regularly. The obvious mismatch caused the UN to increase the size of the peacekeeping force to 3,500 in August, but as the Somali

18

gangs recognized the value of the food aid, they turned to robbing the relief effort. Despite the UNOSOM peacekeepers' best efforts, it became clear that no effective solution to the humanitarian relief crisis could occur without disarming the rival clans.

By 26 July 1992, Security Council Resolution 767 demonstrated that this was not at all clear to the UN. The resolution called for the immediate airlift of food aid to the "triangle of death" in southern Somalia. President George Bush authorized a US operation that would be known as Operation PROVIDE RELIEF. This operation flew nearly 2,500 flights out of Mombasa, Kenya, and although the operation provided nearly 28,000 metric tons of food aid, it failed. The airfields and landing strips in south Somalia had no protection, so looters and even local militias extorted money and supplies for the "right" of landing.[30] US forces gained valuable experience from the operation through working closely with the nongovernment community, but despite the enormous costs of the operation, most of the food never reached the people for whom it was intended. Looting, hoarding, and diversions ensured that while the volume of food coming into Somalia increased, the percentage reaching the needy decreased.[31] The UN peacekeepers' continued inability to control the ports or to protect the food aid led the UN, in December, to accept Bush's offer of 30,000 troops, the UN International Task Force.

Notes

1. Rakiya A. Omaar, *Somalia: A Government at War With Its Own People* (New York: Africa Watch, January 1990).

2. Helen Chapin Metz, *Somalia: A Country Study* (Washington, DC: Library of Congress, 1993), xxi.

3. Ibid., xv.

4. Abdisalam M. Issa-Salwe, *The Collapse of the Somali State: The Impact of the Colonial Legacy*, new edition (London: HAAN Associates, 1996), 3.

5. Ibid. This unit roughly equates to the subclan. The exceptions to this subclan grouping are in the Rahanwein and Digil clans where the primary allegiance is to the broader village (clan) grouping.

6. Omaar, 14.

7. Terrence Lyons and Ahmed I. Samatar, *Somalia: State Collapse, Multilateral Intervention, and Strategies for Political Reconstruction* (Washington, DC: The Brookings Institution, 1995), 14.

8. Issa-Salwe, 72.

9. Ibid., 73.

10. Ibid.

11. I.M. Lewis, *Understanding Somalia: Guide to Culture, History and Social Institutions,* Second Edition (London: HAAN Associates, 1993), 28-31. Although Shermarke's assassination seemed to be motivated by personal concerns, it left a power vacuum.

12. Lyons and Samatar, 14.

13. Mark Bradbury, *The Somalia Conflict: Prospects for Peace* (London: Oxfam, 1994), 9.

14. Omaar, 16.

15. Ibid., 17.

16. Bradbury, 10.

17. Issa-Salwe, 91-92.

18. Bradbury, 11.

19. Issa-Salwe, 94-97.

20. Jama Mohamed Ghalib, *The Cost of Dictatorship: The Somali Experience* (New York: Lilian Barber Press, 1995), 60-62.

21. Issa-Salwe, 98-100. See also Bradbury, 11-12. The actual numbers of killed and refugees vary between sources. With the collapse of the Barre regime, the SNM seceded from Somalia, declaring the northwestern provinces the Republic of Somaliland.

22. Bradbury, 12-13.

23. Issa-Salwe, 107-8.

24. Metz, 51-52. The incident that apparently ended US support was the string of slayings in July 1990. These slayings included members of the Manifesto Group and the Roman Catholic Bishop of Mogadishu.

25. Bradbury, 14. The carrier, USS *Guam*, had been diverted from its station in support of the Persian Gulf war.

26. Metz, xxx. By August 1992, there were 500,000 Somalis in Ethiopia; 300,000 in Kenya; 65,000 in Yemen; 15,000 in Djibouti; and around 100,000 in Europe.

27. United Nations Staff, *The United Nations and Somalia, 1992-1996* (New York: UN Publications, July 1996), 19-20.

28. Ibid., 23.

29. Ibid. The UN estimates that between 300,000 and 500,000 Somalis died from the famine and fighting in 1992 alone.

30. John L. Hirsch, Robert B. Oakley, and Robert Oakley, *Somalia and Operation Restore Hope: Reflections on Peacemaking and Peacekeeping* (Washington, DC: U.S. Institute of Peace Press, June 1995), 24-25.

31. Ibid.

Chapter 2

Operation RESTORE HOPE
Phases I and II, December 1992

Lawrence A. Yates

Between 20 and 26 November 1992, the National Security Council
Deputies Committee convened four times to discuss the worsening crisis
in Somalia. At the meeting on 21 November, the attendees considered three
options for dealing with the famine and civil strife. The least complicated
course of action involved US support for what had been, up to that time,
largely ineffectual UN peacekeeping activities in the war-torn country.
A second option contemplated sending an American-organized military
coalition into Somalia but without US combat units. The last and most
far-reaching scenario envisaged deploying an American-organized and led
multinational force in which armed US troops would play the predominant
role. To the surprise of several at the meeting, the representative from
the Joint Chiefs of Staff (JCS) indicated that, pending the approval of
President George Bush, the Pentagon was prepared to execute this third
option and to support it with a variety of forces, including two American
infantry divisions.[1]

Up to this point, the defense department had voiced strong reservations
about using US ground troops in Somalia, even though congressional
resolutions, state department recommendations, and humanitarian
appeals were urging the Bush administration to take decisive action to
ameliorate the human tragedy brought about by drought and civil conflict.
What, then, had compelled the Pentagon to reverse its position in late
November? To begin with, television newscasts continued to bombard
the American public with graphic footage of starving Somali children
near death, virtual skeletons save for their distended stomachs. Measures
the international community had taken to ease the suffering had thus far
seemed only marginally effective. Certainly, the 564 Pakistani troops sent
to Mogadishu as peacekeepers under UN auspices had been powerless
to stop the thousands of armed bandits and militia who, generally acting
to enhance the power of one warlord or another, routinely seized food
supplies entering the country. As for Operation PROVIDE RELIEF, the US
military airlift of food from Kenya into Somalia, the statistics it compiled
were impressive but well short of what was needed to end the starvation.
Nor could an airlift counteract the violence and anarchical conditions that

prolonged the misery. By late 1992, more than 300,000 Somalis were already dead from famine and famine-related causes. According to some estimates, over 1 million more could expect the same fate, even though the food needed to feed them was already on hand, the supreme irony of the tragedy. But until the bandits, gangs, young gunmen for hire ("morions"), and factional militia could be dissuaded from interfering with humanitarian relief efforts, the starvation would continue.[2]

As pressure grew on the United States to intervene in the crisis, many supplicants pointed out that, in a speech before the UN in October, President Bush had proclaimed the US military's readiness to play an active role in the post-Cold War "new world order." To be sure, neither Bush nor the Pentagon regarded this pledge as an open-ended commitment, but the stipulation that military involvement in overseas ventures would be very selective did not, of itself, preclude action in Somalia. The misery there clearly moved the president and several of his advisers. Moreover, intervention in that country seemed preferable to sending American troops to Bosnia, where ethnic cleansing by Serbs against Muslims had many Arab leaders demanding that Washington take military action to save their coreligionists. This Arab pressure could be deflected, certain presidential advisers believed, if US troops were dispatched to improve conditions in Somalia, also an Islamic country but one whose troubles seemed to pose far fewer risks than those inherent in the complex Balkans crisis.[3]

With these considerations in mind and with an options paper from the Deputies Committee before him, Bush listened on 25 November while JCS Chairman General Colin Powell briefed the proposal for sending US ground forces into Somalia. Powell had been instrumental in shifting the Pentagon's position on this issue, although he had only reluctantly come to believe in the necessity of intervention. "I was not eager to get us involved in a Somalian civil war, but we were apparently the only nation that could end the suffering," he later wrote. Sharing this conclusion and the doubts that went with it were Secretary of Defense Richard Cheney and National Security Adviser Brent Scowcroft. As Scowcroft told the president, "Sure, we can get in. . . . But how do we get out?" An extensive discussion of the ramifications of committing US forces followed. Then Bush, who was spending his last two months in the White House, decided that, if the UN Security Council agreed, the United States would intervene in Somalia at the head of a multinational force in which US troops would represent the largest contingent. That afternoon, Secretary of State Lawrence S. Eagleburger went to New York to inform UN Secretary General Boutros Boutros-Ghali of the president's decision.[4]

24

The administration's offer elicited mixed reactions at the UN. Some officials suspected that America's dominant role in the proposed undertaking would compromise ongoing and future UN operations in Somalia. Also of concern was the US position that the Security Council should invoke, for the first time, Chapter VII of the UN Charter authorizing "peace enforcement"—a term used when the belligerents in a conflict do not request the intervention of outside troops to maintain peace—by "all necessary means," including deadly force. Boutros-Ghali, while mindful of these reservations, was inclined to accept the American proposal, including the request for Chapter VII authority. He opposed, however, President Bush's condition that the US-led coalition be replaced as quickly as possible by a UN peacekeeping force. The UN, Boutros-Ghali insisted, should not increase its commitments in Somalia until the country had been stabilized, a long-term proposition. There followed a week of deliberation during which no consensus emerged on how the US operation would mesh with UN efforts to end the crisis. Nevertheless, on 3 December, the Security Council adopted Resolution 794 in support of a "member state," forming and leading an international coalition that would "establish a secure environment for humanitarian relief operations in Somalia as soon as possible." In effect, the Security Council was endorsing an operation that, like DESERT SHIELD/DESERT STORM, would not be under the UN's formal control. The next day, Bush appeared on television to inform the American people and the world that the United States would send 28,000 troops to Somalia at the head of an American-led multinational force.[5] The operation was code-named RESTORE HOPE.

Planning, Preparation, and Deployment

The plan that Bush approved for military intervention in Somalia had been developed at the US Central Command (CENTCOM), MacDill Air Force Base, Florida. Somalia fell within CENTCOM's area of responsibility, which meant that the unified command, already in charge of Operation PROVIDE RELIEF, would now execute RESTORE HOPE as well. The president's decision to act quickly meant that planning at CENTCOM and subordinate and supporting headquarters would be done in the "crisis-action" mode, entailing severe constraints on the time available to acquire essential intelligence; flesh out the concept of operations and write an operation order (OPORD); coordinate with other participants; identify, schedule, and prepare troop units for deployment; and, in general, make decisions on a variety of complex matters. Referring to this frenetic predeployment period, one commander observed, "It was surprising how little we really knew" about many issues the planners considered crucial.[6]

Under the circumstances, staff officers and commanders preparing for Operation RESTORE HOPE, like their predecessors in other US contingency operations, simply had to make the best use of what little time they had, often basing critical decisions on estimates, guesses, and intuition, with the clear understanding that adjustments would be inevitable once the operation was in progress.

In keeping with crisis-action procedures, General Powell directed CENTCOM's commander in chief (CINCCENT), General Joseph Hoar, US Marine Corps (USMC), to prepare an estimate of the situation. Hoar's staff accomplished this promptly by referring to the Gulf War experience, a recent command post exercise, an off-the-shelf plan that covered humanitarian problems and natural disasters, and the command's continuing experience with Operation PROVIDE RELIEF. CENTCOM's Army component, ARCENT, participated in the process. On 3 December, the day of the Security Council resolution, Hoar briefed his estimate to the National Command Authorities (NCA), after which President Bush approved the courses of action contained therein. Two days later, the command published its OPORD for RESTORE HOPE, containing, among other essentials, a mission statement, a strategy for accomplishing the mission, the composition of the forces to be committed, and the command and control arrangements for them.[7]

The mission statement developed at CENTCOM and coordinated through the interagency process was succinct but indicative of the difficult undertaking upon which US and other forces were about to embark. "When directed by the NCA, CINCCENT will conduct joint and combined military operations in Somalia, to secure the major air and sea ports, key installations and food distribution points, to provide open and free passage of relief supplies, to provide security for convoys and relief organization operations and assist UN/NGOs [nongovernmental organizations] in providing humanitarian relief under UN auspices."[8]

Based on this mission, General Hoar issued his commander's intent and a concept of operations. Combined, they envisaged creating the security essential to moving relief supplies freely into Somalia and throughout designated areas of the country. Only the southern half of Somalia, the "famine belt," would be affected, and it would be divided into eight (later expanded to nine) humanitarian relief sectors (HRSs), each named after the major city or town contained within its borders. In keeping with the press of time, the borders drawn up at CENTCOM reflected US military considerations more than Somali clan and political affiliations within a given area. The HRSs began with Mogadishu in the middle and extended as far north as Belet Uen near the center of the country and as far south as Kismayo (see Map 4). Once the "security and the famine relief situation" had been stabilized in the HRSs, the US-led coalition would turn the responsibility for securing further humanitarian operations in Somalia over to the UN.

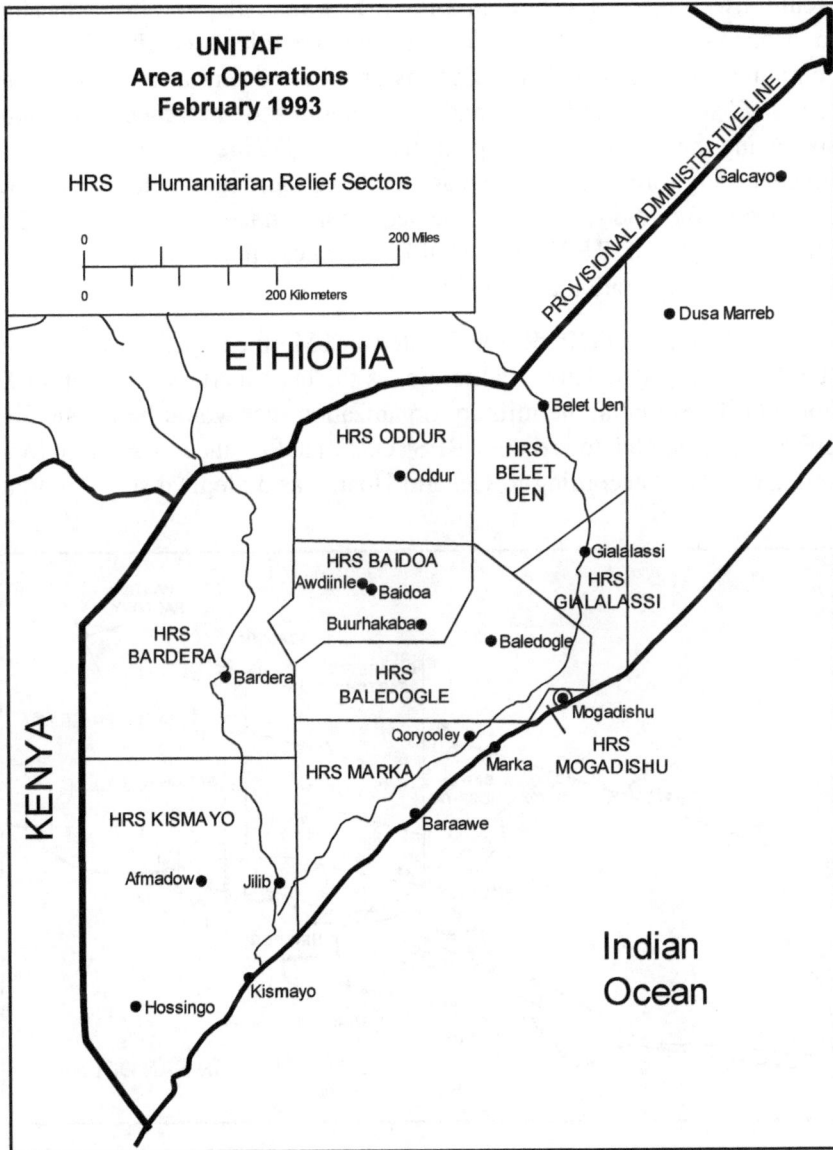

Map 4. HRS Map

Under Hoar's concept of operations, RESTORE HOPE would occur in four phases. In Phase I, coalition forces would deploy to Mogadishu, Somalia's capital. The first troops into the city would create a security zone, secure the airport and port facilities, protect the humanitarian relief supplies in the capital as well as those organizations whose job it was to distribute them, and begin to establish a logistics base. Coalition forces would also seize and secure an airfield in Baledogle, an HRS adjacent to Mogadishu. Phase II would have the coalition securing lines of communication (LOCs) leading to major relief centers in the remaining HRSs. Phase III entailed expanding operations within each HRS and stabilizing the situation to the point that Phase IV, the transition to a UN peacekeeping force, could take place. Although arranged in logical order, the four phases did not have to be sequential; indeed, as CENTCOM's official history of RESTORE HOPE indicates, there would be some overlap as the operation unfolded.[9]

The CINCCENT OPORD designated the I Marine Expeditionary Force (I MEF), Camp Pendleton, California, as the headquarters for Joint Task Force (JTF) Somalia, the military organization that would be physically present in Somalia to execute RESTORE HOPE under CENTCOM's command. This, according to General Hoar, was a "logical step," in that

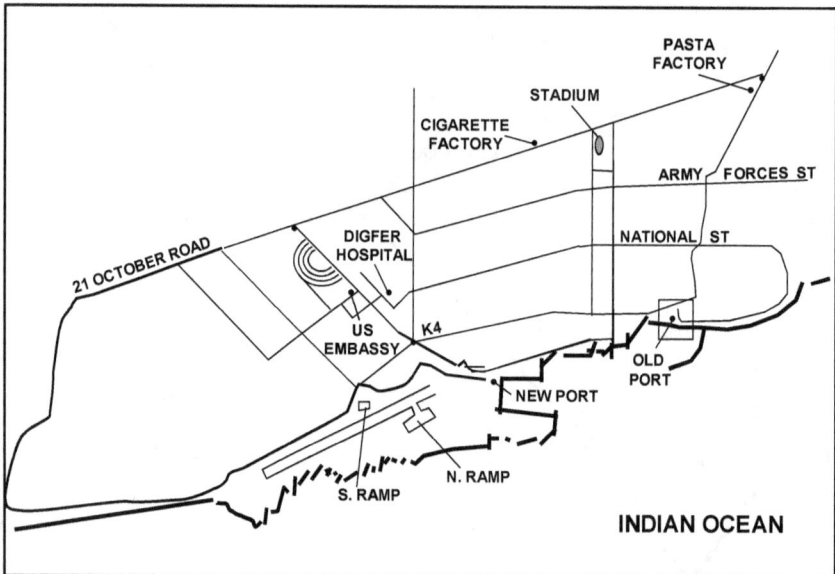

Map 5. Mogadishu during UNITAF

I MEF had "exercised for this type of operation."[10] I MEF's commanding general, Lieutenant General Robert B. Johnston, a veteran of Vietnam, Lebanon, and the Gulf War, learned of this prospective assignment well before he received formal notification, so he and his staff gained some valuable time to address certain critical issues. Johnston was also able to send I MEF planners to MacDill, where they worked with the CENTCOM staff to ensure that the JTF's supporting OPORD meshed with the one CINCCENT was publishing.

One of the first issues Johnston had to confront in his imminent role as commander of JTF Somalia was how to organize the headquarters. He decided on the obvious approach, which was to use the I MEF command element as a core around which he would construct a *joint* staff by bringing in augmentees from subordinate and other Marine commands and from the sister services. This approach was not without its shortcomings, as some sections of the I MEF staff underwent "radical reorganizations" to meet the requirements of a JTF headquarters, creating in the process some operational problems that arriving augmentees, unfamiliar with the setup, only exacerbated. It was, according to one Marine officer, a staff manned to some extent by "strangers." There was also the issue of size. In its early stages, the JTF headquarters grew to more than 800 personnel, the majority being marines, with the Army filling most of the remaining slots. In time, however, about a quarter of these positions would be identified as unnecessary.[11]

Aware of the confusion and dislocations inherent in any period of adjustment, Johnston had followed the most logical course in organizing his JTF headquarters. He also requested capable and experienced officers to head the key staff divisions, and CENTCOM ensured that the requests were honored. Within the command group, a US Army major general served as Johnston's deputy and a Marine colonel as his chief of staff. In the spirit of "jointness," two US Army colonels headed the JTF's J2 (intelligence) and J4 (logistics) shops, with the deputy in each being a marine. The J1 (manpower and personnel), J5 (plans and policy), J6 (command, control, communications, and computer systems), and J8 directorates were headed by Marine colonels, three of whom had US Army deputies (the J5 being the exception). Rounding out the staff as Johnston's director of operations, or J3, was Brigadier General Anthony Zinni, USMC, whose impressive résumé included Operation PROVIDE COMFORT, a humanitarian relief effort to help Kurdish refugees in northern Iraq following DESERT STORM.[12]

Once activated, JTF Somalia had operational control over all forces participating in RESTORE HOPE. The United States provided most of these, including elements from the two principal ground combat units, the 1st Marine Division—a logical choice in that it belonged to I MEF— and the Army's 10th Mountain Division at Fort Drum, New York. The Navy and Air Force also provided essential units and personnel for the undertaking (see Figure 2). To fill out the multinational force, 23 countries contributed troops. Arranging for each of these nations to participate was a time-consuming process that the White House and UN had yet to complete by the time JTF Somalia was set to deploy. Johnston, who would have preferred only "four or five brigades' worth of people" from a handful of countries, thus had to devise his coalition strategy without having a comprehensive list of participating countries or the size, shape, and capabilities of the units they would send. Helping to ease his task, the first states to sign up for RESTORE HOPE sent liaison officers (LNOs) to CENTCOM and JTF Somalia headquarters to facilitate planning and to exchange what essential information was available. Despite the initial holes in the coalition order of battle, Johnston adopted at the outset the general guideline that he would assign the larger, better-prepared foreign units to the HRSs outside Mogadishu while restricting smaller, less-capable units to security missions in the Somalian capital.[13]

At its peak, the force General Johnston controlled contained nearly 39,000 military personnel. In determining how to organize this massive force within JTF Somalia, the general had to choose between two doctrinal models: he could adopt a functional framework, which would mean integrating the units and staffs from different services and different countries, or he could have each US service stand as a JTF component—a Marine Force (MARFOR), Army Force (ARFOR), Air Force Force (AFFOR), and Navy Force (NAVFOR). The latter approach had worked well in the Gulf War and in various contingency operations, while the alternative of a single ground combat element, in the general's mind, would result in "ad hoc, pickup teams" that would not automatically "jell." Thus, with two exceptions—the Air Coordination Authority and the Joint Task Force Support Command, both integrated organizations that were attached directly to JTF Somalia headquarters—Johnston decided to go with service components. To limit his span of control, he also decided that some of the foreign units entering the theater, especially the smaller ones, would be attached to a US service component; the others would answer directly to him (see Figure 3).[14]

```
┌─────────────────────────────────────────────────────────────────────────┐
│ USMC (I MEF)                                                      16,200  │
│        4 Infantry Battalions              26 Heavy Lift Helicopters       │
│        1 Artillery Battalion (30x155mm)   12 Medium Lift Helicopters      │
│        1 Tank Battalion (-) (31xM1A1)     16 Attack Helicopters           │
│        1 Amtrack Battalion (-) (68xLVTP-7) 21 Utility Helicopters         │
│        1 Light Armor Vehicle Battalion (28xLAVS)                          │
│ Army (10th Mountain Division)                                     10,200  │
│        3 Light Infantry Battalions        30 Assault Helicopters          │
│        1 Artillery Battalion (12x105mm)   5 Medium Lift Helicopters       │
│                      (6x155mm)            8 - 16 Armed Lift Helicopters    │
│                                                                           │
│ Air Force                         Tactical Airlift Squadron          600  │
│                                                                           │
│ Navy                              3 Amphibious Ships               1,550  │
│                                                                           │
│ Special Operations Forces         1 Special Forces Battalion         350  │
│                                                                           │
│ Total Personnel                                                   28,900  │
│                                                                           │
└─────────────────────────────────────────────────────────────────────────┘
```

Figure 2. US Forces in UNITAF

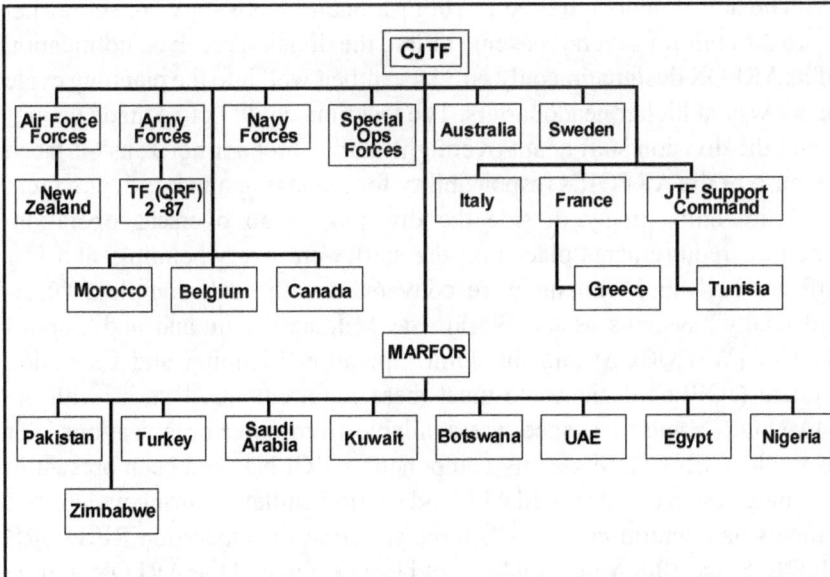

Figure 3. UNITAF Somalia - Command and Control

31

The decision to adopt the component approach to command and control in turn required that another choice be made. Who would serve as commander of each of the two largest components, the MARFOR and the ARFOR? In each case, the officer chosen was the commander of the principal combat unit his service contributed to the operation. Major General Charles Wilhelm, commanding general, 1st Marine Division, became commander, MARFOR, while Major General Steve Arnold, commanding general, 10th Mountain Division, became commander, ARFOR. Being designated as a service component placed additional burdens on both headquarters as the staff in each, besides having to be expanded, was compelled to learn quickly how to deal with an assortment of unfamiliar issues above the tactical level. The 1st Marine Division had something of an advantage over its Army counterpart in making the adjustments. Wilhelm's staff knew as early as 27 November that it was likely to become the MARFOR and was thus able to inject LNOs into the joint planning process in time to contribute to the estimate and courses of action being developed at CENTCOM and, later, at JTF Somalia. An instruction team from the Marine Corps Combat Development Command at Quantico, Virginia, also augmented the 1st Marine Division staff, providing valuable assistance in its transition to a service component.[15]

The adjustments required at 10th Mountain Division were somewhat more difficult for several reasons.[16] First, the division received notification of its ARFOR designation only on 3 December, well into the planning cycle under way at higher headquarters. The lost time could not be made up, nor could the division staff adapt overnight to the "broader horizons" it faced because of the ARFOR's responsibility for managing a major deployment of Army units, many outside the division, to an overseas operation. The new requirements placed on the staff were overwhelming, and few officers in 10th Mountain were conversant with such complex, "user-unfriendly" systems as the Worldwide Military Command and Control System (WWMCCS) and the Joint Operation Planning and Execution System (JOPES) designed to meet these requirements. But, as with the MARFOR, some assistance was available from other organizations. For example, CENTCOM's Army component, ARCENT, had been present in planning sessions at MacDill AFB and Camp Pendleton during which staff officers had determined the US force structure for Operation RESTORE HOPE. Since 10th Mountain had not been designated the ARFOR in time to attend those sessions, ARCENT stepped in to refine the data concerning Army forces and to manage the deployment of the affected units, letting the division provide what input it could through its higher headquarters, the XVIII Airborne Corps at Fort Bragg, North Carolina.

Another problem associated with having a division headquarters serve as an ARFOR centered on the inexperience of 10th Mountain's staff in the joint arena. Thus, the LNOs Arnold sent to Camp Pendleton, like several of the Army staff augmentees who joined them there, were not always prepared to articulate in a joint forum the long-term and short-term requirements of the Army, a "minority service" in JTF Somalia. As Arnold observed later, "We were found to be scratching to try and get Army input into the Joint Task Force OPLAN [operation plan]." Distance further hampered coordination between the JTF and its ARFOR. According to Arnold, he had difficulty finding out "exactly what was being done in California—which is not exactly right out the main gate at Fort Drum, New York."

A variation of this sentiment later found its way into the 10th Mountain's after-action report for Somalia, which complained of "the lack of parallel planning from the strategic to operational to tactical levels." It was a shortcoming that, despite the belated dispatch of LNOs to Camp Pendleton, denied the ARFOR/10th Mountain Division immediate access to updated intelligence; restricted its input on such critical issues as force structure, mission, and end states; and caused last-minute disruptions when decisions made at the strategic or operational level were not communicated immediately to tactical planners.

Despite these difficulties, the joint planning process moved ahead, with Johnston publishing his JTF OPORD on 6 December. Given the synchronization between the CENTCOM and I MEF staffs, Johnston's order reiterated the mission statement and the four-phased concept of operations found in the CINCCENT OPORD of the previous day. The staffs also defined what constituted the "enemy" in Somalia and developed what assessments they could of enemy dispositions, equipment, capabilities, and probable courses of action. In a country that had no functioning government, the armed factions and other gunmen operating in the famine belt clearly presented the most immediate military threat to the troops involved in RESTORE HOPE, but US intelligence officers had only a general idea of the size, leadership, loyalties, and weaponry of the 15 groups analysts identified as being potentially hostile. Initial threat assessments, sketchy as they were, relied heavily on overhead imagery, which offered ample photographs of Somali weapons but little indication of their workability or their owners' intentions. Once coalition forces were on the ground, human intelligence (HUMINT) sources would provide information for a more detailed analysis, but that prospect did nothing to help tactical planners in the predeployment phase.

Thus, while the marines and soldiers set to deploy received a lengthy list of dangers they could expect to encounter, including ambushes, mines, indirect fire, demonstrations, terrorist attacks, and disease, what was less clear was how each Somali faction would respond to the influx of uninvited and well-armed foreign troops into the country. Army officers later criticized strategic planners for failing to consult US Army special forces in Somalia, who, as participants in Operation PROVIDE RELIEF, could have shed some light on the warlords' intentions. In a similar vein, humanitarian relief organizations (HROs) in Somalia expressed surprise that the US military did not contact them for information before executing RESTORE HOPE. Also receiving little attention during the intelligence preparation of the battlefield (IPB) was the degree to which the warring Somali factions were engaged in political maneuvering among themselves at all levels of society. Had analysts better understood this dimension of the crisis, JTF Somalia and the troops under it might have envisioned more clearly the extent to which their mission would take them well outside the realm of strictly military activities.[17]

Within that realm, CENTCOM's threat analysis could not rule out the possibility of US and coalition forces needing to shoot their way into Mogadishu and outlying areas or, once their presence was established, having to contend with daily acts of military defiance. Even if these worst-case scenarios did not materialize, few planners anticipated a completely benign environment, not in a country teeming with weapons, wracked by violence, and dominated by a xenophobic warrior class. Given the probability of some kind of military resistance, how were RESTORE HOPE forces to respond to hostile acts and intentions? To provide guidelines to US troops, especially on the critical question of when to employ deadly force, the CENTCOM and JTF staffs, relying heavily on their staff judge advocates, devised classified rules of engagement (ROE) for the operation that owed much to several reference points: the latitude offered by Chapter VII of the UN Charter, the constraints imposed by international law, and the nontraditional or unorthodox nature of the pending venture.

After the staff work was complete, Hoar and Johnston promulgated ROE that granted every US soldier and marine "the right to use force to defend yourself against attacks or threats of an attack" and to return hostile fire "effectively and promptly." In other words, American troops under Johnston's control could use deadly force not only against "hostile acts" but also against what they perceived as "hostile intent," such as someone they considered unfriendly pointing a weapon at them. Having allowed these basic measures for self-defense, the ROE also placed certain restrictions on the troops, as would be expected in any urban-oriented operation in which thousands of civilians—many friendly or neutral, others hostile—were present. Thus, in the event coalition forces were confronted by civilian rioters or mobs, they were to use only "the minimum force necessary under the circumstances and proportional to the threat." Later, Hoar would explain that the ROE were carefully calculated to convince the Somali factions of the coalition's resolve while giving the "on-scene commander maximum flexibility to determine what constituted a threat and what response was appropriate, including the first use of deadly force." Commanders would also have to determine what constituted the "minimum force necessary" in a variety of situations. In the meantime, 35,000 wallet-size cards containing an unclassified version of basic ROE points were printed at Camp Pendleton for troops in Somalia to use. CENTCOM also made the US ROE available to the coalition forces, who incorporated them with only slight modification into their own ROE.[18]

A more difficult task than devising ROE for operations short of all-out war involves determining the "end state" for such operations. What, in other words, are the conditions that allow one to say that the mission has been accomplished? In the case of Operation RESTORE HOPE, the CINCCENT and JTF OPORDs defined the end state in very general terms: it was the point at which the humanitarian efforts in the country were again functioning in an environment that was stable enough to allow the US-led coalition to turn responsibility for security and relief operations over to the UN (Phase IV in the CINCCENT/JTF concept of operations). But having agreed on this generalization, the planners could not arrive at a set of specific, measurable criteria that would allow the JTF commander or anyone else to know with certainty that the end state had been achieved. Deriving these criteria and determining when they had been met would remain an issue that Johnston's staff had to confront continuously, thus serving as a reminder that no matter how adamantly military headquarters and units demand clear and precise end states before committing to an operation, the complex, dynamic, and ambiguous world in which politico-military endeavors take place rarely proves so accommodating.[19]

Just how complicated the end state issue could be was foreshadowed as the operation was just getting under way. On 11 December, Boutros-Ghali wrote to President Bush, arguing that it was essential for Operation

RESTORE HOPE to disarm all armed factions throughout Somalia. Only then could the secretary general be assured that the environment was secure enough to effect the transition from the US-led coalition to a UN peacekeeping force. The president strongly disagreed, and CENTCOM/JTF Somalia planners deliberately omitted disarmament as a RESTORE HOPE mission or task. As Hoar later explained, "Disarmament was excluded from the mission because it was neither realistically achievable nor a prerequisite for the core mission of providing a secure environment for relief operations." Instead, coalition forces, once on the ground, would attempt only to control the use of various kinds of weapons—"selective 'disarming as necessary,'" in Hoar's words. Furthermore, the selective controls would be enforced only in the southern parts of Somalia occupied by Johnston's forces and not throughout the country. From the beginning of RESTORE HOPE, therefore, the United States and the UN were at odds over the scope of the operation and what it should accomplish. As Johnston later summarized this essential disagreement, "So what we were looking for [was] some short-term fixes, as opposed to trying to solve all of the problems of Somalia."[20] On this basis, it seemed inevitable that the White House and the UN would also disagree, when the time came, over whether the desired end state had in fact been achieved, with a difference of opinion on this point likely to have an adverse effect on a smooth transition from the US-led phase to the follow-on UN phase.

Having some idea of *when* Operation RESTORE HOPE would achieve its end state was a major concern to the Pentagon as well as to President Bush, who, in authorizing the operation, expressed the hope that most US troops would be out of Somalia before President-elect Bill Clinton took the oath of office. Secretary of Defense Cheney quickly dampened the president's unrealistic hopes on this point. Besides, the more pressing issue at hand was getting the troops *into* Somalia, not out. The worrisome question still remained: would coalition forces be able to enter the country peacefully, or would they have to shoot their way in?

Diplomacy provided the answer. As a politico-military operation, RESTORE HOPE needed a ranking statesman on the scene. To that end, Bush appointed Robert Oakley, ambassador to Somalia from 1982 to 1984, to be his special representative in the country. Oakley's expertise on Somalia was unassailable, and while he received no formal guidelines for working with Johnston, his brief was, according to an account he coauthored, "to act as overseer and coordinator of all US civilian activities in Somalia, to provide political advice to UNITAF [a later acronym for Johnston's JTF that stood for Unified Task Force], to act as liaison with the UN special representative [Ismat] Kittani [of Iraq], and to work closely with the NGO community to get humanitarian operations moving."[21]

Oakley immediately demonstrated the indispensable role he would play in the operation. He arrived in Mogadishu on 7 December, the day President Bush ordered CINCCENT to execute Operation RESTORE HOPE. Along with establishing a US Liaison Office (USLO), which provided a formal American diplomatic presence in Somalia, the former ambassador arranged separate meetings with the two key faction leaders in the capital, General Mohamed Farah Aideed of the Habr Gidr subclan and Ali Mahdi Mohamed of the Abgal subclan, each of whom considered control of Mogadishu a critical element in his claim to national leadership. To establish that control, both men maintained or employed armed groups whose weaponry, besides the ubiquitous AK-47 and other small arms, might include rocket-propelled grenades, mortars, some dated artillery pieces, the highly effective "technicals"—jeeps and land cruisers mounted with recoilless rifles, machine guns, and other heavy weapons—and a few US vintage M-41 Walker Bulldog tanks. With this arsenal, the two sides waged war on each other over control of relief supplies and streets and alleyways, in the process killing, extorting, or in many other ways, terrorizing the thousands of noncombatants who inhabited the city. Gunfire, fear, and death were accepted as part of Mogadishu's daily rhythm, and the warriors engaged in the slaughter did not relish outside interference in their internecine conflict.[22]

Oakley's initial diplomatic triumph lay in persuading both Aideed and Ali Mahdi not to resist the arrival of US and coalition forces. After meeting with President Bush's special representative, each leader promised to keep his armed followers away from the proposed landing sites near Mogadishu's new port and airport. A number of observers, both Somali and foreign, praised Oakley's courage and skill but pointed out a downside to his diplomatic feat. In their opinion, his meeting with the two warlords conveyed, perhaps unwittingly, an unspoken message that the incoming multinational force regarded Aideed and Ali Mahdi as legitimate political leaders and that the Americans held these two in higher standing than other Somali political aspirants. (Oakley, in fact, had refused to meet one faction leader, denouncing him publicly as a "cold-blooded murderer.") Johnston, whose troops would be the beneficiaries of Oakley's initiative, had little sympathy for such criticism. "Well, the fact is," he stated later, "the center of gravity is Mogadishu, [and] you've got two major warlords. You had to deal with them. It's that simple." Johnston's staff echoed this sentiment, although many planners wished that Oakley's demarche could have come sooner, in time to adjust the heavy force packages they had designed and deployed on the worst-case assumption that the coalition could find itself engaged in significant fighting.[23]

As it was, the first US combat troops to come ashore as part of Operation RESTORE HOPE did so unopposed. During the predawn hours of 9 December, Navy Sea-Air-Land forces (SEALs), which three days earlier had started conducting clandestine hydrographic and reconnaissance survey missions in the Mogadishu area, slipped ashore near the city's airport. They were followed by 170 marines from the 15th Marine Expeditionary Unit (MEU) (Special Operations Capable) (CENT) attached to the USS *Tripoli* Amphibious Ready Group that had arrived off Somalia the week before. As the SEALs and then the leathernecks crossed the landing beach, they encountered not hostile fire from unfriendly Somalis but a battery of bright lights from camera equipment and a barrage of questions leveled by waiting reporters from the international news media. The chaos and confusion this unexpected spectacle created proved disconcerting to the troops who, at one point mistaking camera flashbulbs for muzzle flashes, almost opened fire. Discipline prevented a tragedy, however, and after some futile efforts to manage the media's disruptive behavior, the marines assembled and moved inland to secure the harbor and airport areas.[24] At 1145, the MEU commander, Colonel Gregory Newbold, declared the airport open, after which a number of his marines went to the American Embassy compound and occupied the site selected for Johnston's headquarters (see Map 2). That headquarters was now called the Combined Joint Task Force (CJTF) Somalia, a title more in keeping with the deploying force's multinational composition. In time, it would receive its final appellation, UNITAF. As the marines secured the embassy, the first plane carrying CJTF headquarters personnel landed at the airport. Operation RESTORE HOPE was under way.

December 1992

Lieutenant General Johnston arrived in Mogadishu the next day. The long list of tasks requiring his immediate attention included setting up his headquarters, establishing contacts with key personnel in the country, managing the influx of US and foreign troops and arranging for their safety, securing critical locations within Mogadishu, assessing the logistic support the operation would require, extending his task forces' (TFs') control into the countryside, and working with HROs to begin getting food to starving Somalis. The initial on-the-ground decisions he and his subordinates made on these and other issues shaped the course of the operation in the months to follow.

38

While addressing these matters, Johnston and his coalition also had to familiarize themselves with the capital itself. Although the headquarters and the deploying troops had no usable maps of the city until well after their arrival, most had received briefings and other warnings of what to expect. Still, when they actually entered Mogadishu, they were appalled at what they found. To be sure, all the physical features of a large urban area were present: public buildings, commercial and business edifices, and a variety of private residences; the matrix of crisscrossing streets, some narrow and primitive, others wide thoroughfares; a major airport and, given the city's coastal location, port facilities; and, of course, the tens of thousands of Somalis living in various neighborhoods and camps around the capital. But with anarchy holding sway in Mogadishu, few public services, such as electricity, running water, and sanitation, were working. The institutions for maintaining law and order were conspicuously absent, as the city's police force and court system had ceased to function. Buildings and homes had been destroyed, others severely damaged and stripped by thieves of any item—wiring, fuel, even corrugated roofs—that could be sold or bartered. Seemingly, every edifice left standing displayed broken windows and shell-pocked walls and doors. Schools were closed, and commercial activity had virtually stopped. Debris, burned-out vehicles, and man-made barricades blocked main avenues, while narrower streets were largely impassable. Vying with these visual images of war, destruction, and destitution was the overpowering stench of garbage, foul sea air, human feces, and death.

Among the inhabitants of Mogadishu, actual starvation was confined to relatively few areas of the city, mainly on the outskirts. Hunger, however, continued to be a widespread problem as long as the factions confiscating the food relief distributed it selectively to their own people. Swelling the ranks of the starving and underfed were those who had fled the famine belt for the city and were surviving as best they could in refugee camps that appeared in almost every open stretch of land. Whether one lived at home, claimed squatter's rights in a vacant dwelling, inhabited a refugee camp, or manned a military compound, the civil war in the capital made daily life precarious. Everyone talked about the "green line" dividing Ali Mahdi's people in northern Mogadishu from Aideed's followers in the south, but, as UNITAF quickly found out, this well-defined physical boundary did not neatly delineate subclan and sub-subclan loyalties. According to a US Marine command chronology, the city "was a hodgepodge of scattered clans, with most people unable to move outside of their immediate neighborhoods." Fear was pervasive, and no night passed without the sound of gunfire being heard somewhere in the city. Given these

39

conditions, it was understandable that many Somalis in the capital greeted the incoming troops with waving arms and smiling faces. Perhaps in some short time there could be a return to something approaching normal life. At least one could hope.[25]

The American Embassy compound where Johnston was setting up his UNITAF headquarters had not been immune from the ravages of the factional conflict in Mogadishu. Evacuated in 1991, much of the multimillion-dollar complex resembled a war area, with stripped and gutted buildings, ankle-deep debris, piles of excrement, and bodies strewn around. The cleanup started at once, and staff officers began to set up shop. Facilities were also created for the other personnel who would work at the headquarters or who would at least visit it regularly. The latter category included political representatives from the USLO and UN, LNOs from the field components and coalition forces, the international news media, representatives from the HROs, and the scores of VIPs who would gravitate to a well-publicized hot spot. With no small amount of physical labor, CJTF Somalia, or as it will be referred to hereafter, UNITAF, quickly became an active, functioning organization. What could not be changed by any amount of toil was the site of the headquarters itself. Located in southern Mogadishu, it was much closer to the part of the city Aideed controlled than to Ali Mahdi's sectors. In the early stages of Operation RESTORE HOPE, Aideed continuously spread the word that this proximity was deliberate and thus provided symbolic evidence that UNITAF favored his claim to national leadership over that of his rivals. Oakley and Johnston went to great lengths to dispel this impression, an unanticipated and irksome annoyance that an accident of local geography had forced upon them.[26]

Besides standing up his headquarters, Johnston moved to address other pressing issues. Recognizing that his mission would be made easier if Aideed and Ali Mahdi continued to honor their pledges not to oppose the intervention, he accepted Oakley's invitation to meet with the two faction leaders on 11 December.[27] It was the first meeting between the warlords since the civil war in Somalia had broken out in full force. Both men agreed to attend only because the site, the USLO building, was located on neutral territory and because a third party, Oakley, had requested the session, thus allowing each leader to avoid the impression that he had been summoned by the other. One topic for discussion centered on ways to prevent unintended clashes between UNITAF troops and the street militia, an issue of primary concern to Johnston. But other, more politically oriented issues were also considered, including the prospects for reconciliation among the warring factions. For this reason, the UN representative, Ismat Kittani, also attended the meeting.

The fact that Johnston remained for the political discussion, even though it ranged far beyond a narrowly defined interpretation of his security mission, was Oakley's doing. Four hours into the meeting, the general complained to Oakley that there were other, more important matters that required his attention. Oakley responded, "No, this is the most important thing you've got to do because they have to understand each other and they have to understand us. It is going to make it much less dangerous as we move ahead." Johnston took the advice and soon acquired the education that went with it: in such a complex environment, one could not hope to compartmentalize political and military matters, much less Somalia's short-term and long-term needs. Consequently, the UNITAF commander was soon telling interlocutors that "it became a much more complicated mission than I ever contemplated. It was more heavily diplomatic than it was military." In an organizational recognition of this fact, he and Oakley established a committee in which they or their representatives would meet daily to coordinate policy. In this way, they could speak with one voice in sending "a clear message" to the factions.[28]

At one point during the 11 December meeting with Aideed and Ali Mahdi, the two archenemies asked that they and their delegations be left alone to confer together. To Oakley's surprise, the private discussions produced a breakthrough of no small significance: a seven-point agreement that each leader signed after the news media had been called in. Among the seven points were calls to end hostilities between the two sides, to cease "all negative propaganda," to break down "the artificial lines" in the capital, and to move each leader's forces and technicals to locations outside the city within 48 hours. In another positive development, Somali leaders requested that a permanent "joint" committee be set up so they and USLO/UNITAF officials could meet daily. Oakley agreed. In his opinion, the dialogue such a forum promised would help the interested parties promote understanding, clarify positions, and avoid surprises.[29]

Oakley later wrote that the signing of the seven-point accord "was the starting point of the US strategy for creating a benign security environment" in Mogadishu. As implemented, that strategy followed a general pattern in which UNITAF and USLO officials, through a combination of persuasion and coercion (one verbal form of the latter being a series of pointed reminders of what US firepower had accomplished in the recently concluded

Gulf War) began pressuring the two warlords and their lieutenants to implement the agreements they had reached and to initiate additional steps that would help end the civil strife, further the humanitarian relief effort, and ultimately set the stage for national reconciliation. In taking this approach, Oakley, Johnston, and their deputies looked first to what they perceived as the two principal points of the 11 December agreement—the cease-fire and the removal of each faction's heavy weapons from the city's streets. Somewhat surprisingly, the cease-fire agreement actually held except for a few minor incidents. The movement of the factions' heavy weapons, including technicals, into designated cantonment areas took until the end of December. Once that was accomplished, UNITAF warned each side that any such weaponry caught on the streets would be "fair game."[30]

While UNITAF and USLO pursued their strategy, Aideed and Ali Mahdi devised their own ways to manipulate the situation that now confronted them. To begin with, each sought to exploit the newly established dialogue for his own purposes while both projected themselves "as responsible national leaders worthy of U.S. support." To illustrate this self-serving maneuvering, both warlords warned UNITAF about the threat of terrorist attacks it faced from the Somali National Islamic Front (NIF), a faction composed of Islamic "fundamentalists" receiving outside support from Iran and Sudan. Aideed even went so far as to propose coordinated military operations in which Johnston's forces and his own would move against the NIF in Mogadishu and elsewhere. UNITAF and USLO, while taking the terrorist threat very seriously and making it a target of intelligence gathering, refused Aideed's offer, thus avoiding "being sucked into an unnecessary confrontation with Islamic groups or developing an anti-Muslim image." In Mogadishu, the NIF and other like-minded groups spewed out propaganda against the United States, the UN, and UNITAF, but the dreaded terrorist attacks never materialized. The whole episode demonstrated, however, the lengths to which the various factions would go in their efforts to manipulate and ingratiate themselves with the powerful military coalition now in their country.[31]

While Johnston was being introduced to the complex political side of his mission, he was also handling more conventional military matters. One involved the arrival of the multinational force under his command, another the continuation of Phase I operations. After the marines had secured Mogadishu's airport on 9 December, a company of French paratroopers landed. Two days later—the day of Johnston's meeting with Oakley, Ali Mahdi, and Aideed—Major General Wilhelm and the MARFOR command element arrived in the capital, as did the 1st Battalion

(-), 7th Marines, with a reinforced rifle company. The battalion's presence in Mogadishu freed a company from Newbold's 15th MEU to mount a heliborne assault to seize an airfield located about 50 miles from the capital in the Baledogle HRS. Because planners believed the facility would take pressure off Mogadishu's airport, they had made taking Baledogle a Phase I objective. To accomplish it, marines flew into the HRS on 13 December. Shortly thereafter, 10th Mountain Division troops from Company A, 2d Battalion, 87th Infantry, landed and, after setting up a TF 2-87 command post, relieved the Marine company.

The prompt arrival of US Army soldiers at Baledogle belied the difficulties the 10th Mountain Division had encountered in deploying the force.[32] There were, of course, the numerous problems the division experienced as the ARFOR, the time crunch of crisis-action planning, the dearth of timely and precise information, and the staff's inexperience in the joint arena and with joint programs. Other complications also arose. Early on, staff officers anticipated that the entire division would deploy, but they later learned that only the 2d Brigade, in its rotation as the division ready brigade, would be sent initially. Moreover, the brigade would deploy with only two of its three battalions—the 2-87th and the 3-14th—a decision that staff officers at Fort Drum blamed on the "arbitrary" ceiling of 10,200 that the secretary of defense had set for the number of US Army troops that could participate in RESTORE HOPE. Both battalions were short of equipment and personnel, but the division's roundout National Guard brigade helped stock the deficient inventories, while personnel shortfalls were handled by the "temporary change of station" process.

During all this, the first train carrying 10th Mountain materiel slated for Somalia departed for the port of Bayonne, New Jersey, on 7 December. As for the troops poised for deployment, they were scheduled to begin leaving Fort Drum on 19 or 20 December. The Air Force assured ARFOR planners that they would have 28 C-141 transport aircraft available each day to get the troops and the priority equipment and supplies to their destinations. Then, on 10 December, the day after the Marine landing at Mogadishu, Arnold and his staff received orders from Johnston's headquarters that a few 10th Mountain units needed to be in Baledogle on the 13th, in effect moving up their departure date by seven days. To make matters worse, the Air Force could only provide three C-141s for the deployment, causing the 2-87th staff to trim drastically the assets it could deploy. This airlift shortage went beyond the immediate deployment to Baledogle, as the division also learned that it would have only 12 C-141s a day, not 28, to move what remained. This meant that some priority materiel would have to be sent by sea. The first two trains that could have carried some of that equipment to the port of Bayonne, however, were already loaded with other items, and one of them had already departed.

Despite these last-minute obstacles, TF 2-87 managed to get airborne and, after a stopover in Egypt, arrived in Baledogle on schedule. That same day, an advance team from Fort Drum arrived in Mogadishu where its leader, Brigadier General Lawson W. Magruder II, the assistant division commander for operations, established liaison with the marines and prepared to receive other 10th Mountain units. These troops began deploying on 15 December, one day before most of the Marine forces started arriving in country. From this point on, Mogadishu airport had to handle a near-continuous stream of US and foreign troop transports, commercial airliners, and assorted aircraft carrying humanitarian aid and military supplies. This increased traffic taxed the facility's air control capabilities to the maximum. Aggravating matters was the ripple effect of the congestion, as planes awaiting permission to land at the airport often had to adjust aerial refueling schedules or use intermediate staging bases. Not until later in the month, after personnel arrived from the Third Marine Aircraft Wing, did Johnston have the people with the expertise to man a joint air control authority (ACA) that could draw up and enforce a strict schedule for arrivals and departures. The fact that the ACA was responsible for commercial as well as military flights only added to its burden.[33]

When Marine and Army units landed, the MARFOR and ARFOR, respectively, assumed responsibility for getting them squared away. Initially, incoming foreign forces that fell under UNITAF or MARFOR control did not receive similar assistance. Johnston, at first, had no comprehensive plan for their employment but often determined assignments only after the units arrived. When possible, he adhered to his desire to confine the smaller coalition elements to security duties in Mogadishu, especially around the airport. Political considerations often intruded, as was the case with the Italian contingent, which Johnston "was not immediately disposed to have . . . in Mogadishu" where, given Italy's colonial experience and its leanings toward Ali Mahdi, the troops risked "polarizing the factions" while alienating younger, anti-imperialist Somalis. While grappling with these mission-oriented considerations, the general also had to confront other, more basic concerns surrounding the growing influx of foreign units. Where would they find billets and staging areas? Where would they get supplies? Who would help them establish liaison with higher headquarters? Who would brief them on their mission and inform them of ongoing developments? How would language barriers be overcome?

The organizational answer to these questions came on 17 December when Major General Wilhelm formed a coalition forces support team (CFST) of more than 50 marines under a full colonel. The team's mission was "to assist newly arrived coalition forces by orienting them to the military situation and the UNITAF structure, coordinating their initial logistical requirements, and providing liaison between their forces and U.S. units." In practice, this translated into developing a set of formal procedures that could then be "tailored to meet the needs of each contingent." These procedures included providing vehicles and communications to support liaison activities; in-processing the forces; building a "transient area" to house arriving units; finding the units staging areas; and presenting each group with tailored briefings containing the pertinent information concerning operations, intelligence, and ROE. Sharing information was a two-way proposition, with CFST personnel relaying what intelligence the coalition forces had to the MARFOR G2 while assessing for UNITAF "the capabilities, political restraints, and views of the commanding officer of each national contingent." Finally, the CFST made sure that the foreign units received any supplies and equipment they needed.[34]

This last requirement depended on the tremendous logistic effort that began soon after the first marines came ashore. Initially, supplies came from the MEU's service support group and from pre-positioned ships. At least two of the ships, however, could neither fit into the harbor nor unload their cargo in rough waters off the coast. Still, very soon after the marines secured the port area on 9 December, one pre-positioned supply ship, the *Lummus*, was unloading its cargo, an arduous and at times less than efficient process given the deplorable condition of the port and the need for trained personnel to manage the offloading. Meanwhile, mechanical problems significantly delayed two of the nine ships transporting priority materiel for the 10th Mountain Division. Other ships carrying heavy combat equipment and weapons, such as artillery, reached Mogadishu only to learn that their cargo would not be unloaded because UNITAF had downgraded the threat facing the coalition. Further complicating supply efforts at the beginning of Operation RESTORE HOPE was that many trained logisticians could not obtain priority seating on the troop transports flying to Mogadishu. The Army's 7th Transportation Group, for example, did not reach the city "until 50 percent of the ARFOR units had already deployed."

In time and with a great deal of effort, the supply situation improved. The port began to operate smoothly after 54 acres had been cleared—in some cases bulldozed—to upgrade its facilities. By the end of December, the docks were handling both military and humanitarian aid cargoes. The Mogadishu airport also streamlined its logistic operations, while the airfield at Baledogle performed its designated role as a second airhead, albeit one in need of frequent repair. To sustain Operation RESTORE HOPE over the long haul, CENTCOM established, under Johnston, the JTF Support Command (JTFSC), a functional organization built around the staff of the US Army's 13th Corps Support Command, headquartered at Fort Hood, Texas. (The fact that the JTFSC was composed exclusively of Army personnel was no small irritant to the ARFOR commander, who believed it should have been placed under his control.) The JTFSC would assume its critical role on D+50. Until then, the marines retained primary responsibility for logistic support, while a Navy rear admiral, with the help of several humanitarian relief personnel, orchestrated use of the port.[35]

As UNITAF established control over the airport, port, and coalition headquarters in Mogadishu and as the buildup of coalition forces accelerated, Johnston concentrated on what he considered to be his "primary mission," securing his troops. The means of achieving force protection in Mogadishu were diverse, beginning with fortifying and continuing to reinforce one's compound, base, checkpoint, or outpost—procedures left to troop commanders, engineer units, and troops. Surprise security inspections from higher headquarters also served as an inducement to keep defenses credible. Another force protection measure was to make sure that UNITAF troops going on patrols or convoys were trained and armed to defeat any military action taken against them. In a similar vein, shows of force reminded the faction leaders of the massive military power UNITAF could turn against them. This was a point Johnston could emphasize during his frequent meetings with these leaders, especially Aideed and Ali Mahdi, as he tried to persuade them to keep their armed followers under control.

The meetings also allowed Johnston to keep faction leaders informed about what weapons they could display in public without risk of drawing coalition fire. To the general's relief, President Bush had not made disarmament a UNITAF mission. A more feasible approach was "weapons control," which meant getting the factions' most dangerous weaponry off the streets. Toward that end, the 11 December agreement between Aideed and Ali Mahdi to place their heavy weapons in designated cantonment areas was a promising start but one that still left the warlords and bandits with small arms and a variety of larger weapons. UNITAF's ROE addressed these circumstances:

> Crew served weapons are considered a threat to UNITAF forces and the relief effort whether or not the crew demonstrates hostile intent. Commanders are authorized to use all necessary force to confiscate and demilitarize crew served weapons in their area of operations. . . . Within areas under the control of UNITAF forces, armed individuals may be considered a threat to UNITAF and the relief effort whether or not the individual demonstrates hostile intent. Commanders are authorized to use all necessary force to disarm individuals in areas under the control of UNITAF. Absent a hostile or criminal act, individuals and associated vehicles will be released after any weapons are removed/demilitarized.[36]

One question this passage from the ROE raised was whether troops could fire on technical vehicles or armed Somalis on sight. Johnston decided against such an interpretation. As a rule, commanders, while expected to assess the risk involved, were not to authorize "all necessary force" until an armed vehicle or individual had been approached and challenged. Given the low level of violence UNITAF forces were encountering, the decision seemed sound. According to one source, "The UNITAF ROE were welcomed by the coalition countries, and generally accepted by Marines and Soldiers of UNITAF as effective and reasonable."[37]

Psychological operations (PSYOP) offered Johnston a less traditional means of force protection. The CINCCENT OPORD had emphasized the importance of employing PSYOP, and within a week of landing in Mogadishu, Army experts in the field joined with USLO officials to publish a Somali-language newspaper and to set up a radio station that broadcast in Somali. The intent of both media was to enhance coalition security by countering hostile propaganda and by calming the fears of many Somalis concerning the purpose and scope of Operation RESTORE HOPE. Additional PSYOP measures included using loudspeaker teams and translators on most UNITAF operations and dropping leaflets over the city (and later over the outlying areas) to inform and, when need be, instruct the local population. As a precautionary measure, PSYOP personnel consulted with Islamic religious leaders in Somalia to ensure that the information UNITAF intended to disseminate would not offend Muslim sensibilities.[38]

As a last resort, force protection could entail the actual use of force, not to change the balance of power between the two main faction leaders but to demonstrate to both the futility of armed resistance. Thus, when technicals located northwest of the embassy compound opened fire on three US helicopters on 12 December, the Marine crews returned fire, destroying two of the armed vehicles and an armored personnel carrier. After the shooting, Oakley called Aideed and Ali Mahdi and said, "I assume that these were not your people, and I'd appreciate it if you'd go on the air with your radios and tell everybody that this was not done by you, that you're not having a war with us. Otherwise it's going to be very dangerous for you." Both leaders did as the special envoy suggested. In this case and others, the use of force was not isolated from diplomacy but an integral part of it. "We never broke off the dialogue," Oakley later reported, a fact that in his mind "avoided building up the most dangerous thing in operations of this kind—an adversarial mentality."[39]

The effectiveness of the various methods Johnston used to enhance force protection depended to a great extent on his intelligence people's ability to formulate a more thorough and accurate threat assessment once coalition forces were on the ground.[40] The US predeployment IPB, the MARFOR G2 quickly discovered, contained critical gaps: "The information on the political situation," he observed, "was sketchy and simplistic at best." The ARFOR staff, once in Mogadishu, echoed this sentiment: "Applying traditional warfighter considerations to Somalia failed to capture the unique character of the operation." Major General Arnold, the ARFOR commander, was even more critical: "So the strategic level IPB was not particularly good. We didn't know much about Mogadishu. We didn't know much about Somalia. We didn't know much about clans, and we didn't know a hell of a lot about the personalities, although we had some information on the clan/faction labels." To this, Zinni, the UNITAF J3, added his succinct observation: "I didn't know Somalis from salamis."

Overhead imagery showed Zinni where each faction located its heavy weapons, but he knew next to nothing about the leaders who owned the weapons, the way they interacted with one another, and, in general, the way Somali society and politics worked. When he entered the country, he later confessed, he naturally brought the individualistic mind-set common to Americans, only to encounter a society geared to communal, not individual, values. In the course of surmounting his initial ignorance of Somali beliefs and values, society, customs and traditions, politics, clans and factions, and personalities, Zinni became a fervid advocate of "cultural intelligence." "All of these societies are tremendously complex," he said in an interview. "Their fabric is complex. Their traditions are complex. Their methods of interrelationships and communications are complex. You have to learn something new every day . . . and every time you learn

48

something, you get better." Johnston made the same points in interviews he gave, noting that "this is a very, very complex environment," in which it was essential for him to know "the political subtleties of clan loyalties [and] of faction leaders who . . . have clan loyalties." Oakley, too, agreed. Without cultural intelligence, he argued, one lacked a meaningful context in which to place the programs, events, issues, negotiations, and activities that arose in the course of any politico-military operation.

Having identified the need for an armed force to understand the foreign society in which it was operating, Zinni lamented the US military's inability to transcend its traditional mind-set in providing relevant predeployment information. "We never do a good job of cultural intelligence," he observed, "of understanding what makes people tick, what their structure is, where authority lies, what is different about their values, and their way of doing business." In the case of Somalia, a near-immediate recognition of this shortcoming resulted in a high-priority task to "determine the nature of the clan and factional alliances within Mogadishu and outlying areas, a task made all the more difficult by the volatile nature of these relationships." As anticipated, an intensive HUMINT effort helped to fill the gaps in cultural intelligence, but before that effort could realize its true potential, it required proficient translators, several of whom were native Somalis living in the United States, as well as counterintelligence teams, few of which were on hand at the outset of the operation. By the end of December, however, these much-in-demand specialists, including many American civilian translators under contract and in uniform, were arriving in country and, along with other duties, working to improve HUMINT networks and procedures. Through "low-level source operations, debriefs of indigenous personnel, screening operations, interrogations and threat analysis via interpreters, humanitarian agencies, official contacts, and firsthand observation," HUMINT allowed intelligence analysts to give Johnston a much better appreciation of what he faced politically and culturally, as well as militarily, not only in Mogadishu but also in the outlying HRSs.

Johnston used this cultural intelligence not only to anticipate better the kinds of threats his forces faced and the kinds of responses that might be appropriate and effective but also, in conjunction with other sources of information, to help the troops adjust more readily to their new, unfamiliar environment. Before and during deployment, many US units had been briefed on Somalia's history and current crisis, but as one company commander observed, the overviews they received were very superficial. Thus, one tasking for PSYOP personnel was to disseminate more detailed information to the troops once they arrived in country. Newsletters and fliers served this purpose, as did a pamphlet the Army quickly published, *The Soldier in Somalia*. Zinni praised the pamphlet as "an outstanding piece of work," a highly accurate "good first cut and appreciation of the environment" that, even if it missed some nuances, at least got the troops better informed on the society and culture in which they were operating. As related to force protection, the idea was that a marine or soldier who understood something of Somalia's culture could interact better with the local population, if only by avoiding the kinds of unintended slights and behavior that might unnecessarily trigger hostility and violence. Most US forces readily grasped this point, realizing from the outset that maintaining a professional and cordial bearing toward the locals, even if one regarded them with suspicion or disdain, would likely expedite the accomplishment of UNITAF's mission.[41]

That mission remained establishing a secure environment in which humanitarian relief could reach those Somalis who needed it. If Johnston devoted special attention and employed a variety of means to protect the force entrusted to him, he did not allow his preoccupation with that issue to interfere with the essential tasks the troops needed to perform. In mid-December, those tasks included increasing the security environment in Mogadishu while, in line with Phase II of the general's concept of operations, sending UNITAF units into the unoccupied HRSs. The security issue in the capital could be addressed in part by having coalition forces expand their military presence beyond the enclaves and main supply routes (MSRs) over which UNITAF had asserted its control in the first days of the operation. To that end, Major General Wilhelm, his deputy, and his operations cell at MARFOR headquarters produced a four-phase program, the first phase of which envisaged using combat engineers and Seabees to clear obstacles from Mogadishu's MSRs. This action allowed coalition vehicles to move more freely around the city. Not insignificantly, clearing the MSRs would also give the Somalis easier access to street markets once the urban environment became safe enough for people to venture out at will.[42]

Although the MARFOR plan for opening the MSRs was ready by late December, Wilhelm did not execute it until Johnston had moved to occupy and, to some degree, secure the HRSs outside Mogadishu and Baledogle. From the beginning of Operation RESTORE HOPE, Johnston had been under pressure to send troops into the interior. With coalition units landing in full sight at Mogadishu's airport, the news media and several HROs began asking why those forces were not rushing to the famine-stricken areas. The dire situation, they charged, demanded urgent action. Even in the Pentagon, gratuitous remarks began to surface about the marines being "too slow." It was, in Johnston's words, as if people were saying, "Just send a half a dozen Marines up there and everything [will] be wonderful." Such wishful thinking, while stemming from noble sentiments, made for unsound military advice. To rush into an operation invited unforeseen and possibly disastrous consequences. "We don't do business that way," the general proclaimed. As far as UNITAF headquarters was concerned, RESTORE HOPE was on schedule. Until he had a concrete plan, a better threat assessment, and adequate firepower, Johnston tried to resist what he perceived as increasing pressure on him to launch the next phase of his plan prematurely.

As one commentator summarized the situation, "From the humanitarian perspective, the Marines were moving at a glacial pace. From the military perspective, however, the Marines were 'smokin.'" The impasse broke after a week. The agreement between Aideed and Ali Mahdi, the lack of resistance in Mogadishu, and, as Johnston candidly admitted, the mounting calls for action caused him to accelerate his original timetable for moving into the outlying HRSs. As he revealed in a later interview, "I did not want that media pressure to be translated into JCS pressure to make us do things militarily. So, I was anxious to sort of move the tempo and the momentum to the extent we could do it and still secure the force."[43]

Movement into the countryside began in earnest three days after marines seized the Baledogle airfield. On 16 December, US Marine and French units calling themselves TF Hope mounted an air-ground assault on the airfield at Baidoa, the town called the "city of death" because of the ravages of famine, disease, and war it had suffered. Upon their arrival, coalition officers, including civil affairs personnel, began conferring with the town elders, and the next afternoon, the first UNITAF-escorted convoy in the interior got under way with 14 armed vehicles moving from the airfield to the town to deliver food to a local orphanage. One journalist described the show of force as "embarrassing overkill," but to a US Marine officer on the scene, the "light display of authority [demonstrated] that we can carry out our mission." The success of the Baidoa operation led Johnston to declare that Phase I of RESTORE HOPE, establishing and securing lodgments in and around Mogadishu, had been completed.[44]

As TF Hope moved on Baidoa, UNITAF was planning similar operations into Kismayo and other HRSs. What made Kismayo important—so much so, in fact, that the operation was given a higher priority than originally intended—was that it contained a large port and an airfield, both of which Johnston desperately needed to supplement Mogadishu's facilities for handling incoming troops and materiel. UNITAF also needed to establish an armed presence in the city and HRS because of the continued fighting there between General Said Hersi "Morgan," Siad Barre's son-in-law, and Omar Jess, an Aideed ally who controlled the city and its valuable port. The port's importance determined the method used to establish UNITAF's presence, as Johnston directed US Navy elements off the coast to mount an amphibious operation to seize the city. He also placed the commander of a Belgian parachute battalion in charge of the landing force, which included a US Marine rifle company and two Belgian platoons. Like the marines, the Belgians had "sound experience in amphibious doctrine," and on the morning of 20 December, after Navy SEALs had reconnoitered the beach area, the landing force came ashore and took its objectives without incident. The Belgian commander and the amphibious TF commander then met with Jess, who, while protesting the presence of "colonial" Belgians, made no attempt to resist the incoming force. After several days, ARFOR units under Brigadier General Magruder's TF Kismayo relieved the marines—the Belgians stayed in the HRS—and assumed responsibility for security in the city.[45]

Throughout the rest of December, the other HRSs were secured in operations that, in general terms, bore a striking resemblance to one another. UNITAF would assemble a joint or multinational force on the basis of what units were available and the capabilities of each, plan the operation with staff officers and LNOs from the units involved, and issue a fragmentary order to the appropriate commanders. Before the order's execution, Oakley (or his representative) would travel to the HRS and meet with "a broad cross-section of the local population." In each case, he repeated what he had done so effectively in Mogadishu. He talked to the clan elders, military commanders, religious and local political leaders, and women's groups, reassuring them of RESTORE HOPE's benevolent intentions and America's respect for Islam, and, if necessary, persuading those in charge not to resist inserting foreign troops. An airdrop of PSYOP leaflets often followed to reinforce this dialogue. Then came the military operation in which the designated units would make their way by air, land, or sea—or some combination of the three—to the objective, landing first at an airfield (and, if on the coast, a port), securing the facility, and then moving patrols into the central city. Despite the near certainty of a peaceful entry, the troop insertion was planned as a combat operation, with fire support, medical evacuation, long-range communications, and air support on hand to support the combat element. Once the troops had secured the area, however, further PYSOP initiatives were conducted to emphasize again the peaceful nature of RESTORE HOPE. In this manner, all nine HRSs (the ninth being a late addition of Marka to the original list of eight) had UNITAF troops on the ground by the end of the month, providing security for humanitarian relief efforts. Some HRSs, including Mogadishu, were occupied by US and foreign units under the MARFOR; others such as Kismayo and Belet Uen were secured by US and foreign units under the ARFOR. Over time, the initial division of responsibility between UNITAF's two main components changed frequently, generally without friction. MARFOR-ARFOR cooperation across HRS boundaries also became routine, with common sense often overriding doctrine if the former promised to avoid complications or friction.[46]

As coalition forces consolidated their presence in Mogadishu and moved into the other HRSs, they made contact with the HROs throughout southern Somalia. It was these 50 or so groups that UNITAF was there to protect as they went about the dangerous business of receiving and delivering food and other supplies throughout the famine belt. Providing that protection, however, proved more difficult than expected. The charters of some humanitarian groups prohibited them from working with the military. Other HROs preferred not to work with the military or feared that such ties would undermine their credibility with some of the people they sought to serve. In some cases, an HRO's way of doing business clashed with the military's approach. There was also the matter of security. Some humanitarian groups had hired Somali gunmen with their technicals to guard convoys and relief sites, even though these "guards" often turned around and plundered or extorted the organizations they were being paid to protect. From the UNITAF perspective, the presence of these armed security forces contradicted the command policy of getting heavy weapons off city streets. Johnston's troops, however, could not disarm these "technical advisers" without leaving the HROs that employed them completely defenseless. UNITAF's initial efforts to exchange its protection for that of the local gunmen enjoyed some limited success but only when the HROs involved agreed to relocate their headquarters within areas coalition troops controlled, something that some groups would not or could not do.[47]

To improve operational coordination between the military and the HROs, as well as to help bridge the "cultural gap" between the two groups, Johnston and Oakley requested that a Civil-Military Operations Center (CMOC) be set up in Mogadishu and collocated with the Humanitarian

Operations Center (HOC) at the UNOSOM headquarters—a nod to the UN's long-term responsibility for relief operations—10 minutes from UNITAF's headquarters at the embassy. According to the account of Operation RESTORE HOPE by Oakley and John Hirsch, UNITAF's political adviser:

> The objective was to share information on the latest security developments; explain UNITAF ground rules and operational plans; coordinate humanitarian assistance activities, especially the protection for food convoys within Mogadishu and moving to the interior; and provide an opportunity for information exchange, coordination, and cooperation on humanitarian operations generally.[48]

Initially, the CMOC in Mogadishu served mainly as a forum in which the marines received and coordinated HRO requests for convoy security. Quickly, however, the organization became the focal point for UNITAF-HRO interaction on a variety of security issues. Some of these issues, such as continuing to use armed Somalis for HRO protection, proved difficult to resolve. For some HROs, the CMOC seemed more a liaison organization, given that the military representatives had to report back to UNITAF, than "an operations center at which people solved problems at the same table." Thus, the CMOC/HOC arrangement never quite bridged the cultural gap or ended the friction between the military and the humanitarian groups. But on the whole, the results were more positive than negative, with the CMOC receiving high praise. Several civilian veterans of humanitarian operations claimed that it offered the best NGO-military interface they had ever witnessed. Johnston shared this view, directing the forces under his control to set up local CMOCs whenever they established their presence in an HRS.[49]

UNITAF forces had established that presence in all of the HRSs by the end of December, weeks ahead of schedule, allowing Johnston to declare Phase II of Operation RESTORE HOPE completed on 28 December. Three days later, the last of the major US Marine combat units arrived in Mogadishu. In looking to the months ahead, the prospects were mixed. On the negative side, UNITAF involvement in securing the humanitarian relief mission was only getting started, and southern Somalia as a whole was not yet secure. Indeed, UNITAF troops throughout their first month on the ground routinely became targets of factional violence, mostly in the form of inaccurate but annoying sniper fire, occasionally punctuated by something more serious. On the positive side, UNITAF had made its presence felt, the humanitarian relief program would soon kick into high gear, and in most areas, including Mogadishu, the violence showed signs of subsiding as faction leaders accepted the fact that they were outgunned by the coalition force. The threat of a serious military challenge to UNITAF forces thus seemed remote. On New Year's Eve and New Year's Day, President Bush made a morale-building visit to the troops, reassuring them that their mission was "limited" and that they would not "stay forever."[50] Operation RESTORE HOPE was definitely on track. It was now just a matter of taking the momentum built up in Phases I and II and applying it to Phases III and IV of the mission. Many troops who had deployed to Somalia had missed Christmas with their families and friends. It seemed highly unlikely that they would miss Easter as well.

Notes

This chapter is based on unclassified material ranging from published works to official histories, after-action reviews (AARs), and documents. Of special assistance in writing this and the following chapter was a draft of a manuscript on UNITAF being prepared for publication by Colonel Dennis P. Mroczkowski, USMCR, Retired. Mroczkowski graciously allowed me to use the manuscript, which has the working title *The United States Marines in Somalia: With the Unified Task Force During Operation Restore Hope*. As my citations indicate, I referred to this work often.

1. Robert B. Oakley, "An Envoy's Perspective," *Joint Force Quarterly* [hereafter *JFQ*] (Autumn 1993), 45; John L. Hirsch and Robert B. Oakley, *Somalia and Operation Restore Hope: Reflections on Peacemaking and Peacekeeping* (Washington, DC: U.S. Institute of Peace Press, 1995), 42-43.

2. Sources differ as to the number of Somalis who died from starvation and disease during 1991 and 1992, but most place the number over 200,000 or 300,000. For this account, I relied on those figures cited in Lynn Thomas and Steve Spataro, "Peacekeeping and Policing in Somalia," *Policing the New World Disorder: Peace Operations and Public Security*, Robert B. Oakley, Michael J. Dziedzic, and Eliot M. Goldberg, eds. (Washington, DC: National Defense University Press, 1998), 181. Thomas and Spataro cite UN sources for the figures they use.

Some accounts maintain that by the time the Bush administration considered military intervention in Somalia, the worst of the famine had passed, although disease caused by starvation was on the rise. This point was made not to argue that the US intervention was unnecessary, only that it was late in coming. All accounts agree that Operation RESTORE HOPE saved thousands of Somalis from dying of starvation and disease. See Chris Seiple, *The U.S. Military/NGO Relationship in Humanitarian Interventions* (Carlisle Barracks, PA: Peacekeeping Institute, U.S. Army War College, 1996), 106; Scott Peterson, *Me Against My Brother: At War in Somalia, Sudan, and Rwanda* (New York: Routledge, 2001), 52.

3. Hirsch and Oakley, 40-42. Of course, not everyone offering advice came to accept the arguments for intervention. *U.S. News & World Report*, for example, printed excerpts from a message from the American ambassador in Kenya to the State Department warning against embracing "the Somali Tarbaby." The chaotic situation in Somalia, he stated, was beyond "the quick fix so beloved of Americans." *Associated Press* story, 5 December 1992.

4. Hirsch and Oakley, 43; Oakley, 45; Colin L. Powell and Joseph E. Persico, *My American Journey* (New York: Random House, 1995), 564-65.

5. Hirsch and Oakley, 44-47. The text of UN Security Council (UNSC) Resolution 794, 3 December 1992, can be found in Ibid., 177-81. The text of President Bush's speech is contained in *U.S. Department of State Dispatch* (4 January 1993), 5.

6. Oral History Interview RHIT-JHT-048, Major General Steven Lloyd Arnold, 26 February 1993, Mogadishu, Somalia, interviewed by Major Robert K. Wright, Jr., USAR, and Captain Drew R. Meyerowich. Arnold was commanding general of the US Army 10th Mountain Division.

7. Hirsch and Oakley, 42-43; I Marine Expeditionary Force (MEF) Command Chronology, 27 November 1992 to 28 February 1993, section 3, "Chronological Listing of Significant Events," copy in archives of the U.S. Marine Corps Historical Center, Navy Yard, Washington, DC; Jay Hines, Jason D. Mims, and Hans S. Pawlisch, *USCENTCOM in Somalia: Operations PROVIDE RELIEF and RESTORE HOPE* (MacDill AFB, FL: U.S. Central Command History Office, November 1994), 21; Robert B. Oakley and David

Tucker, *Two Perspectives on Interventions and Humanitarian Operations*, Earl H. Tilford, Jr., ed. (Carlisle Barracks, PA: Strategic Studies Institute, 1997), 4. The NCA consists of the president and the secretary of defense or their duly deputized alternates.

8. The Operation RESTORE HOPE mission statement is quoted in Major General Waldo D. Freeman, USA; Captain Robert B. Lambert, USN; and Lieutenant Colonel Jason D. Mims, USA, "Operation Restore Hope: A US CENTCOM Perspective," *Military Review* (September 1993), 64.

9. Hines et al., 22-23.

10. Joseph P. Hoar, "A CINC's Perspective," *JFQ* (Autumn 1993), 58.

11. On organizing the JTF headquarters, see Katherine A.W. McGrady, CRM 93-114, *The Joint Task Force in Operation Restore Hope* (Alexandria, VA: Center for Naval Analysis, March 1994), 4-5.

In an interview with Army historians during Operation RESTORE HOPE, Johnston expressed some second thoughts about trying to create a "totally purple" staff in the midst of crisis-action planning. Better, he reflected, to ask for only those officers from other services who are essential. As examples, he cited the wisdom of having Army officers for the intelligence and logistic sections and an Air Force officer for strategic airlift. But he questioned whether a Marine staff director should have an Army deputy or vice versa just for the sake of integrating the JTF. The bottom line: "We're trying to validate, What the hell does a joint JTF headquarters look like for an operation like this?" Oral History Interview RHIT-JHT-085, Lieutenant General Robert B. Johnston, USMC, 12 March 1993, Mogadishu, Somalia, interviewed by Lieutenant Colonel Charles H. Cureton, USMCR, and Major Robert K. Wright, Jr., USAR.

12. The selection of the key staff directors is covered in more detail in Mroczkowski, chapter 2.

The potential for friction in the JTF headquarters arising from the fact that Zinni outranked the other staff directors, including Johnston's chief of staff, all of whom were full colonels, never materialized. According to Zinni, Johnston believed that the large coalition force that would participate in RESTORE HOPE made it essential that he have a general officer as his J3. Oral History Interview RHIT-JHT-081, Brigadier General Anthony C. Zinni, 11 March 1993, Mogadishu, Somalia, interviewed by Lieutenant Colonel Charles H. Cureton, USMCR, and Major Robert K. Wright, Jr., USAR.

13. Oral History Interview RHIT-JHT-085.

14. Ibid.; Mroczkowski, chapter 2.

15. I MEF Command Chronology, 27 November 1992 to 28 February 1993, section 2, "Narrative Summary," 1-2.

16. The account of the difficulties the 10th Mountain Division encountered in assuming the role of ARFOR is based on Center for Army Lessons Learned (CALL), *Operation Restore Hope* (Fort Leavenworth, KS: CALL, 16 August 1993), I-10-13, IV-2-3, 5-6; U.S. Army Forces Somalia, 10th Mountain Division (LI), *After-Action Report Summary*, 2 June 1993, 4-5, 18.

The issue of designating a division as an ARFOR is controversial, with many arguing that the staff is simply not large or experienced enough to handle the additional responsibilities. The 10th Mountain Division maintained that a division was, in fact, capable of serving in that capacity but only if given timely notification, additional staffing (especially for deployment and scheduling purposes), and adequate time for planning along doctrinal (meaning *parallel*) lines. See CALL, IV-15-18; U.S. Army Forces Somalia, 10th Mountain Division (LI), 6.

17. This brief summary of the threat assessment is based on Mroczkowski, chapter 3; Task Force Mountain briefing slides on Operation RESTORE HOPE, no date; U.S.

Army Forces Somalia, 10th Mountain Division (LI), 3-5; Oral history interview with David Dawson, 29 January 2003, MacDill AFB, Florida, interviewed by Dr. Larry Yates, hereafter cited as Dawson interview; Seiple, 111.

18. Mroczkowski, chapter 3; Lieutenant General Robert Johnston, USMC, briefing slides on United Task Force Somalia, no date; Freeman et al., 64-65; Hoar, 58; I MEF Command Chronology, section 2, 2; Colonel F.M. Lorenz, USMC, "Rules of Engagement in Somalia: Were They Effective?" *Naval Law Review* (1995), 61-78; Colonel F.M. Lorenz, USMC, "Law and Anarchy in Somalia," *Parameters* (Winter 1993-94), 30.

19. Mroczkowski, chapter 3; CALL, I-4.

20. Hirsch and Oakley, 47; Hoar, 58; Oral History Interview RHIT-JHT-085.

21. Hirsch and Oakley, 49-50.

22. Ibid., 54; Oakley and Tucker, 4. For a gripping depiction of the violence, terror, and slaughter that took place daily in Mogadishu during the civil war between Ali Mahdi and Aideed, see Peterson, 19-35.

23. On the criticism surrounding Oakley's "embracing" Aideed and Ali Mahdi by meeting with them, see Ibid., 58-59. Johnston's reaction is in his Oral History Interview RHIT-JHT-085. Several ARFOR staff officers voiced criticism, not of Oakley's achievement but of the failure to employ HUMINT assets in Somalia to determine the factions' passive intentions well before the ambassador's visit.

24. Several Army officers watching the landings on television together were "sickened and outraged" by what they regarded as the journalists' irresponsible behavior and the risks the media thus created for the landing party. As one of the group later wrote, "I vowed privately that if anyone did that to me, I'd break every light set out there and maybe a few cameramen too." What was not well known at the time was that a US official had told the journalists where the landing would take place, and the press had received guidelines on how to behave when the troops came ashore. One journalist claimed that Oakley had directed the reporters to the landing sites. Oakley, in turn, later placed responsibility at the feet of "U.S. military sources eager for good publicity but who had failed to inform the landing teams that the media would be on hand." In any case, as one observer noted, it was "a made-for-TV event." See Martin Stanton, *Somalia on $5.00 a Day: A Soldier's Story* (Novato, CA: Presidio Press, 2001), 75; Dawson interview; Peterson, 54; Oakley and Tucker, 4.

For a concise overview of the role special operations forces, including Navy SEALs, played in Operation RESTORE HOPE, see U.S. Special Operations Command (USSOCOM), *USSOCOM History* (MacDill AFB, FL: USSOCOM History and Research Office, nd), 43-45.

25. Mroczkowski, chapter 4; I MEF Command Chronology, section 2, 2-3.

26. Mroczkowski, chapter 4; Hirsch and Oakley, 60. One source indicates that improvements to the embassy compound during the course of UNITAF and UNOSOM II came to $50 million. See Peterson, 79.

27. Unless otherwise noted, the account of the 11 December meeting and its ramifications is contained in Hirsch and Oakley, 55-59.

28. For Oakley's advice, see Robert Oakley, "The Urban Area During Support Missions Case Study: Mogadishu—The Strategic Level," *Capital Preservation: Preparing for Urban Operations in the Twenty-First Century*, Russell W. Glenn, ed. (Santa Monica, CA: RAND, 2001), 324. On Johnston's realization of the politico-military nature of his assignment, see his Oral History Interview RHIT-JHT-085. See also Mroczkowski, chapter 5.

29. The seven-point agreement is reprinted as an appendix in Hirsch and Oakley, 183. On the origin and usefulness of the USLO/UNITAF/Somalia committee, see Oakley, "The Urban Area During Support Missions Case Study: Mogadishu—The Strategic Level," 324.

30. Besides Hirsch and Oakley, see Mroczkowski, chapter 5.

31. Hirsch and Oakley, 84-85.

32. This summary of the problems ARFOR/10th Mountain Division planners encountered in getting the first troop units to Somalia is based on Oral History Interview RHIT-JHT-048; CALL, 4-11, I-2-3, II-4-5, IV-1-6; Stanton, 71-72; U.S. Army Forces Somalia, 10th Mountain Division (LI), 1, 4-6, 18.

33. Mroczkowski, chapter 5; Memorandum for Record, Commander, UNITAF Somalia, to Potential Users of Somali Airspace, Subj: Control of Somali Territorial Airspace, no date, copy obtained from U.S. Army Center of Military History (CMH), Washington, DC; I MEF Command Chronology, section 2, 2-3, 19; McGrady, 55-59.

34. The summary of how UNITAF and the MARFOR handled incoming foreign troops, including the CFST's mission and activities, is based on Johnston's Oral History Interview RHIT-JHT-085 and I MEF Command Chronology, section 2, 44-46. David Dawson, who as a Marine captain served briefly in Mogadishu as the UNITAF historian and for a longer period as the MARFOR historian, tempers these accounts with his own observation that many US staff officers and troops involved with the coalition knew little of such basics as the proper names of ranking foreign commanders and the proper designations of the units they commanded. While some soldiers and marines simply dismissed foreign troops who were not well equipped, well trained, or highly motivated, others tried to work closely with them, providing them incentives for playing a more active role when possible. See Dawson interview.

35. For the account of logistics in Operation RESTORE HOPE, see Ibid.; Kenneth Allard, *Somalia Operations: Lessons Learned* (Washington, DC: National Defense University Press, 1995), 46-50; Mroczkowski, chapters 2 and 4; Hirsch and Oakley, 59; Oral History Interview RHIT-JHT-085; Oral History Interview RHIT-JHT-048; CALL, 6-7, II-1-5; Oakley and Tucker, 6. In the last publication cited, CALL concluded that the "nature of the operation was such that [combat support], [combat service support], and Civil Affairs units should have had an equal, if not greater, priority during deployment than the combat units." CALL also supported Arnold's position that the JTFCS, composed entirely of Army elements, should have been placed under ARFOR and that the failure to do so, besides violating doctrine, severely disrupted ARFOR's airlift allocation. Transports originally assigned to deploy 10th Mountain units were taken from ARFOR's allotment to transport the JTFCS, which, again, was not under ARFOR's control.

36. Lorenz, "Rules of Engagement in Somalia: Were They Effective?" 64.

37. Ibid. For a fuller discussion of disarmament versus weapons control, see the next chapter.

38. Mroczkowski, chapter 5; Hirsch and Oakley, 61-63; Johnston briefing slides.

39. Oral History Interview RHIT-JHT-085; CMH, *Resource Guide, Unified Task Force Somalia, December 1992-May 1993, Operation Restore Hope* (Washington, DC: CMH, 1994), 108; Oakley, "The Urban Area During Support Missions Case Study: Mogadishu—The Strategic Level," 325-26.

40. This summary of intelligence requirements that emerged once Operation RESTORE HOPE commenced is based on I MEF Command Chronology, section 2, 22-23; CALL, 5-6, I-5; U.S. Army Forces Somalia, 10th Mountain Division (LI), 3-4, 30-31; Oral History Interview RHIT-JHT-048; Oral History Interview JHT-RHIT-081; briefing by Major General Anthony Zinni, Fort Leavenworth, Kansas, 1994, hereafter cited as Zinni briefing; Oral History Interview RHIT-JHT-085; Oakley, "Urban Area," 318; Interview with Colonel Stephen Spataro, 24 February 2003, Fort Leavenworth, Kansas, interviewed by Dr. Larry Yates.

41. Oral History Interview JHT-RHIT-081.

42. I MEF Command Chronology, section 2, 6-7.

43. Seiple, 122-25; Oral History Interview RHIT-JHT-085.

44. Mroczkowski, chapter 4; Hines et al., 25; Peterson, 62.

45. Oral History Interview RHIT-JHT-085; Mroczkowski, chapter 4; CMH, 110-13.

46. Hines et al., 24-27; Hirsch and Oakley, 69, 71; Mroczkowski, chapter 4; U.S. Army Forces Somalia, 22.

One case in which the common-sense rule prevailed was in determining command and control arrangements for convoys leaving an HRS controlled by ARFOR or MARFOR troops and entering an HRS controlled by the other component. Rather than engage in elaborate handoffs, it was determined that whoever was responsible for a convoy's security when it set out would remain the responsible party after it crossed the boundary.

47. Zinni briefing. The term "technicals," referring to the armed vehicles employed by Somali bandits and factional militia, was a fallout of the NGOs referring to the armed personnel they hired for protection as "technical advisers."

48. Hirsch and Oakley, 66.

49. I MEF Command Chronology, section 2, 3; Seiple, 113-30; CMH, 117.

50. Seiple, 108.

60

Chapter 3

Operation RESTORE HOPE
Phases III and IV, December 1992-May 1993

Lawrence A. Yates

Phase III of Operation RESTORE HOPE, the "stabilization phase," contained the essence of the UNITAF mission—providing security for the effort to get food and other forms of humanitarian relief to Somalis suffering throughout the famine belt. This segment of the operation, as expected, overlapped to some degree with the first two phases and would continue until UNITAF gave way to UNOSOM II on 4 May 1993. The transition that day from a US-led coalition to a UN peace-keeping force in Somalia signaled another milestone: the completion of RESTORE HOPE's fourth and final phase.

Stabilization

As 1993 opened, optimism ran high that UNITAF could accomplish the last two phases in its concept of operations expeditiously. Phases I and II, entailing the lodgment of coalition forces in Mogadishu, Baledogle, and the main cities and towns of the outlying HRSs, had been successfully executed against minimal resistance. The matrices of color-coded indicators that US staff officers devised to measure progress, or the lack thereof, pointed with confidence to the future. Through a determined yet flexible approach, it seemed the coalition could consolidate its initial gains, extend UNITAF's reach into the more isolated areas of each HRS, work with UN officials on the handoff to UNOSOM II, and then, having been instrumental in ending a human tragedy, withdraw without further ado.

In discussing the means to achieve these goals, Brigadier General Anthony Zinni, UNITAF's director of operations, separated the myriad of activities engaging coalition forces and other outside organizations in Somalia into three broad categories: military, humanitarian, and political. Military concerns dealt mainly with security issues; humanitarian activities, while concentrating on immediate relief measures, occasionally addressed the long-term requirement to reconstruct parts of the country; and political initiatives sought to achieve limited but utilitarian accommodations among the warring factions while supporting, when possible, the broader and more precarious process of national reconciliation. Activities in all three categories took place at different political and societal levels and in

61

different geographical areas, thereby complicating matters and requiring some decentralized execution of general policies. Thus, while Zinni maintained that "These three tracks have to work exceptionally close to each other, and in parallel," he would find occasion to lament that this was not always the case.[1] Still, if the parties involved could achieve some progress along each track, it was possible that the situation in Somalia could be stabilized to the point that the follow-on UN peace-keeping force might anticipate a fair chance of success for its much more complex and comprehensive mission of nation building.

The military element. Of Zinni's three categories, UNITAF naturally concentrated on the military track, especially the requirement to provide security for its own forces and for an assortment of disparate groups: the HROs and NGOs engaged in humanitarian efforts; the officials tackling diplomatic problems; VIPs on the scene and a host of visiting dignitaries, prominent Somali political, military, and religious leaders; and the Somali people themselves. The methods used to achieve this security varied, as did the levels of success attained. From the outset, the coalition employed the strategy of "deconfliction," as Zinni termed it, one facet of which began with presidential envoy Robert Oakley's pre-intervention meetings with Aideed and Ali Mahdi and expanded once Lieutenant General Robert Johnston, the UNITAF commander, joined the talks after his arrival. This dialogue with faction leaders and their representatives continued throughout RESTORE HOPE and found its organizational underpinning in two committees created early in the process. One, the political committee, provided the venue for Oakley and other USLO officials to meet regularly with prominent Somalis in Mogadishu. The second, the security committee, included military officers from each of the factions, with Zinni and his staff usually representing UNITAF. Discussions in the security committee addressed numerous topics, with one aim being to anticipate and defuse "potential conflicts" and "potential confrontations." Negotiations were often delicate, with Zinni striving to "separate the politics from the security issues," a "very difficult" procedure given their close relationship but a necessary one if UNITAF hoped to avoid the impression of "showing favoritism to one side or the other." Maintaining UNITAF's impartiality was, according to Zinni, "hard work." "Many of the factions would like us to condemn their adversaries or to openly show that we are siding with them," he observed. "We want a sense of cooperation with each of the factions from a military and security perspective." The pursuit of this goal produced a generally productive dialogue in both committees, enabling Oakley to conclude later that, despite recurring difficulties, the "strategy of seeking cooperation, avoiding direct confrontation if possible, and gradually increasing pressure on all factions seemed to be working."[2]

One issue discussed in the security committee was variously called "weapons control," "weapons collection," or "selective disarmament," all terms UNITAF employed as an alternative to "total disarmament," which Johnston, from the outset, had no intention or mandate to implement. As noted in the previous chapter, he and his superiors fully understood that any attempt to disarm the warring factions completely would have encumbered UNITAF with a host of unwanted and near insurmountable challenges. To begin with, coalition forces were confined to southern Somalia and could not disarm the factions there without placing them at a disadvantage vis-à-vis their rivals to the north. Similarly, a disarmament program in UNITAF-occupied areas of the south would have to be implemented in a way that would avoid giving an advantage to one faction over another. Such an impartial and simultaneous approach in so complex a political and military environment was not feasible during the short time UNITAF planned to be in the country.

Posing another obstacle to complete disarmament, there were simply too many weapons in Somalia. During the Cold War, first the Soviet Union and then the United States had flooded the country with arms, and Somali fighters had grown accustomed to the vast array of firepower made available to them. "If you think the National Rifle Association has a fixation regarding weapons," Oakley once remarked, "it's nothing compared to the Somalis. It's part of their manhood. And they learn how to use them." Personal security also bonded a Somali male with his weapon. As Zinni later recounted, Aideed relied on the AK-47 and pistol he carried to protect himself and his family. He and tens of thousands of other Somali males, imbued with a warrior mentality and confronted by daily threats, could not surrender these small arms without placing themselves and their relatives in grave danger. Nor could UNITAF hope to find all the weapons caches in Mogadishu or any other part of the country. In the estimate of Major General Steven Arnold, the 10th Mountain Division commander, "We think that we would be here for ten years to disarm Somalia and not be finished."[3]

Given these conditions, Johnston, Oakley, and Zinni, with the backing of CINCCENT, advocated a more realistic approach, one of placing restrictions and controls on the weapons faction leaders had in their inventories and on the streets. In Mogadishu, the 11 December agreement between Aideed and Ali Mahdi to remove their technical vehicles to cantonments, or Authorized Weapons Storage Sites (AWSS), where coalition forces could monitor them, served as a promising start, and both warlords had complied with the agreement by the end of December. In mid-February, Ali Mahdi took the additional step of relinquishing his cantoned technicals to UNITAF, signifying to Oakley that the Somali leader would thereafter seek to further his influence through political means. At the same time, however, many of Aideed's technicals disappeared from his AWSSs, having been relocated to undisclosed areas outside the city. This development troubled Johnston and Oakley, but not to the point of recommending punitive action "so long as [the weapons] posed no threat to UNITAF forces or humanitarian operations and so long as UNITAF was able to confiscate weapons found in the course of its operations without setting off a fight with the faction that owned them."[4] Their assessment reflected the view that the coalition's weapons control policy served as both a force protection measure and a means to create the secure environment mandated in the RESTORE HOPE mission.

Beyond Mogadishu, weapons control proceeded with an eye to local conditions. Recognizing that each HRS had its own "personality," Johnston's headquarters promulgated general guidelines for dealing with the problem, then left it for subordinate commanders throughout the south to develop more specific policies based on circumstances prevalent within a given area. Thus, after Task Force (TF) Hope flew into Baidoa, Colonel Newbold, aware of UNITAF's guideline that weapons would be confiscated if they posed a threat to coalition forces, concluded that "it would be impossible to create a secure environment as long as the bandits continued to openly carry weapons." He therefore applied a strict interpretation to the guidance when he informed local leaders that his troops would "seize any weapon seen on the streets of Baidoa." Two days later, after TF Hope marines came under fire from a nearby compound, the colonel's men surrounded the facility, seized the arms present, and began an even more aggressive policy of confiscating weapons, one that went well beyond what was then being implemented in Mogadishu.[5]

US Army units in the outlying HRSs also tailored weapons control policy to local circumstances. UNITAF's general guidelines again provided a baseline, to which the soldiers soon appended a checklist approved by Major General Arnold on 31 December. Arnold's directive was referred to as the "4 NOs": no bandits, no checkpoints (erected by armed Somalis for purposes of extortion), no technical vehicles, and no visible weapons. In the general's opinion, these rules "would be simple to remember and translate well," lent themselves easily to a PSYOP campaign, and could actually be enforced. Originally designed for the Marka HRS, the 4 NOs became the basis for more specific policies in all US Army-controlled areas.[6]

Throughout the UNITAF area of operations, enforcing selective weapons control involved a variety of measures ranging from diplomatic pressure, shows of force, and area sweeps, to raids on unauthorized arms caches and, when necessary, the use of significant military force against flagrant violators. In determining what particular approach to take, UNITAF tried to strike a delicate balance. When political prudence dictated, weapons-toting Somalis might be stopped or detained, only to be released still clutching their weapons. Similarly, coalition troops might keep a known weapons cache under observation but not raid it. In contrast, a serious provocation might precipitate a strong military reaction. Such had been the case in mid-December when technical vehicles firing on Marine helicopters had been quickly destroyed in an impressive display of retaliatory fire. In January, an even more serious incident occurred in which a Marine convoy in Mogadishu received fire from two AWSSs under Aideed's control. Major General Wilhelm, the MARFOR commander, branded the shooting "a flagrant violation of the cantonment area agreement" and sought to punish those responsible. Retaliation was swift. That night, a reinforced Marine task force, backed by AH-1W Cobra attack helicopters, moved LAVs and organic anti-tank weapons into positions surrounding both compounds. At dawn, following PSYOP broadcasts at one of the sites, the Somalis inside allowed the marines to enter and seize the weapons present. At the second site, the Somalis resisted, so "Marine ground and air forces opened fire, and after a heated exchange of fire silenced all opposition." The next day, in a follow-up operation, marines conducted "the first sweep and clear operation of a major arms market" in the capital. Zinni then went to Aideed and offered him a choice: more of the same or a return to the strategy of "deconfliction." The warlord readily agreed to the latter option.[7]

The AWSS incident served as a reminder that Johnston would not shrink from using the firepower available to him when he believed a situation demanded decisive action. (The incident, according to Oakley, also deflated Aideed's bogus but well-publicized claims that coalition forces favored his faction over Ali Mahdi's.) But such levels of violence were rare. Militarily, the faction militias and other armed Somalis chose not to mount a serious challenge to the powerful force under Johnston's control. UNITAF headquarters tumbled onto this basic fact soon after it became operational. Once coalition troops were on the ground, aggressive reconnaissance and "eyes-on-target" patrolling, the manning of checkpoints and strongpoints, the conduct of cordon and search or search and clear operations, and the cultivation of HUMINT sources generated the intelligence that staff officers needed to update their threat assessments. The revised calculations indicated that the most likely military peril facing friendly forces was not a firefight, much less an all-out assault, but burning tires, thrown projectiles such as bottles and bricks, frequent sniper and small-arms fire, and occasional mortar, RPG, and artillery rounds, all of which, while dangerous and sometimes deadly, did not produce heavy casualties and generally did not require a massive response. In the context of this threat reassessment, a mortar and recoilless rifle barrage directed at coalition troops on New Year's Eve (after which the MARFOR submitted an urgent request for two AN/TPQ-36 counterbattery radars) and the AWSS firefight in January stood as atypical occurrences—tests, perhaps, of UNITAF's resolve. A firm response generally discouraged, or at least deferred, further provocations, as demonstrated when Aideed swiftly acquiesced to Zinni's ultimatum following the AWSS episode.[8]

By the middle of December, according to a MARFOR command chronology, "It was clear that a smaller force than originally envisioned would suffice" in Somalia, and that "large mechanized forces and heavy fire support would not be needed." As a consensus emerged within Johnston's headquarters that the various groups of armed Somalis did not pose a serious military challenge to the coalition, the general, his staff, and commanders had to determine what weapon systems and equipment were really required to establish a secure environment in areas under UNITAF control. They soon concluded that mortars, attack helicopters, armored personnel carriers, antitank weapons, and small arms were essential for accomplishing the mission. Systems geared to heavy operations, however, such as Abrams battle tanks, CH-47 Chinook transport helicopters, and field artillery, were deemed expendable. Arnold, for one, estimated that the ARFOR did not need 17 percent of its materiel. On the basis of this kind of advice, Johnston proceeded to cancel or reload onto ships many of the weapons and equipment that he no longer thought necessary. In several instances, his decision to return what he considered to be nonessential invited severe criticism from those who had shipped the materiel at great expense.[9]

UNITAF's reevaluation of the threat it faced also affected troop deployments and dispositions. Some RESTORE HOPE units scheduled for a late arrival in Somalia, such as the 1st Battalion, 1st Marines, and the 1st Tank Battalion, were simply canceled. Leathernecks from the 3rd Battalion, 11th Marines, on the other hand, made it ashore but learned they would be without their field artillery. The battalion's artillerymen became provisional infantry serving in security roles, thus giving credence to the motto, "Every Marine a Rifleman." Further into Operation RESTORE HOPE, more adjustments were made. In mid-January, for example, the 3rd Battalion, 9th Marines, redeployed from Mogadishu to Camp Pendleton, allowing Wilhelm to reorganize the placement of MARFOR combat units by putting "a more mechanized force in the open terrain of the Bardera HRS with a less mechanized force in the urban terrain of Mogadishu."[10]

The capital generally remained the most volatile area occupied by UNITAF, and Wilhelm continued to implement the four-phase program his staff had devised in December to stabilize and pacify the city. By the end of 1992, combat engineers and Seabees had managed to clear several of Mogadishu's main streets, preparing the way for coalition units to establish a formidable presence in the capital and, when necessary, to take direct action against hostile elements and other targets. In anticipation of such measures, Wilhelm stood up Task Force *Mogadishu* under the command of his deputy, Marine Colonel Jack Klimp. The 15th MEU (SOC) and the 7th Marines were also available to help out. In early January, UNITAF movement into the western part of the city began, with initial activities concentrating on intensive patrolling, punctuated by a weapons sweep or some other major operation every two days. In a related maneuver, elements from the 3rd Battalion, 11th Marines, under Lieutenant Colonel Ed Lesnowicz, Jr., occupied a strongpoint just outside the New Port, establishing there a permanent presence that the marines hoped would curb the area's well-known criminal activity. Some TF Mogadishu units also pushed on into northern Mogadishu, where they came under frequent but mostly inaccurate sniper fire, especially in the vicinity of the soccer stadium and the 21 October Road. Some of this harassment abated, however, as a result of the forceful message UNITAF sent in its swift and violent response during the AWSS incident.[11]

The active patrolling, the sweep and clear operations, and the creation of 24-hour strongpoints "began to bring a clear improvement in Mogadishu" by mid-January. This assessment prompted Wilhelm to launch Mogadishu II, a two-phase plan that, in the words of the Marine command chronology, sought "to turn Mogadishu back into a functioning city." To that end, the general's staff placed specific areas of the capital into one of two categories: those sections that required stabilization through a continuation of assertive operations, and those sections that had been normalized to the point where coalition troops could exercise a "benevolent presence" and engage in "humanitarian civic assistance."

An example of the second category was the area around Lesnowicz's strongpoint, which fell along the so-called green line separating Aideed's and Ali Mahdi's factions. Soon after the marines effected an around-the-clock presence along the volatile boundary, "the local inhabitants began to reemerge and life in this neighborhood began to return to normal."[12]

As a consequence of TF Mogadishu establishing a presence in various parts of the city, personal contacts between coalition forces and the indigenous population increased dramatically. While many Somalis in the capital seemed to welcome the foreign troops, that sentiment was far from universal, thus resulting in "an environment where a marine on patrol at night might be met by a waving, smiling crowd on one corner and gunfire on the next." Aggravating these person-to-person contacts was the behavior of many Somali males, including children, who according to reports filed by coalition troops would try to steal almost any item that was not firmly secured. As a further complication, UNITAF forces ran into a cultural barrier that, for many, appeared too incomprehensible to overcome.

Under such conditions, extensive contact with the Somali people began to exact a psychological toll on the troops. It was not long before many UNITAF personnel in Mogadishu and the outlying HRSs began referring to the Somalis as "skinnies," or using other derogatory terms. In some cases, behavioral indicators of a negative attitude appeared in just a matter of days, or even minutes. A journalist on the scene recounted how one newly arrived marine "put on a happy face" as he held at bay Somali children swarming around planes on the airfield. Within 30 minutes, the same marine was cursing the children and chasing after them, "the transformation from benevolent cop to tough-guy law enforcer complete." The Marine command chronology put it another way: "Many Marines began to grow increasingly impatient with the naturally curious Somalis, particularly when Somalis crowded them." Recognizing the stress many of the troops were feeling, and concerned that frustrated marines could end up hurting or alienating the people they were there to help, Wilhelm issued a "30-Day Attitude Adjustment Message" that reminded MARFOR troops of the friendly intentions of 90 percent of the population. The message also directed his men to take "a brief stand down" periodically for "a few moments of relaxation" before returning to the task of "being simultaneously friendly and vigilant."[13]

The UNITAF command made other adjustments to minimize the friction arising from direct personal contact between coalition troops and the Somali people. PYSOP programs sought to convince the locals that coalition forces were there to help not harm them. As for the children the troops considered "undisciplined," if not out-and-out thieves, some marines had taken to carrying whipping sticks to keep the ubiquitous youths at bay. But administering beatings to kids neither enhanced the warrior ethic and self-esteem of the marines nor endeared them to the indigenous population. A more effective approach, it was found, was to ask or hire Somali elders to keep the youngsters under control and, when necessary, to punish them. In the hands of the elders, a stick—a symbol of authority in Somali culture—served as a traditional and acceptable disciplinary instrument.[14]

In general, then, creating a secure environment in Somalia confronted UNITAF with a dilemma: the mission required that coalition forces establish a presence throughout the HRSs and interact with the Somali people, but such contact often produced friction, a friction that could best be reduced by limiting the contact, especially in highly populated areas such as Mogadishu. One organizational solution to this dilemma surfaced early in the intervention when UNITAF and USLO addressed the issue of reconstituting a Somali police force.[15] If Somali policemen could perform some of the law-and-order, security, and interpersonal tasks then being discharged by coalition forces, the result might not only be a more secure environment, but also one in which inevitable tensions between the local populace and foreign troops could be reduced. As Oakley later commented about indigenous policemen, "They spoke Somali; we didn't. They understood the body language; we didn't." Not only would a common language and culture enable Somali police to interact effectively with the population, but by providing a sort of buffer between coalition troops and the people, a resuscitated police force would, in effect, serve the cause of force protection. Furthermore, in terms of law enforcement, a police force could deal with the petty crimes rampant in urban areas like Mogadishu, thus freeing UNITAF to target, in Zinni's words, the "gross problems of violence." The logic for resurrecting the Somali police force thus seemed irrefutable. That did not prevent the initiative from becoming, like disarmament, a highly controversial issue.

Prior to the civil war, the Somali national police force had been an effective organization of between 15,000 and 18,000 members with a reputation for fairness and impartiality. Once factional violence in the country began escalating, however, the police found themselves outgunned by the warring parties. Simply as a matter of self-preservation, many policemen in southern Somalia returned to the towns and villages of their subclans and families to weather the storm. With the arrival of UNITAF on the scene, the worst seemed to have passed, and several "retired" police officers led by General Ahmad Jama, the last chief of the national police, approached Oakley, USLO officials, and representatives from General Johnston's headquarters with the request that a police force be reestablished in areas controlled by the international coalition. What was needed, they made clear, was assistance in the form of uniforms, money, and training, and some degree of protection from the factions that would almost certainly try to take charge of a resuscitated force. Oakley was receptive to the idea and recommended that the rebuilding process begin at the district level and work its way up to regional commands.

At first, Johnston did not embrace Oakley's viewpoint. Resurrecting a Somali police organization was simply not part of UNITAF's mission. Indeed, many civil affairs personnel whose expertise Johnston could have employed to help revive such an organization had early on been dropped from the RESTORE HOPE operation plan. Higher up the chain of command, CENTCOM and the Pentagon viewed the project, with its obvious overtones of nation building, as another example of "mission creep." There were also laws, specifically Section 2420, Chapter 32 of the US Code (Foreign Assistance; Miscellaneous Provisions), that prohibited the use of funds for the US military to train, advise, and support foreign police and other law-enforcement agencies. Reinforcing these American doubts and restrictions, the UN opposed the idea for fear that a newly constituted police force would be perceived as simply another armed element contributing to Somalia's internal strife. Furthermore, the UN representative on the scene, keenly aware that UNOSOM II's mandate would be nationwide, argued that creating a *national* police force should precede setting up *local* police authorities, the opposite of Oakley's position.

Having voiced their misgivings, practically all the opponents of a revived Somali police force soon changed their minds. Johnston was one of the first. From the time of his arrival, he had done what he could to prevent his combat troops from becoming "policemen," but just being in Mogadishu, manning checkpoints, providing installation security, and escorting convoys had often required them to perform a variety of police-like functions. In talks with Oakley and others, Johnston came to see that a Somali police force, according to one account, "would eliminate the need for UNITAF troops to serve as police, not only freeing them for other duties but avoiding confusion about their role and reducing friction with the local population, thus minimizing casualties on both sides." In his own words, Johnston articulated a related benefit: "To the extent that you can get somebody other than the warlords providing security, then you enfeeble the warlords."

Washington took longer to accept the merit of these arguments. Twice President Bush's people rejected Oakley's entreaties on the matter, prompting the special envoy to fire off yet another message warning that, absent Somali policemen, the coalition was "going to get people killed patrolling in dark alleys." Just hours after the cable reached the president's national security adviser, a US marine was, in fact, killed in a Mogadishu alleyway. Upon the heels of the incident, Oakley and UNITAF received White House permission to move forward on the police force, although the US government initially offered no material assistance for the undertaking.

Once authorized, the process of reestablishing the Somali police got under way in several UNITAF-controlled areas, with the main effort—as was often the case with other issues as well—taking place in the capital. There, Somalis on the political committee agreed to establish a police committee and presented names of 10 "former police officers" to serve on it. To guarantee that the 10 men—only six of whom turned out to have had police experience—were acceptable to Aideed and Ali Mahdi, Oakley consulted with both leaders to ensure a balance of "individuals from their subclans and other influential Mogadishu subclans." The two warlords voiced support for the undertaking, but from the outset, each maneuvered within the committee to gain control over the new force. Their schemes, generally, were stymied, in part by timely intelligence UNITAF received from US interpreters assigned to committee members and in part by the determination of the former policemen on the committee to create a professional force isolated as much as possible from disruptive political influences.

While officially UNITAF had no formal responsibility for what was touted as a community-controlled Somali police force, Brigadier General Zinni served as an adviser to the committee, on call to apply his influence in helping to resolve the most serious problems. Of the various Somali and coalition personnel who met daily to address the issue, the key American participant was US Army Lieutenant Colonel Stephen Spataro, the UNITAF provost marshal. As the "top cop" in Johnston's command, Spataro had arrived in Somalia advocating the need for an indigenous police force, perhaps contracted, to perform various security functions. Told by Oakley (with Johnston's blessing) to pull a Somali police force together, Spataro's main task on the committee was to help turn the concept into a practical plan.

In a memorandum to Zinni, dated 27 January 1993, Spataro spelled out the committee's conclusions and recommendations up to that point. Contrary to Oakley's advice, many on the committee had started out wanting to reestablish a national force. Aideed and Ali Mahdi favored this approach, in that the power of either would be enhanced through control of a *national* organization. While others on the committee shunned this self-serving political calculus, they shared Jama's opinion that only a national force could hope to contend with Somalia's political crisis. The obstacles to creating such a national institution, however, were enormous, so the committee soon lowered its sights to the more practicable goal of getting the police functioning in Mogadishu. A force of a little over 3,000 was projected. For a variety of reasons (including the need to circumvent the law prohibiting US military personnel from training police), Spataro referred to the proposed organization as the Auxiliary Security Force, or ASF. Its logistic requirements could be "bare bones"—some trucks, radios, uniforms, and small arms—although Spataro thought that, for the force to be truly effective, it would need much more support. The committee also agreed on how the ASF would be divided geographically throughout the city. As for the composition of the force, membership would consist of policemen technically still on duty and others who would be put back on the job if they had had two years of training. There were many loose ends to tie up, Spataro noted, and this would "have to be done at the JTF level and also at the worker level."[16]

With the help of old police records, the committee set about the work of vetting ASF members. It also undertook the difficult task of writing a handbook for police operations. Meanwhile, Zinni, Spataro, Oakley, and even the White House began seeking out the financial and logistic support the ASF would need. Through a number of avenues, assistance was solicited, commitments made. The World Food Program, for example, agreed to provide food to the families of police personnel. Various NGOs also made contributions, and belatedly the UN even made funds available for operating the ASF (although UN officials refrained from promising ASF members a position in the national police organization that presumably would be established after the transition from UNITAF to UNOSOM II). Italy proved especially generous in its support, providing uniforms among other contributions, and so did the Netherlands and Germany. UNITAF stripped technicals of their crew-served weapons and converted them into police vehicles, while Somali and US military engineers set about rebuilding Somali police stations, using material provided from several sources. In addition, UNITAF also turned over its own surplus vehicles and radios, most left over from the Gulf War, to the fledgling force.

While Johnston helped to find sources of assistance, he still tried to set limits on the support UNITAF would offer the ASF directly. To this end, he initially opposed a request to have coalition units help protect the new force from armed militia and bandits. As time passed, however, the logic of the situation again compelled him to reverse his position. For one thing, the concern that, in providing protection, UNITAF would be drawn into a series of firefights with militia groups seemed to subside when both Ali Mahdi and Aideed approved the plan for an ASF. Moreover, the protection the ASF requested increasingly came to be regarded as a reasonable price to pay for the services the new force offered. Once on the streets, the police proved adept at controlling crowds and traffic, patrolling, securing key facilities such as ports and airfields, and arresting criminals. Also, at Oakley's insistence Spataro dispatched 100 Somali policemen to replace the marines along the "green line," a move that brought some stability to that troubled boundary. Given the important role of the ASF in promoting a more secure environment and in freeing coalition forces to perform other mission-essential tasks, Johnston consented to providing it some UNITAF protection. By late February, armed coalition contingents could be found near each newly reopened police station in the capital. From these locations, UNITAF troops could provide the ASF communications, moral encouragement, and, when need be, fire support.

Even as the ASF demonstrated its value, its supporters recognized that a police force alone represented but one element in the larger formula for law and order. For the ASF to be effective, there would have to be jails in which to incarcerate convicted criminals and people suspected of crimes or awaiting trial, a penal code to enforce, and courts to apply the law fairly and consistently. In other words, as with the police force, the penal and judicial systems would have to be reconstructed from the severe damage inflicted on them during the civil war. The task would be extremely difficult and invite accusations of nation building, but US officials on the scene once again concluded that helping to rebuild some Somali institutions was inextricably linked to creating the secure environment that would facilitate the RESTORE HOPE mission.

As part of the more comprehensive approach to law and order, UNITAF arranged to open a prison in the capital (and holding facilities in the outlying areas under its control). It also held meetings with Somalis

73

who had been lawyers and judges and, in early March, supported a conference, hosted by the US Information Service (USIS), that brought together jurists throughout the city to discuss reviving the judicial system. When Aideed and Ali Mahdi objected to the undertaking as usurping the work of the political committee on which they were represented, they were told that "USIS and UNITAF—setting the stage for UNOSOM II—simply wanted to bring together a broad group of Somali jurists." Although this explanation lost some of its plausibility when UNOSOM officials failed to attend the meeting, 43 Somalis did show up, some only after armed UNITAF soldiers had escorted them through sections of Mogadishu deemed hostile. When the jurists agreed to adopt the pre-Barre 1962 Somali Penal Code as the basis for a revived judicial system, UNITAF reproduced and distributed copies of that important document. Johnston also made his command's judge advocate general available to offer advice on legal matters. Yet, despite these promising developments, progress on rehabilitating the penal and judicial systems in Mogadishu proved glacial, thus leaving for UNOSOM II the critical challenge of trying to institutionalize the mechanisms for law and order in the capital city.

The successes and failures, accomplishments and frustrations that characterized work on the police, penal, and judicial systems in Mogadishu were experienced as well in the other HRSs. Initially, the ASF was authorized 2,000 policemen for the areas under UNITAF control outside the capital, and efforts were made to adapt the judicial system in some HRSs to local custom and conditions. By all accounts, the Australians were the most successful in this endeavor. In Baidoa and the Bay region, they brought in the civil affairs and legal experts needed to set up a functional law and order program. In close cooperation with community leaders, Australian troops in one location built a police station, jail, and courthouse all within a single compound. The setup imparted such a sense of security that the area became "a center of communal activity." More to the point, the newly restored and integrated system actually worked. In one particular case, the ASF and Australians teamed up to capture a notorious bandit leader and bring him to trial—a boost to the credibility of the police, lawyers, and judges involved in the case. US officials who applauded the overall Australian achievement sometimes qualified their praise by observing that, in certain areas, the presence of only one clan simplified law and order activities to a degree not found in such faction-ridden HRSs as Mogadishu. But other admirers spoke without condition, attributing the Australians' success to the fact that they "had a full civil affairs program and they implemented it. UNITAF did not and had to improvise."

Back in Mogadishu, activation of the ASF "meshed" with preparations the MARFOR staff was making for inaugurating a Mass Distribution Site (MDS) program.[17] Specifically, UNITAF would flood the city with grain, to be distributed at 35 locations. The goal was not only to get the grain into the hands of the people but to do so in a way that would "break the back" of the black market that flourished as a result of faction-generated food shortages. The program kicked off in early February, with the ASF assuming responsibility for crowd control at all 35 distribution points (with coalition forces providing backup support at 27). ASF participation in the MDS, while limited, served several purposes: it reduced the chances for "disastrous confrontations" between MARFOR troops and the people, it provided the new police force with a "manageable task," and it allowed coalition forces and the police to work together in such a way as to confer legitimacy on the latter. The venture also provided the ASF an opportunity "to prove its mettle." During the first day of the program, in an incident technically unrelated to the distribution of food but occurring near an MDS checkpoint, refugees belonging to the Mursade clan tried to resettle an area in which the Habr Gidr had come to reside. After violence erupted, MARFOR units, State Department officials, and clan elders arrived on the scene. Once they had imposed a degree of calm, about 100 Somali police took charge, managing to resettle the refugees without further bloodshed. The dangers involved in these and other assignments were reflected in the casualties the ASF suffered in its initial operations: two killed and six wounded.

Standing up the ASF, together with the implementation of weapons control measures, the dialogue with faction leaders, and periodic demonstrations of military power, did not exhaust the methods by which coalition forces sought to establish and maintain a secure environment in southern Somalia. In late December, after marines had moved into Baidoa, their commander, Colonel Newbold, in essence ignored UNITAF guidance to leave humanitarian projects to the HROs and initiated a civic action program in the sector. His reasoning was basic: He "knew that the best protection for his force was the goodwill of the locals. He also knew that the Somali people had trouble understanding the concept of neutrality, and that if his Marines and sailors did not actively assist the inhabitants of Baidoa, they ran a strong risk of being perceived as enemies." Thus, on Christmas Eve, Newbold launched Project Hand Clasp, in which his troops helped construct or repair schools and orphanages, along with some other facilities. As the work progressed, the morale of the marines improved, as they "were eager to do more than just escort convoys to help those in need."[18]

Seeing the link between civic action and security, other HRS commanders followed Newbold's example and began planning projects of their own. The effort ultimately spread to Mogadishu, as well, where on 14 January, Newbold kicked off Operation RENAISSANCE. Designed to stabilize the section of the city between the international airport and the port, the operation employed a combination of active patrolling and limited medical and dental treatment for the Somalis in the area. Soon thereafter, Major General Wilhelm implemented Mogadishu II, which also emphasized "humanitarian civic assistance" in areas thought to be "normalized."[19]

For the most part, the civic action and civil affairs activities undertaken by the marines and by the US Army units that came after them were decentralized programs, allowing officers in each HRS to determine what would work best at the local level. In late December, three 4-man Civil Affairs teams from the Army's 96th Civil Affairs Brigade arrived in country. In Arnold's opinion, they were "force multipliers," working with the CMOC in Mogadishu and branching out when possible to do what they could in the countryside. Thanks to the CA teams, Arnold said in an interview, the town of Marka had been transformed from a violent town into one with a burgeoning marketplace and some political stability. This stood in contrast, he believed, to the "great difficulty" experienced in those HRSs where UNITAF units attempted to formulate goodwill projects without the aid of the CA teams. In contrast with CENTCOM's predeployment decision to cut many civil affairs personnel from the OPLAN, Arnold lamented that he should have asked for more teams and insisted on giving them, together with CI elements, a high deployment priority.[20]

The humanitarian element. In implementing a variety of measures to create a more secure environment in southern Somalia, UNITAF made it safer for its forces to concentrate on their main objective—ensuring that humanitarian aid reached Somalis in the famine belt. Because that principal mission necessitated daily coordination between the coalition and the various relief agencies on the scene, the Humanitarian Operations Centers (HOCs) and, within them, the Civil-Military Centers (CMOCs) set up in December continued operating throughout the course of RESTORE HOPE, with the parent organization in Mogadishu providing general policy guidance for its counterparts in other HRSs. In general, the HOC remained the forum in which military officers and civilian officials met to exchange views, coordinate operations, and monitor the evolving situation, while the CMOC, manned by UNITAF staff officers, processed HRO requests for military support. Within this framework, the initial division of labor between UNITAF and the HROs remained largely unchanged. Coalition forces would secure ports and airfields, protect humanitarian convoys, and guard relief distribution points, while relief agencies would distribute food, run clinics, and tackle a number of long-term projects. If there was a blurring of the line on occasion, it usually occurred when the military got involved in distributing food or providing medical treatment to the locals.

While the HOC/CMOC arrangement would be hailed as the organizational solution to civil-military interaction in Somalia, the record of accomplishment it compiled during the course of RESTORE HOPE was mixed. On three of the key issues the participants addressed—convoy escorts, general security, and weapons policy—only the first, while experiencing some coordination difficulties, could be considered highly successful, with coalition troops escorting on an average of 70 convoys a month. In the process, many of the relief groups discovered that they could expand the geographical reach of their activities by working closely with Navy Seabees and the Army Corps of Engineers, both of which had the capabilities to build and repair roads and improve airfield and port capabilities.[21]

The condition of the roads was of particular concern. Getting supplies from the port cities and airfields out to the HRSs, and from a central town in an HRS into the hinterland, required a functioning transportation network. The airlift of some supplies to the interior served as a temporary expedient but not as a long-term substitute for ground convoys. Yet in many areas, roads were nonexistent or in such disrepair or rudimentary condition that they could not support heavy trucks and military vehicles. To complicate matters, many roadways concealed mines implanted by the warring factions. Before routine convoy operations could be mounted with limited risks and maximum effectiveness, these various impediments had to be addressed and, where possible, removed. Army and Marine engineers and Navy Seabees were given the task, and during the course of RESTORE HOPE, compiled an impressive record. Nine airfields were repaired and maintained to accommodate the coalition's heavy transport aircraft, and 2,500 kilometers of main supply routes were constructed or repaired. In addition to this, the engineers built base camps for the troops in the interior and took part in various civic action programs—building or repairing schools, orphanages, and hospitals; digging wells; and setting up medical clinics.[22] In that these activities had the concomitant effect of improving the country's infrastructure, concerns about mission creep and nation building once again surfaced. But as in other cases, US officials on the scene quickly defended such measures as being essential to the fulfillment of UNITAF's principal mission.

As the transportation infrastructure improved and the roads became safer, and as more coalition forces inundated the countryside, the number of humanitarian relief convoys accompanied by armed escorts increased from a trickle to a steady flow by the end of January. What disruptions they experienced owed more to mechanical breakdowns and media vehicles weaving in and out of the columns than to Somali gunmen. By the end of January, ARFOR reports indicated that food was reaching virtually all the famine-stricken areas in southern Somalia.[23] UNITAF was well on its way to accomplishing the humanitarian portion of its mission, although the situation was far from perfect. A comprehensive solution to one major problem, the security of the HROs, proved elusive. UNITAF troops, try as they might, simply could not provide protection to all the humanitarian groups and personnel taking part in the relief effort. Many relief agencies remained scattered around Mogadishu or the countryside—there were 585 HRO offices, warehouses, residences, feeding centers, and clinics in the capital alone—and, as a matter of expediency, continued to rely on Somali "technical advisers" for their security. These bandits and faction-aligned gunmen, in turn, continued their practice of looting and extorting money and supplies from the relief organizations they were hired to protect. HRO personnel who attempted to stop the thievery ran the risk of being beaten or shot.

Responsible for the safety of the humanitarian workers but not wanting to mount an all-out challenge to "technical advisers" throughout the south, UNITAF sought a compromise that would permit private Somali security guards to work for the HROs but only if they carried pink identification cards and limited their weaponry to small arms. The new "pink card" system quickly ran into trouble. To begin with, IDs lacked the holder's photograph, thus enabling many security guards to pass the cards around, with the result that unauthorized personnel gained access to HRO compounds. Another problem with the system arose in Mogadishu, where not all marines pulling guard duty were familiar with carding procedures and thus ended up confiscating the weapons of legitimate security people. In an attempt to rationalize the process, some UNITAF tactical units began issuing cards on their own, a measure that had the contrary effect of increasing the confusion until word got around that only IDs issued by Johnston's headquarters were valid. At the end of February, UNITAF revamped verification procedures and began issuing a "blue card" that bore a photograph of the authorized holder. As with the pink card program,

Somalis engaged as convoy escorts or guards could only carry small arms. The blue cards introduced many improvements over the old system, but violations and mistakes continued to plague the overall effort, with still too many Somali security personnel being deprived of the weapons that permitted them to protect humanitarian relief materiel. Left with perhaps a rifle or two for its defense, an HRO whose security guard had just been disarmed could be expected to lodge an angry protest with the nearest CMOC.[24]

These and other types of complaints often exacerbated the negative stereotypes that permeated relations between the military and relief workers from the outset of Operation RESTORE HOPE. In the eyes of too many US officers, the HROs were populated with left-wing, antimilitary, disorganized, self-righteous "do-gooders." Reciprocating, too many relief workers viewed most officers as right-wing, insensitive, inflexible, "balls-to-the-wall" control freaks who exhibited little understanding of the situation in Somalia or what was required of them to alleviate the widespread suffering. Over time, the need to work together and the organizations set up to facilitate civil-military interaction helped to erode the stereotypes and to mitigate much of the friction, even though the "cultural gap" was never bridged entirely. Fortunately, according to one participant, "Tension between the military and HROs during Restore Hope had little operational impact."[25]

The political element. The third realm of UNITAF activities, according to Zinni's schema, encompassed *political* matters, an integral part of RESTORE HOPE, but an aspect of the operation that Johnston and his staff initially regarded as beyond the military's purview. That impression did not survive the command's first few days in Somalia. The meetings between Johnston, Oakley, and the faction leaders in Mogadishu constituted one early example of political engagement. Another derived from Oakley's early forays into the countryside as he paved the way for the insertion of UNITAF forces. On these trips, the special envoy not only consulted local leaders on the military reasons for his visit but, looking to the future, also began laying "the groundwork for the revival of local political institutions." He had broached this subject with Somali leaders he conferred with in Baidoa—one of the first HRSs after Mogadishu and Baledogle to be occupied—and he subsequently made references to the "Baidoa model" when talking about the political arrangements he had in mind. Essentially what he was offering local and regional communities was a chance to choose their own leaders. In Baidoa and other areas, this translated into an opportunity to restore traditional councils while expelling those officials that Aideed's lieutenants in the hinterland had imposed on local and regional authorities. Given the risks involved, UNITAF's presence within each HRS was critical to this "ground up" approach to political restructuring. To begin with, coalition troops and Civil Affairs teams provided a security umbrella under which political authority could be restored to "traditional community leaders." Further, by working with local and regional councils on a variety of humanitarian issues, UNITAF helped confer legitimacy on these traditional governing bodies. As the ARFOR after-action report put it, UNITAF "assisted in empowering the elders within the villages to return to the peaceful operation of village councils." Not all local and regional leaders embraced the process. Of these, some rejected it categorically and others paid only lip service to it, but nearly all feared the retribution that might befall them once UNITAF withdrew its troops. Other leaders, however, rallied behind the idea. Major General Arnold, in reviewing the situation in the Marka HRS, lavished praise on "a vibrant city that's run by a community council that was helped set up by Civil Affairs; that's got clan representation, elders representation. . . . so we've gone back to the traditional leadership. And it's been orchestrated by the Civil Affairs and away from self-appointed government officials who were really the biggest crooks in town."[26]

While these measures contributed to the local and regional stability that UNITAF found it in its interest to promote, the UN was pursuing the goal of long-term political stability at a higher level by initiating the first major steps toward *national* reconciliation. In early 1993, at the UN's request, leaders from all the warring factions agreed with varying degrees of enthusiasm to meet in Addis Ababa, the capital of Ethiopia.[27] The first meeting was scheduled for early January, and USLO and UNITAF helped set the stage. In Mogadishu, within the security committee headed by Zinni, UNITAF raised various issues with Somali militia leaders as a way of "laying the groundwork for a bigger discussion." Meanwhile, Oakley used the forum provided by the political committee to bring faction leaders together to discuss their differences before the conference convened. Oakley performed another service as well. On 3 January, after UN Secretary-General Boutros Boutros-Ghali arrived in Mogadishu en route to Addis Ababa, Aideed's followers staged an all-out demonstration in the capital, a display of the faction leader's distrust of the UN and his personal dislike of Boutros-Ghali, a Coptic Christian who, during Somalia's recent civil war, had been Egypt's deputy foreign minister at a time when that country was supporting Siad Barre. Aideed also threatened to boycott the Addis Ababa conference, but Oakley used cajolery and persuasion to change his mind. As a UN concession to help the warlord save face, the sessions scheduled to begin on 5 January were labeled "preparatory."

Contrary to the gloomy expectations of many, not only did the two-day conference convene on schedule, but the delegates chose to continue their deliberations after it adjourned, producing between 8 and 15 January a series of general agreements on several important issues. Among other things, the conferees called for a countrywide cease-fire that would be monitored by UNITAF and UNOSOM, the cantonment of all heavy weapons in designated compounds, the demobilization of the factional (as opposed to legitimate) militia, and the disarmament of other armed elements. The consensus on these issues was fragile, causing Johnston, in hopes of furthering the cause of weapons control, to insist that the UN arrange follow-up meetings in Mogadishu for the purpose of identifying additional cantonment sites and establishing timetables for implementing other aspects of the accords.

During the first two months of 1993, then, UNITAF and USLO tried to advance political stability in Somalia from the bottom up, while the UN sought to foster the same objective from the top down. Zinni, for one, viewed the opposite approaches as complementary. As he remarked at the time, "So from the grassroots level up, and from the top down . . . we have to work both sides. There has been some discussion that you ought to choose one route or the other, and I think that is wrong to go one way. You have to work it from both ends."[28] In the meantime, all parties received frequent reminders as to the urgency of the situation. For although UNITAF exerted a mitigating effect on the turmoil in southern Somalia, violence continued to be a daily fact of life. Coalition forces escorting convoys, manning checkpoints, or patrolling city streets came to regard as routine the sniper fire directed against them. More serious were those episodes in which the violence escalated and threatened to get out of control. In those instances, Johnston generally responded quickly and decisively with counterforce, the best way to settle things down and send a strong message at the same time. Occasionally, however, political prudence dictated other courses of action.

The worst episode of escalating violence to affect UNITAF erupted in the Kismayo HRS in late February. Its origins, which antedated Operation RESTORE HOPE, lay in the military operations mounted by General Said Hersi "Morgan," Siad Barre's son-in-law, to wrest control of the city of Kismayo and its port from his principal rival in the area, Omar Jess, an ally of Aideed. The arrival of UNITAF forces in Mogadishu and then in Kismayo temporarily halted the fighting, but on 24 January it broke out again when Morgan attacked Jess' militiamen who were guarding a weapons compound some distance outside the city. UNITAF charged Morgan with violating the Addis Ababa cease-fire agreement and issued him an ultimatum to withdraw his troops but to leave his technical vehicles behind. When Morgan failed to comply, ARFOR elements, in this case a Belgian battalion supported by four US helicopters, destroyed six of the technicals, four howitzers, an armored vehicle, and a rocket launcher. After this, major fighting in the HRS went back on hold.[29]

About a month later, however, on 22 February, small groups of Morgan's men slipped past UNITAF positions and infiltrated into the center of Kismayo, where they tracked down several followers of Jess and mounted raids on buildings occupied by Jess' militia. Jess and his men fled the city, in the process looting some humanitarian warehouses they had been guarding and shooting at Belgian soldiers in the area. Major General Arnold, the 10th Mountain Division commander whose troops were in the Kismayo HRS, ordered Morgan to leave the city. Johnston and Oakley followed up the next day with an angry ultimatum: Morgan had until midnight 25 February to move his men and equipment out of the city to designated locations. "If any of your forces are found outside of these locations on February 26 or thereafter," the written warning continued, "they will be engaged. Any weapons located will be destroyed." Johnston and Oakley also ordered Jess "to canton his men and arms at locations near Jilib." As a show of force, UNITAF deployed a theater quick-reaction force to Kismayo to conduct security and weapons control operations.[30]

Both faction leaders complied with the ultimatums. But repercussions from the violence in Kismayo quickly spread to Mogadishu, where Aideed was already in a belligerent mood.[31] One source of his displeasure was the political reform being implemented by USLO and UNITAF from the bottom up. As Aideed's lieutenants in the countryside saw their power base being threatened through the "empowering" of traditional local and regional leaders, they began pressuring their own leader in Mogadishu to reverse the trend. In the midst of this disquieting news, Aideed received word that his ally Jess had been arrested while making an unauthorized trip from Mogadishu to Kismayo, an incident that was reported to have infuriated Aideed. Consequently, when the fighting broke out in Kismayo, the warlord was ready to vent his anger. Encouraging him to do so were erroneous news reports, spread by Reuters and the BBC, that UNITAF had conspired with Morgan in the attack on Jess' supporters in the city.

On 24 February, shortly after sunrise, Aideed's followers began demonstrating at the US embassy compound and at other locations within his sectors of Mogadishu. The crowds threw rocks and Molotov cocktails, burned tires, and established barricades at various locations. Major General Wilhelm ordered coalition helicopters to monitor the demonstrations and to be prepared to provide support to UNITAF ground units, but, due to a lack of intermediate maintenance, only half of the requested aviation assets were fit to fly. As it turned out, it was not a critical deficiency, as the demonstrations spent themselves before any air support was required. Still, the day was a costly one, as three marines were wounded and two Somali policemen in a grain convoy were killed. The next day, Nigerian forces at the strategic K4 traffic circle came under attack, in part because of their small numbers, in part because Nigeria had given sanctuary to the deposed Siad Barre. UNITAF had received warning of the attack and had sent marines to reinforce the Nigerians. The firefight lasted 4 hours, during which three more marines were wounded. That afternoon, two companies of marines and one company of the Botswana Defense Force were able to sweep and clear the area around K4.

While the firefight produced few casualties, its psychological impact on UN officials and HROs in Mogadishu was traumatizing. Again the news media heightened the anxiety by claiming that the demonstrations and fighting had been citywide, when in fact the most threatening activities had been confined to an area of a dozen or so blocks. While wanting to prevent widespread panic and to stop the disorder but knowing that the estimated 200 demonstrators were mostly unarmed civilians, Johnston, Zinni, Oakley, and UNITAF's political adviser John Hirsch decided that the best course of action, once the coalition had provided additional armed security for UN and HRO locations in the city, was to wait out the violence in hopes that it would subside on its own. Influencing their decision were intelligence reports that Aideed had momentarily lost control of the situation. It would be pointless, perhaps even counterproductive, to send him an ultimatum to which he would be powerless to accede. Within two days, the wait-and-see approach seemed to have paid off, as order—or what passed for it—returned to the city.

Mogadishu would not see another violent flare-up during the remainder of UNITAF's stay in Somalia. Indeed, by the end of February, less than a week after the demonstrations had subsided, the marines could still describe Mogadishu in positive terms as "a changed city."

Gunmen no longer roamed the streets; gunfire was seldom heard at night; markets were beginning to flourish; civil authority was beginning to return. . . . During February, the citizens of Mogadishu began to once again sit outside their homes in the evenings, playing dominoes, visiting small cafes, or simply walking and talking with their neighbors. Criminal activity still occurred, but Mogadishu was well on its way to returning to normal.[32]

This optimistic portrayal of capital life, while not quite idyllic, was echoed in progress reports emanating from many of the HRSs where operations similar to those mounted in Mogadishu had produced positive results in feeding and caring for the local population and in providing oppressed Somalis greater security. But success in the outlying areas created at least one unanticipated problem in the capital: the overcrowding of coalition forces. Some coalition units never left Mogadishu once they had arrived. Others returned to the city after they had secured their HRSs. Since all coalition forces in the capital tended to congregate in secure areas, the resulting congestion raised concerns about friendly fire. After a few close calls, the MARFOR set up the Vital Area Security Committee to try to keep the various forces from running afoul of one another. The committee, which met weekly, "included all the compounds in northwest Mogadishu, had each compound submit an overlay of its defensive fire plan and then coordinated to reduce the probability of friendly fire incidents . . ."[33]

The ability to solve these sorts of problems, combined with the progress UNITAF had made in accomplishing its mission, raised expectations that, despite an occasional violent episode, the coalition forces under Johnston would soon be able to turn operations in Somalia over to the United Nations. By the end of February, almost a month after Johnston had declared that UNITAF had accomplished its Phase III objectives, planning for the transition was taking place, but at a fitful pace.

Transition

The violence that rocked Kismayo and Mogadishu in late February had occurred as the second round of the Addis Ababa talks, specifically the National Reconciliation Conference, was getting under way. As was the case after the preparatory conference in January, the delegates reached agreements on weapons control and a cease-fire, as well as on an accord outlining the framework for a long-term political settlement to the country's crisis. Johnston showed a keen interest in the outcome of both rounds of talks, focusing intently on the pledges concerning weaponry in areas occupied by UNITAF. Following the initial agreements in January, he had sent one of his staff, Colonel Pete Dotto, to UN-sponsored meetings at which the participants sought to draft a workable plan that would translate promises to limit weapons into reality. Throughout the process, Johnston reminded everyone that, while UNITAF would *assist* in executing any concrete plan, the UN would have to accept overall responsibility for long-term implementation, in that the process under discussion would continue to have ramifications well after Operation RESTORE HOPE had given way to UNOSOM II. To the surprise of many, Ismat Kittani, Boutros-Ghali's representative in Mogadishu, refused on behalf of the UN to accept responsibility. The UN later changed its position, but by then, as Hirsch and Oakley have noted, precious time had been lost.[34]

This particular issue, which had divided the Bush administration and the UN from the outset of RESTORE HOPE, revolved around the tremendous differences between a program of comprehensive disarmament throughout Somalia, which the UN demanded, and one of selective arms control within the area of southern Somalia controlled by UNITAF. The gap between the two approaches had not been bridged after Bill Clinton replaced Bush in the White House in late January. Instead, the issue continued to fester to the detriment of the "seamless" transition that was supposed to characterize the handoff of operations in Somalia from UNITAF to UNOSOM II. That transition constituted Phase IV of Johnston's mission and was inextricably linked to the concept of "end state." As previously noted, the end state incorporated into the CINCCENT and JTF OPORDs for Operation RESTORE HOPE had been defined only in general terms as an environment in which UNITAF could turn operations in Somalia over to the UN. Determining the specific indicators that would show when the end state did in fact exist fell to Johnston's staff once RESTORE HOPE was under way. At first, a set of objective measurements seemed elusive. By early 1993, however, the staff had devised indicators based on regarding Mogadishu and other Somali cities as being analogous to American urban areas. US cities experienced violence daily, yet they were not considered unstable or lacking in overall security. Applied to RESTORE HOPE's end state, the analogy suggested that the area occupied by UNITAF should be considered secured once "organized" violence, as opposed to criminal violence, had been placed in check. The staff drew up a matrix with five categories: resistance, humanitarian relief, infrastructure, populace, and transition actions. The criteria for measuring progress or the lack thereof in each category was published with the matrix. It was then up to each HRS commander to submit a weekly report, often incorporating additional criteria developed at the local level.[35] Taken as a whole, the reports correctly reinforced the view that UNITAF was making progress at an unanticipated pace, so much so that in early 1993, Johnston's headquarters concluded that RESTORE HOPE was approaching its end state and that the time had come to begin planning for the transition to UNOSOM II.

There was one major flaw in this reasoning. Boutros-Ghali did not agree. His convictions concerning the need for a comprehensive program of disarmament, which he had conveyed to President Bush in mid-December, were only buttressed by the anti-UN demonstrations that had greeted and embarrassed him when he had visited Mogadishu en route to Addis Ababa on 4 January. That experience had convinced him that Somalia was still a very violent, unstable country, more than ever needful of something well beyond the limited scope of UNITAF's weapons control. Until the United States accepted this reality and the responsibility that went with it, he concluded, planning for the transition to UNOSOM II would be premature; UN forces would be courting almost certain disaster. Consequently, UNITAF encountered "a series of delays by the Secretary General that may have been detrimental to the transition process in the long term." Against this procrastination, Johnston managed to make only limited yet not insignificant headway during Boutros-Ghali's brief stay in Mogadishu. In a meeting with the secretary-general and Kittani, the general impressed upon them the fact that, for UNITAF to be supportive during the crucial transition period, it was imperative that the UN at least name the UNOSOM II force commander and provide him a staff. In February, Boutros-Ghali acceded to that one appeal, naming Lieutenant General Cevik Bir of Turkey the UNOSOM II commander. The United States, in turn, selected Major General Thomas Montgomery to serve as Bir's deputy. Later, with Kittani stepping down for medical reasons, the Clinton administration, at Boutros-Ghali's request, put forward US Navy Admiral Jonathan Howe (retired), a former deputy national security adviser to President Bush, to become the senior UN representative on the scene for UNOSOM II.[36]

In late February, both Bir and Montgomery arrived for two days of meetings in Mogadishu. The timing was bad, in that their visit coincided with the demonstrations and firefight that erupted in the capital as a result of the violence in Kismayo. By coincidence, just as Johnston was assuring the two generals that the threat level in Mogadishu had been reduced to mere annoyances, the headquarters in which the briefing was being given came under attack, leaving Montgomery, for one, questioning much of what he had just heard. Within a month, both Bir and Montgomery returned to Mogadishu for further meetings, and for the next six weeks Bir would work alongside Johnston. At no point during this time did either Bir or Johnston have a comprehensive plan to guide them. Nor were the two generals able to "twin" their staffs, largely because a UNOSOM II staff was virtually nonexistent at that time. The UNITAF commander vented his frustration in an official interview: "But I am very unhappy with what I view as being an absence of a strategy on the part of us, JCS, CENTCOM, to create a game plan with some milestones. . . . What is the strategy that will help us make the UN move?" As late as April, with only a few weeks to go to the announced transition date of 4 May, Boutros-Ghali still refused to permit detailed planning for the handoff until UNITAF yielded on the disarmament issue, something Johnston had no intention of doing given the limited scope of his mission and the additional forces he would need to execute the kind of nationwide operation the secretary-general had in mind.[37]

As the transition date neared, numerous critical problems remained unaddressed or unresolved. Which coalition forces in UNITAF would remain for UNOSOM II? What new forces would be added? What would their capabilities be? How and where would they deploy? What military operations would they conduct once they arrived? How would they interact? Would they serve readily under UN command or would they bring their own national agendas? These and many other related questions went begging for an answer. Of the important issues that had been resolved, one concerned the extent of US military support for UNOSOM II. Bush had made a commitment in general terms before RESTORE HOPE got under way, and Clinton intended to honor it. Both administrations played a role in determining the specifics, which in final form amounted to keeping around 4,200 US military personnel in Somalia to provide logistic and communication support and another 1,300 soldiers from the 10th Mountain Division (and a MEU on call, if needed) to serve as a quick-reaction force.[38]

Sometime before the transition date, Admiral Howe flew to Mogadishu. Before leaving Washington, he had conferred on several occasions with Oakley, who had returned to the United States after completing his service as special representative in early March. Howe had taken the advice Oakley proffered to heart, but when the retired admiral arrived in Mogadishu, it became clear that he also shared Boutros-Ghali's views on the need for comprehensive disarmament of the Somali factions before Operation RESTORE HOPE ended. With that in mind, he tried to persuade Johnston and Zinni to keep UNITAF in Somalia until sometime in June, but neither yielded to his entreaties. Howe then turned to his highly placed contacts in Washington to bring pressure on the White House to support his position, but the ploy only precipitated a bureaucratic tug-of-war that CENTCOM and the JCS, supporters of Johnston's viewpoint, won. On 4 May, RESTORE HOPE formally ended, and UNOSOM II, with its mandate for nation building, began. For many who had witnessed the incomplete and at times acrimonious and incoherent transition, the new UN-led coalition seemed vulnerable, at least as it struggled to get started, and ill prepared and poorly resourced to assume its broad mission. Key UNOSOM II staff positions had yet to be filled (Montgomery estimated that only 27 percent of the staff were present in Somalia on the 4th) and key military units had yet to arrive or even be notified that they would be deploying.[39] Given Aideed's animosity toward the UN, Boutros-Ghali, and any approach to nation building that would leave the warlord marginalized, those monitoring the situation assumed that any violent response to the new operation would be initiated on his orders.

Conclusions

Judged by the criteria set forward in the CINCCENT and JTF OPORDs, Operation RESTORE HOPE was a resounding success. The worst of the famine in southern Somalia was over, thanks to the acceleration of humanitarian relief operations following the arrival of coalition forces. As one indication of UNITAF's effectiveness on this front, US authorities terminated Operation PROVIDE RELIEF, the airlift of food out of Kenya, in February 1993. By the time UNOSOM II assumed responsibility for the food program in early May, the relief community had declared the "emergency" in Somalia over.

In the process of ameliorating the human tragedy in southern Somalia, RESTORE HOPE also set the stage for UNOSOM II's follow-on efforts to work for political stability *throughout* the country. At the time of the transition, the rampant violence that had plagued many areas of southern Somalia, especially in Mogadishu and Kismayo, had been reduced dramatically, and UNITAF's weapons control policy had succeeded in removing crew-served weapons, RPGs, and the dreaded technical vehicles from the streets of most cities. A food for weapons program had enjoyed some limited success in reducing the number of small arms on the streets as well. Johnston's headquarters had also helped to implement or enforce agreements made among the warring parties on two critical issues, a cease-fire and the cantonment of the objectionable weapons. And the command had assisted in standing up a police force whose performance enhanced security in Mogadishu and the outlying HRSs. Meanwhile, UNITAF engineers and civil affairs personnel had built and repaired miles of Somalian roads; engaged in de-mining operations, dug wells, built or repaired schoolhouses and other public buildings; improved the capabilities of ports, airports, and other critical facilities; and provided medical assistance to the population. In most of the HRSs, UNITAF marines and soldiers had initiated civic action and other programs designed to win over the population, and these same troops, in line with USLO's strategy of stabilizing Somali politics from the ground up, had also played a part in local politics by "empowering" various elders seeking a return to more traditional and democratic forms of local government. If many of these activities could be construed as improving Somalia's infrastructure, thus constituting a low-level dose of nation building, Johnston by 4 May had ceased to mind or make excuses. All had worked toward the accomplishment of his mission.

Upon the general's return to the United States, President Clinton, "in a photogenic ceremony on the White House lawn," personally praised him and those he commanded for a job well done. "You have proved," Clinton said, "that American leadership can help to mobilize international action to create a better world." What the president did not say was that this benevolent achievement had been accomplished at an "acceptable" price in terms of American casualties. Eight US military personnel had been killed in action, 10 killed in accidents, and 24 wounded. Oakley estimated that somewhere between 50 and 100 Somalis were killed as a result of actions taken by coalition forces during RESTORE HOPE.[40] One lesson seemed clear: with the right combination of good intentions, professional leadership, sound judgment, and overwhelming power, it was possible for the United States to intervene militarily in dangerous situations in such a way as to be effective while keeping its troops largely out of harm's way.

Not all the verdicts on RESTORE HOPE were so positive. Some UN personnel were predictably critical of UNITAF's record in Somalia. As one UN humanitarian official in Baidoa reportedly said, "The Americans could have done 10 times more than they have done. Fifty times. They thump on their chests, but the biggest part of the job has yet to be done."[41] There was a logic behind this bitter outburst, one that had been raised by critics of the US intervention at the outset. To send forces to Somalia simply to see that starving people were fed did little if anything to remove the underlying causes of that human tragedy. A lasting solution to the country's crisis required a long-term program geared to political reconstruction and nation building, two areas touched upon but never embraced by UNITAF.

Stepping outside the contemporary debate to draw conclusions about Operation RESTORE HOPE, one might begin with the obvious observation that it was a "political-military" endeavor. This is not offered in the Jominian sense that political authorities set policies and objectives, then give the military a free hand in achieving them. Rather, in RESTORE HOPE (as in numerous contingency operations), the success of the operation was as dependent on diplomacy as it was on military action, political considerations (as opposed to military necessity) often dictated military policies and activities at the operational and tactical levels, and commanders from general officers down to platoon and squad leaders often found themselves engaged in undertakings that tested their political savvy and diplomatic skills. This should have been anticipated, in that UNITAF's principal mission was not to fight and destroy the warring factions in Somalia, but rather to provide security for the humanitarian relief efforts aimed at alleviating the famine. That UNITAF accomplished this mission expeditiously was due largely to the ability of coalition officers, starting with Lieutenant General Johnston, to adapt quickly to the political aspects of the operation and, in doing so, to forge a strong working relationship with the civilian diplomats and political operatives on the scene. The relationship between Johnston and Oakley was indicative of this essential interaction. Oakley could not have achieved what he did on the political front without Johnston standing behind him as the man who could assist the contending parties or, when necessary, punish them. Johnston could not have fulfilled his mission at an "acceptable" cost without Oakley's diplomatic troubleshooting and expertise. It helped matters, of course, that Johnston, Oakley, Zinni, Hirsch, and other military and civilian officials also got along personally and, for the most part, were working in harmony rather than at cross purposes. Organizationally, the intertwining of political-military concerns was represented in the close relationship established between UNITAF and USLO: UNITAF had a political adviser, USLO was assigned military LNOs, and the daily meetings between the two elements became standing practice. The Humanitarian Operations Centers also provided an organizational framework for political and military operators to work together, in this case bringing into the process nongovernmental relief agencies as well.

The predominant role of diplomacy and political considerations in Operation RESTORE HOPE resulted largely from the fact that the warring Somali factions, their survival instincts aroused, avoided any sustained military confrontation with the clearly superior UNITAF forces. Once that point was established, the door was open to the strategy of "deconfliction"—talk backed by military force—that was applied to especially good effect in Mogadishu. This strategy had widespread repercussions for UNITAF. It allowed Johnston to accelerate both the deployment schedule for units coming into Somalia and the schedule for moving those units into the designated HRSs, and to stop the buildup of forces and materiel well short of what would have been required for all-out combat. It also necessitated that he, Zinni, and others in his headquarters (and at other echelons as well) who would be doing the talking acquire information that shed light on the country's politics, history, leadership, society, and culture, not generally topics singled out by military intelligence for in-depth coverage. Above all else, deconfliction made it easier for Johnston to accomplish his mission, while generally keeping his forces out of harm's way. On the negative side, the strategy did open the door for faction leaders such as Aideed and Ali Mahdi to use the process's political and military forums to further their own agendas, something that Oakley and Johnston constantly had to guard against.

While the UNITAF commander and staff learned to operate within the framework of deconfliction, they had to make other major adjustments as well. As Operation RESTORE HOPE unfolded, Johnston found himself authorizing military involvement in several endeavors not listed in his mission statement or implied tasks. A partial inventory of the unanticipated undertakings initiated or supported by UNITAF includes helping to set up a Somali police force, executing civic action programs, working for local political reform, assisting in the resettlement of Somali refugees, negotiating with clan elders and religious leaders, and performing tasks that could be interpreted as falling into the category of nation building. By the early 1990s, the military had a term for the kind of activities that took commanders beyond a strict interpretation of their mission—"mission creep." What was not clear at the time of RESTORE HOPE was whether mission creep was a phenomenon inherent in a dynamic situation, and thus something that commanders and their staffs needed to anticipate and adjust to, or whether it was an insidious process that commanders could avoid through thorough planning and operational discipline.[42] Historically, the former view seems more plausible. In the case of the United States, contingency operations since the founding of the Republic have had to adapt tasks and missions to the logic of a changing situation. To cite but one example of this phenomenon in Somalia, Johnston initially resisted

91

the proposal to help reestablish a Somali police force, but the realization that this initiative, although not found in his OPORD, would actually work to enhance the security of his own forces while improving the prospects for stability in Mogadishu presented him with a logic that quickly overcame his objections. Talk in some military quarters today of avoiding or even abolishing mission creep thus seems, from a historical perspective, nonsensical.

As an unorthodox operation, RESTORE HOPE required military commanders and staffs to interact on a daily basis, not just with their diplomatic counterparts, but with a host of HROs, the news media, and, of course, the Somali people. Working with each of these groups posed various challenges, but for the first two, at least, UNITAF had an organizational response to facilitate the interaction: the HOC/CMOC for the HROs and the Joint Information Bureau for the media. But a constructive working relationship demanded more than an organizational forum in which to conduct business. It also required for many in uniform an attitudinal adjustment, a recognition of the cultural gap that separated their profession from the others and the different perceptions fostered by that gap. According to several after-action reports, many officers made the adjustment, in some cases by overcoming or suppressing their own biases against civilian "do-gooders" and the "headline-hungry" press and by curbing the ingrained military tendencies that foster the kind of "take-charge" attitude almost certain to alienate many civilians. Also helping to bridge the gap was the fact that it is often (but not always) easier to dislike someone in the abstract—a journalist, say—than it is once you have worked together face-to-face.

Interacting with the Somalian people required its own set of adjustments. Most Somalis were friendly, but many were not. No physical line divided the one group from the other. And while many were curious about the foreigners in their country, few felt any deep-seated compulsion to adopt the cultural norms the outsiders brought with them. If anything, they believed, the reverse should be the case, a proposition not readily accepted by all the coalition troops. But even with the best of intentions on both sides, the cultural gap could generate hostility or misunderstanding. One anecdote illustrates the point. A US company commander in one of the HRSs was invited to a local meeting of the town elders. As she entered the room, the door behind her was slammed shut and locked. Fearing for her safety, her first inclination was to reach for her 9mm pistol, but she resisted the impulse. Later she learned that closing and locking the door was local custom, done routinely at every meeting once all the participants were in the room.

Given the cultural differences, the nonlinear nature of the "battlefield," and the daily contact UNITAF troops had with Somalis, Johnston and other commanders did what they could to minimize the chances of unintended incidents between their troops and the population. But in the uncertain, at times ambiguous environment of Somalia, they also sought to protect their troops through a variety of means: promulgating rules of engagement that allowed the use of deadly force in self-defense; issuing operating procedures carefully crafted to enhance safety in various activities such as escorting convoys and guard duty; ensuring that all base camps, enclaves, and strong points were well defended; providing preventive medical treatment against disease; and negotiating with local leaders to remove or reduce potential causes of friction. Commanders protected their troops in another way as well—by demonstrating or using the overwhelming force they had at their disposal. Johnston himself had employed this method as a response to several major provocations. Invariably, the demonstration or use of force had produced the desired effect. While Somali militiamen were warriors, most were not martyrs.

Some of these general observations concerning RESTORE HOPE were included in the after-action reports published by various units and other military organizations soon after the operation ended. But most of the so-called lessons learned that appeared within the US military were oriented toward specific services, mainly the Marine Corps and the Army. These two "land" services contributed the majority of the troops and staff officers who participated in RESTORE HOPE, and not surprisingly, many of their service-specific lessons overlapped. Both services, for example, experienced disruption during the preparatory phase of RESTORE HOPE, when headquarters staffs had to be fleshed out or learn new duties to meet the additional responsibilities placed on them: I MEF becoming the JTF, 1st Marine Division the MARFOR, and 10th Mountain Division the ARFOR. In many cases, staff officers lacked the qualifications for what they were being asked to do. This was particularly true at the ARFOR and MARFOR level, where divisional staffs suddenly had to deal with strategic and operational issues, with joint planning, and with the deployment of nondivisional units, all within a constricted and constantly changing set of deadlines. Compounding the problem for the Army was the lack of personnel trained in articulating the Army's service-specific requirements to a joint headquarters. Over time, however, adjustments were made, and problems solved.

Many of the other service-specific lessons also emphasized the need for flexibility and adjustments. The initial gathering of intelligence did not address many issues that UNITAF would confront once inside Somalia; nor did the intelligence existing at CENTCOM and the JTF during the planning phase filter down to the tactical level in a timely way. In time this changed, but not until many units had deployed. Once UNITAF forces began arriving in Somalia, they had to adjust to the fact that there would be little organized resistance to their presence. That meant jettisoning much of the heavy weaponry they brought with them, except where such items, say a heavily armored vehicle, could be used for psychological purposes. Units stationed inside cities and towns had to hone their skills in urban operations. Among many specific techniques, this meant learning that roadblocks set up to confiscate weapons were most effective when moved every few hours. It also meant learning that time-honored methods for clearing rooms in a house or building had to be modified in a town or city where much if not most of the population was friendly. As one company commander put it, "there are so many civilians around that when you go crashing through doors there's a potential to massacre innocent civilians."[43]

Once the humanitarian relief picked up, the troops providing protection for the food convoys had to determine what mix of vehicles, weapons, troops, air cover, translators, engineers, and PSYOP personnel would be most effective given the threat in a particular area. If a convoy had to traverse long distances, the conditions of the roads had to be checked and adequate long-range communications established. When such an operation involved a handoff in command and control from MARFOR to ARFOR, or vice versa, the procedures had to have been arranged to make the transition as smooth as possible. In almost every case, trial and error led to the necessary adjustments being made.

To conclude, the success of Operation RESTORE HOPE can be related to a plethora of complex factors, many of which may still not be known. Of those that are, several compete for top billing. UNITAF by-and-large had experienced commanders and staff officers who, while lacking a precise method of measuring their end state, understood their mission and were not reluctant to exercise the resolve and flexibility needed to achieve it. This determination, when combined with overwhelming force and the willingness to use it against a determined but outgunned opponent, set the stage for a successful outcome. Fog and friction were present in every phase of the operation and at every level in UNITAF, but adjustments were made, initiatives seized, reason and judgment applied. As a result, the groundwork was laid for further progress. That it would be achieved under UNOSOM II, however, was by no means certain.

Notes

This chapter is based on unclassified material ranging from published works to official histories, after-action reports (AARs), and documents. Of particular assistance in writing this chapter was a working draft of a manuscript on UNITAF being prepared for publication by Colonel Dennis P. Mroczkowski, USMCR (Retired). Mroczkowski graciously allowed me use of the manuscript, and as the notes below indicate, I referred to it often. Many of the issues I treat in this chapter are covered in much more detail in the colonel's manuscript, the working title of which is *The United States Marines in Somalia: With the Unified Task Force during Operation Restore Hope*. Readers interested in the operation can only look forward to publication of his work.

1. Oral History Interview JHT-RHIT-081, Brig. Gen. Anthony C. Zinni, 11 March 1993, Mogadishu, Somalia, interviewed by LTC Charles Cureton, USMCR, and Major Robert Wright, Jr., USAR.

2. Ibid. and John L. Hirsch and Robert B. Oakley, *Somalia and Operation Restore Hope: Reflections on Peacemaking and Peacekeeping* (Washington, DC: United States Institute of Peace Press, 1995), 82.

3. Robert Oakley, "The Urban Area During Support Missions Case Study: Mogadishu—The Strategic Level," in Russell W. Glenn, ed., *Capital Preservation: Preparing for Urban Operations in the Twenty-First Century* (Santa Monica, CA: RAND, 2001), 311; Oral History Interview RHIT-JHT-048, Major General Steven Lloyd Arnold, 26 February 1993, Mogadishu, Somalia, interviewed by Major Robert K. Wright, Jr., USAR, and Captain Drew R. Meyerowich; Briefing by Maj. Gen. Anthony Zinni, Fort Leavenworth, KS, 1994.

4. Hirsch and Oakley, 58-59.

5. I Marine Expeditionary Force (MEF) Command Chronology, 27 November 1992 to 28 February 1993, Section 2, "Narrative Summary," 4, 37, copy in archives of the U.S. Marine Corps Historical Center, Navy Yard, Washington, DC.

6. U.S. Army, Center of Military History (CMH), *Resource Guide, Unified Task Force Somalia, December 1992-May 1993, Operation Restore Hope* (Washington, DC: U.S. Army Center of Military History, 1994), 120; Arnold Oral History Interview RHIT-JHT-048.

7. I MEF Command Chronology, Section 2, 9-10; U.S. Army, CMH, *Resource Guide*, 124; briefing by Maj. Gen. Anthony Zinni, 1994.

8. Oakley, "Urban Area," 325; I MEF Command Chronology, Section 2, 7; Zinni Oral History Interview JHT-RHIT-081.

9. I MEF Command Chronology, Section 2, 7, 18; Johnston Oral History Interview RHIT-JHT-085; Arnold Oral History Interview RHIT-JHT-048. Regarding what weapon systems were needed and which were not, the ARFOR AAR did suggest that an AC-130 and unmanned aerial vehicles might be useful in some future operation, meaning UNOSOM II, but this was a suggestion, not a prediction.

10. I MEF Command Chronology, Section 2, 7, 12.

11. Ibid., 6-10.

12. Ibid., 11. Which of the two categories a particular area of Mogadishu fell under was based on an evaluation that constituted the fourth phase of Wilhelm's original plan for securing the capital. As for establishment of a continuously manned strongpoint, the I MEF narrative makes it clear that this action was based on the Marine experience with the Combined Action Program (CAP) in Vietnam. CAP marines actually lived in the village or hamlet they were assigned to protect, thus avoiding the pattern followed by conventional

line marines of occupying an area during the day only to leave it at night, thus allowing the Viet Cong to move back in a reassert their influence.

13. Ibid., 10. The episode recounted by the journalist is in Scott Peterson, *Me Against My Brother: At War in Somalia, Sudan, and Rwanda* (New York: Routledge, 2001), 55.

14. On the use of sticks, see Peterson, 55; and Oral History Interview, David Dawson, 29 January 2003, MacDill AFB, Florida, interviewed by Dr. Larry Yates. In one well-publicized incident, a marine shot and killed a Somali youth who, as it turned out, was only trying to steal the marine's sunglasses.

15. Unless otherwise cited, the account of UNITAF's involvement in the reestablishment of a Somali police force is taken from Zinni Oral History Interview JHT-RHIT-081; Oral History Interview, Colonel Stephen Spataro, 24 February 2003, Fort Leavenworth, Kansas, interviewed by Dr. Larry Yates; Hirsch and Oakley, 87-92; Mroczkowski, Chapter 5; Martin R. Ganzglass, "The Restoration of the Somali Justice System," *Learning from Somalia: The Lessons of Armed Humanitarian Intervention*, edited by Walter Clarke and Jeffrey Herbst (Boulder, CO: Westview Press, 1997), 20-29; Oakley, "The Urban Area During Support Missions Case Study," 332-37; and Lynn Thomas and Steve Spataro, "Peacekeeping and Policing in Somalia," *Policing the New World Disorder: Peace Operations and Public Security*, edited by Robert B. Oakley, Michael J. Dziedzic, and Eliot M. Goldberg (Washington, DC: National Defense University Press, 1998),175-214.

16. Memorandum from Provost Marshal to J-3, "Auxiliary Security Force," 27 January 1993, copy in PMO/ASF folder, USACMH.

17, A summary of the MDS program can be found in I MEF Command Chronology, Section 2, 13-14.

18. Ibid., 5-6.

19. Ibid., 6, 11.

20. Ibid., 38; Arnold Oral History Interview RHIT-JHT-048; Thomas and Spataro, "Peacekeeping and Policing in Somalia," *Policing the New World Disorder,* 187 note. According to one account, the initial plans for RESTORE HOPE called for the activation of eight to 10 Reserve Civil Affairs units (from 200-300 personnel) to help restore the government, mainly by rebuilding the police and the judiciary system. Given the limited mission set by President Bush, however, and the limited time to accomplish it, the JCS opposed this part of the plan. CINCCENT was also reluctant "to risk any political action in Somalia." Thus, only three dozen CA specialists deployed, compared with the 1,000 used in Kuwait (and Panama after JUST CAUSE). Walter Clarke and Jeffrey Herbst, "Somalia and the Future of Humanitarian Intervention." *Learning from Somalia: The Lessons of Armed Humanitarian Intervention*, edited by Walter Clarke and Jeffrey Herbst (Boulder, CO: Westview Press, 1997), 244-45.

21. Hirsch and Oakley, 67-68; Jonathan T. Dworken, "Restore Hope: Coordinating Relief Operations," *Joint Forces Quarterly* (Summer 1995), 14-20. Dworken's article provides a succinct overview of the HOC/CMOC organization, the issues requiring military-HRO coordination, and the friction arising from differences in "organizational culture" between the military and the relief organizations. Except where noted, the remainder of this section is based on Dworken's observations.

22. I MEF Command Chronology, Section 2, 9; Lt. Gen. Robert Johnston, USMC, briefing slides, *Unified Task Force Somalia*, no date.

23. I MEF Command Chronology, Section 2, 39; U.S. Army Forces Somalia, 10th Mountain Division (LI), *After Action Report Summary*, 2 June 1993, 2.

24. Zinni Oral History Interview JHT-RHIT-081; I MEF Command Chronology, Section 2, 43-44.

25. Dworken, 20.

26. Hirsch and Oakley, 69-72, 75, 83-84; U.S. Army Forces Somalia, *After Action Report Summary*, 2; Arnold Oral History Interview RHIT-JHT-048.

27. This overview of the "preparatory" sessions of the conference on national reconciliation at Addis Ababa is taken from Hirsch and Oakley, 93-95; and Mroczkowski, Chapter 5.

28. Oral History Interview JHT-RHIT-081.

29. U.S. Army, CMH, *Resource Guide*, 136-37; U.S. Army Forces Somalia, *After Action Report Summary*, 23. Between its arrival in HRS Kismayo and the fight on 25 January, the Belgian battalion had seen six of its soldiers wounded in 10 different grenade attacks on its positions.

30. Hirsch and Oakley, 76-77; U.S. Army, CMH, *Resource Guide*, 151; Written statement, R.B. Johnston and R.B. Oakley [to Morgan], 23 February 1993, CMH archives; U.S. Army Forces Somalia, *After Action Report Summary*, 24.

31. The account of the violence in Mogadishu following the factional fighting in Kismayo is based on Hirsch and Oakley, 77-79; CMH, *Resource Guide*, 152-53; I MEF Command Chronology, Section 2, 15-17.

32. I MEF Command Chronology, Section 2, 17.

33. I MEF Command Chronology, Section 2, 12-14.

34. Hirsch and Oakley, 95.

35. Mroczkowski, *Marines in Somalia*, working draft, Chapter 5.

36. Hirsch and Oakley, 108-10; Montgomery Report, *United States Forces Somalia, After Action Report* (Washington, D.C.: US Army Center of Military History, 2003), 233.

37. Hirsch and Oakley, 105, 108; Johnston Oral History Interview RHIT-JHT-085; Oral history interview with Lieutenant General Thomas Montgomery, USA (Ret.), 17 February 2002, interview conducted by Dr. Robert Baumann; Telephone interview with Lieutenant General Thomas Montgomery, 11 July 2003, interview conducted by Lawrence A. Yates. With respect to the threat assessment presented by Johnston to Bir and Montgomery, one should note that three months later, Oakley was quoted as making a similar prognosis for a much wider audience. "There will be violence in Somalia for a long time, but it will be low-level violence," he predicted. "The cycle [of anarchy and starvation] has been broken." *Time*, 17 May 1993, 42.

38. Hirsch and Oakley are adamant in their account that the Bush administration was first to commit US troops to UNOSOM II (beginning with the Cheney-Powell press briefing on 4 December 1992) and that Clinton honored and elaborated that commitment. Conventional wisdom, of course, has it that Clinton was solely responsible for committing US forces to Somalia beyond RESTORE HOPE.

39. Ibid., 111; Montgomery telephone interview.

40. *Time*, 17 May 1993, 42; Hirsch and Oakley, 82.

41. *Time*, 17 May 1993, 42.

42. This uncertainty on how to regard "mission creep" can be found in the Center for Army Lessons Learned volume on RESTORE HOPE. On one page, the phenomenon is treated as something commanders should anticipate and prepare for, on another page as something they should avoid. *Operation Restore Hope*, Center for Army Lessons Learned, 5, I-15.

43. *Operation Restore Hope*, Project Report, MCCDC Collection and Lessons Learned Project, 2-C-3.

Chapter 4

UNOSOM II

Robert F. Baumann

The story of the UN Operation in Somalia (UNOSOM II) is largely that of a mission that began with one purpose and ended with another. As a result of a meeting of key players in Addis Ababa in March 1993, the UN undertook the Herculean task of nation building in Somalia, a process that unleashed a whirlwind of trouble. Assembled as a peacekeeping force with the broad objective of influencing conditions across Somalia as a whole, UNOSOM II soon found its attention and resources concentrated overwhelmingly on an increasingly tense and explosive situation in Mogadishu. Eventually, combat operations superseded routine peacekeeping duties, and a manhunt displaced the initial strategy.

Based on UN Security Council Resolution 814, approved 26 March 1993, the turnover of the Somalia mission from the Unified Task Force (UNITAF) to UNOSOM II commenced. The UNOSOM II plan of operations, Operation Plan (OPLAN) 1, affirmed that the situation in southern Somalia had substantially improved: "Southern Somalia itself has transitioned from total anarchy, with the assistance of UNITAF, to a much more stabilized state ready to take the next steps supported by UNOSOM II throughout Somalia."[1] Later on, regarding this assessment with the benefit of hindsight, the command of UNOSOM II would find it unreasonably sanguine, particularly in light of the expanded mission, embracing the broad problems of nation building and extended territorial responsibilities. Alert to the difficulties associated with such a vast mandate, the UNITAF command worked steadfastly to circumscribe its own obligations as narrowly as possible. This approach served the muscle-bound UNITAF well, enabling it to avoid encumbrance by a myriad of tasks for which, as a blunt instrument of military power, it was not ideally suited.

Consequently, the redesigned mission passed to an eclectic hodgepodge of military formations that collectively bore the UN imprimatur. Certainly, the circumstances of transition from the US-led UNITAF to UNOSOM II were even less favorable than first appeared to be the case. As noted by Special Representative of the UN Secretary General in Somalia, Admiral Jonathan T. Howe, "the early May change of command marked the transformation of the force from one dominated by a superpower with more than 20,000 troops of its own on the ground to one led by a weak organization of many small contingents, the largest being 4,000 Pakistanis still waiting for a portion of their equipment."[2] As the mission grew larger, capabilities diminished. Scholar John Hillen noted, "It was incredible to many involved that the Security Council could pass such an overreaching resolution."[3]

The OPLAN rested on a robust list of 21 assumptions, several of which addressed the environment in which UNOSOM II forces would operate. Assumption 12 asserted, "The primary threat to security will be isolated lawlessness, armed looters, and small scale inter-factional fighting. Areas that were declared 'secure' under UNITAF will remain so." Assumption 20, moreover, maintained that an "interim auxiliary security force composed of former police officers" would assume responsibility for securing key traffic routes and relief centers. Neither of these conditions was close to realization. Finally, assumption 21 noted that creating a neutral Somali police force was an indispensable precondition to success.[4] The overarching logic of these assumptions was that Mogadishu would remain calm and that the maintenance of order would slowly but surely become the Somalis' business. UNOSOM II would watch over the nation-building process within the context of a standard peacekeeping operation.

The UNOSOM II mandate, stated in Resolution 814 under Chapter VII of the UN Charter, included eight broad tasks:

- Monitoring the factions to maintain peace.
- Preventing and responding to outbreaks of fighting.
- Controlling heavy weapons.
- Confiscating small arms from those who were unauthorized to possess them.
- Securing all ports and lines of communication.
- Protecting UN personnel and installations.
- Continuing mine-clearing efforts.
- Repatriating refugees and displaced persons.

At the Secretary General's guidance, military operations consisted of four phases:

- Assuming operational control from UNITAF.
- Deploying and assuming operational control across Somalia.

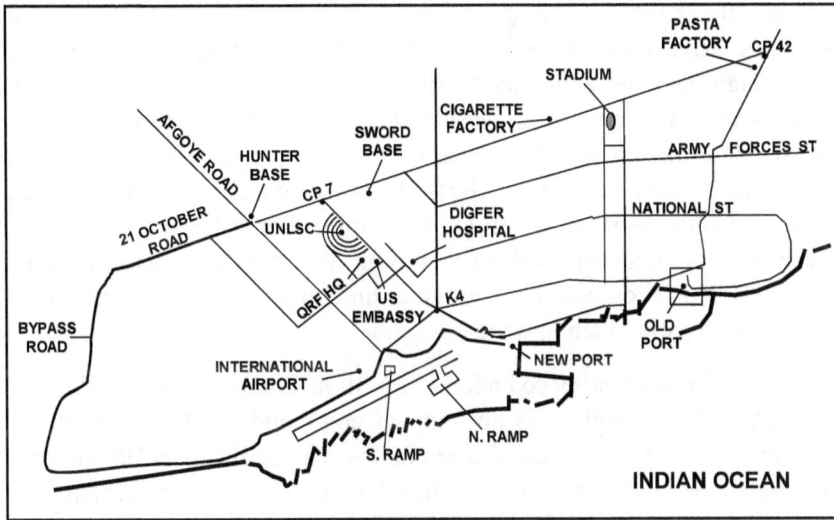

Map 6. Mogadishu during UNOSOM II

- Scaling down military activity and turning greater authority over to civil officials.
- Redeploying or reducing UNOSOM II forces.[5]

OPLAN 1 stated the military mission succinctly: "When directed, UNOSOM II FC [force commander] conducts military operations to consolidate, expand, and maintain a secure environment for the advancement of humanitarian aid, economic assistance, and political reconciliation."[6] As such, UNOSOM II faced the expansive challenge characteristic of international peace operations of the 1990s. While exercising maximum restraint, it was to maintain basic public safety—typically a difficult, if not always dangerous, task—while diplomats sought to perform the major miracle of mitigating hostilities between implacably bitter adversaries. The remarkable supposition that such chasms could be bridged found no starker reflection than the attempt to forge mixed police forces pledged to political neutrality and an ethos of Western-style professionalism after a crash training course spanning weeks not years. Moreover, such amazingly ambitious programs unfolded against a political backdrop of international impatience to quit the scene and forge ahead to other, not necessarily greener, pastures.

Even in the process of its birth, UNOSOM II faced extraordinary challenges. The UN named Turkish Lieutenant General Cevik Bir the force commander of UNOSOM II. The authorized strength of the force

101

was roughly 28,000 soldiers, a total drawn from more than 20 contributing countries. This sounded good in concept, but in reality, it was a motley assemblage, and the anticipated fifth brigade, the Indians, would reach Somalia only in September. During the interim, the force commander would dilute his strength in the capital to cover broader responsibilities around the country.[7] US Army Major General Thomas Montgomery acted as Bir's deputy as well as serving as commander, US Forces Somalia. Faced with the daunting task of assuming the Somalia mission in May, the UNOSOM II command had minimal time to prepare and at first only a skeletal staff with which to do it.

Unity of command posed another question. Analyst Norman Cooling asserted, "There simply was no unity of command or effort in Somalia during UNOSOM II . . . unity of command was jeopardized by US attempts to operate independently outside of the UNOSOM II command structure."[8] At the same time, some felt US Forces Somalia itself was not a genuine headquarters since its staff officers were actually part of a UN command. Command and control responsibilities for US ground forces ultimately fell to the 10th Mountain Division's aviation brigade, although it did not have all of the capabilities normally associated with such a role.[9]

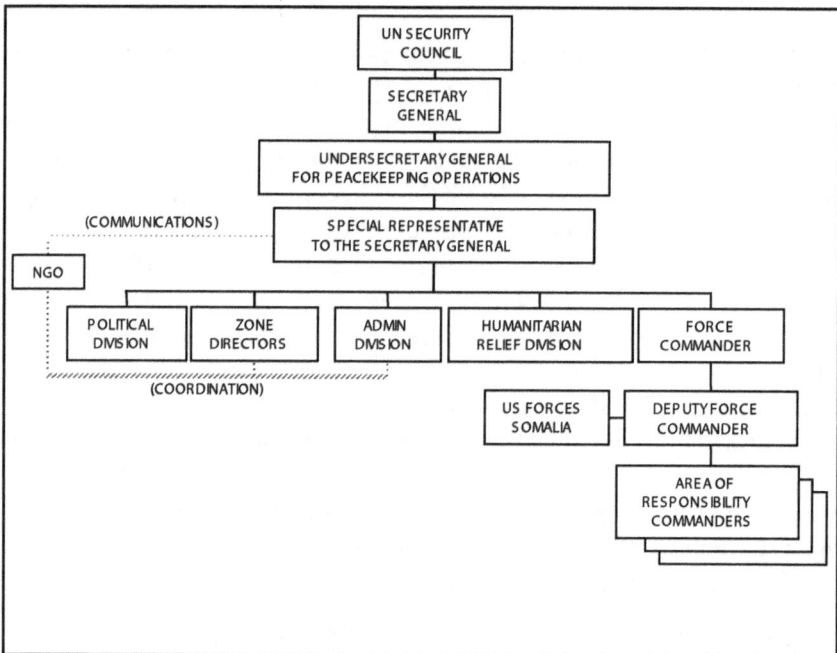

Figure 4. UNOSOM II Command Structure

Still, Montgomery and Bir began a hasty effort to assemble a functioning operations team tailored roughly to a European model. Identifying the component forces of the coalition and pinning down their reporting dates was as much an act of diplomacy as it was of planning. With no force of its own, the UN first had to appeal for contingents from nations that were willing to participate to execute its varied missions. Even then, it lacked any means by which to compel member states to fulfill their promises.

Attempting to size up the developing mission in late February, Montgomery and the commander in chief, US Central Command (CINC-CENT), Lieutenant General Joseph Hoar, joined Lieutenant General Bir in Somalia for a meeting with Lieutenant General Robert B. Johnston and the UNITAF staff. The occasion included a dinner with Ambassador Robert Oakley and Osman Atto, General Mohamed Farah Aideed's deputy. Despite the effects of jet lag, Montgomery could hardly fail to notice the din outside during the formal briefing on UNITAF. Smoke and the distinctive scent of burning rubber wafted into the meeting room. Moments later the sound of machine guns and helicopters precipitated a brief adjournment of the session. The disturbance occurred at a particularly awkward moment. Reflecting the position of both the Army and the Clinton administration, Johnston was anxious to return the Somalia mission to UN control. However, the official transfer of authority depended on UN authorities agreeing that the situation in Somalia was stable and secure. In point of fact, the turmoil in the streets outside the meeting reflected the outbreak of a riot rather than pitched combat, but it was a decidedly inauspicious omen nonetheless.[10]

Undaunted, Johnston put the best possible face on the situation. Later on in May, on the eve of the official transition of authority, Bir pressed Johnston once more for a "worst-case assessment." The UNITAF commander estimated that street demonstrations, such as the one that greeted Montgomery upon his previous visit to the Somali capital, were probably the most violent incidents to be expected.[11] Events later proved this assessment, on the basis of which the UNOSOM force commander concluded that he could spread his disparate units out across Mogadishu, to be unduly optimistic. For the time being, however, it was the foundation for Bir's and Montgomery's sense of the local threat. This misperception would prove hard to correct. The UNOSOM II staff's understanding of actual conditions suffered from a poor transfer of the intelligence mission that left it scrambling for detailed information on the politics and outlook of Somali factions. This occurred for three reasons. First, most of the US

Central Command (CENTCOM) Intelligence Support Element (CISE) departed with UNITAF, with the result that presence in the streets shriveled from several dozen to only a few collectors. Furthermore, as conditions became more dangerous, intelligence gathering in the streets of some parts of the city, such as the Bakara Market area, became too dangerous.[12] Second, despite the presence of Montgomery and a number of American staff officers, releasing highly classified intelligence information to a non-US command raised security concerns. The reverse was sometimes true as well. According to one UNOSOM II staff officer, "There also wasn't a good exchange of information between the Pakistani brigade with responsibility for security in South Mogadishu and the CISE."[13] Third, the UN, and therefore many of its international staff officers, harbored a cultural aversion to the very idea of intelligence gathering during a nation-building operation. Another change with adverse consequences was the abrupt rupture of established personal relationships between the UNITAF leadership and the local factions. UNOSOM II lacked the extensive personal lines of communication to Aideed that Johnston and Ambassador Oakley had carefully nurtured.[14]

Part of the problem may have stemmed from Aideed's relationship with the UN. Oakley later commented, "Certainly in my talks with Aideed he made it clear he did not trust [Boutros] Boutros-Ghali in particular and the United Nations in general." In this instance, the personal history between the two old adversaries played a role. Years earlier when serving as the deputy foreign minister of Egypt, Boutros-Ghali supported Siad Barre's government of Somalia that Aideed and others subsequently toppled.[15] By the same token, some in the UN felt that unrest which had been building under UNITAF had already reached a boiling point.[16]

Among those with a valuable perspective on the transition of command was Major Frank Gorski who served under UNITAF and helped plan the turnover to UNOSOM II. Having worked extensively in Somalia with both the Belgian and Italian contingents, Gorski was not a captive of the American point of view. He thus observed the regional nuances of the mission as well as the varied approaches of different coalition members. In particular, he noted a sudden and sharp change in public opinion in February following a firefight near the infamous K-4 circle in Aideed's sector of the capital. According to Gorski, natives who only days before had freely passed him information were hurling insults at him. Still, in late April, Gorski surmised that, in general, the Somalian situation was relatively stable.[17] In Montgomery's view, the essence of the situation was that UNOSOM II had a nation-building mission that undermined the authority of the warlords. He summarized, "That [to build a nation] was not in the best interest of the warlords, who wanted, each of them, to control, and of course Aideed was the strongest of the warlords."[18]

Even so, UNOSOM II assumed the mission as scheduled on 4 May 1993. Of particular significance was the order to form the Army Forces (ARFOR) as the quick-reaction force (QRF) in Mogadishu and turn over command of humanitarian relief sector (HRS) Marka to the Pakistani contingent. The QRF was under Montgomery's tactical control but would remain under the operational control of Hoar at CENTCOM. Retired Admiral Howe, the UN Secretary General's man on the scene, later suggested that this arrangement was less than optimal: "What they [the QRF] did had to be blessed in Washington or at least by the Central Command. And so therefore it was not necessarily a force that the commander General Bir could control, necessarily, or even General Montgomery, if he wanted to do something, it required a lot of constant liaison back and forth."[19]

Although it was not obvious at first, the QRF, formed from units of the 10th Mountain Division (Light), would play an ever-expanding role. As outlined in OPLAN 1, the QRF mission consisted of three essential parts. First, it was to provide a military response capability to deal with attacks or apparent threats to UNOSOM II forces. Second, it was to stand ready

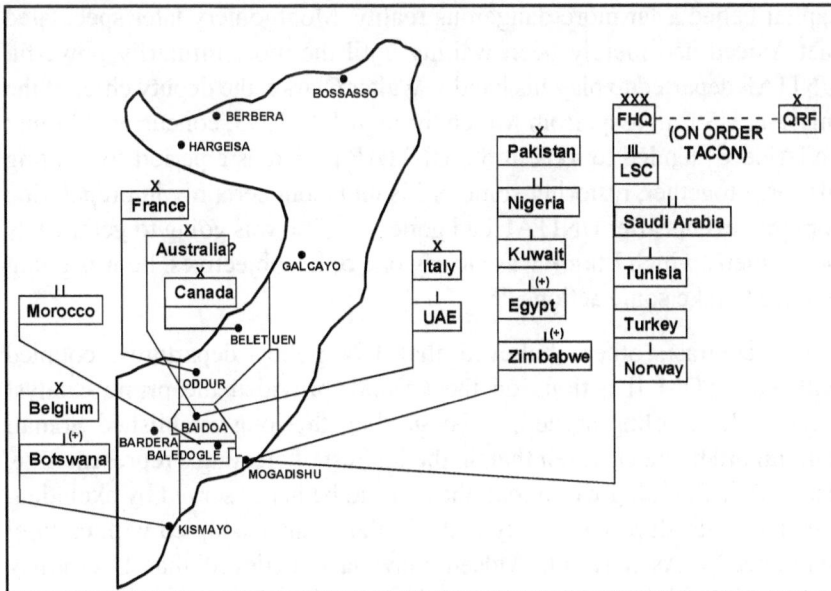

Map 7. UNOSOM II - Force Structure, 4 May 1993

105

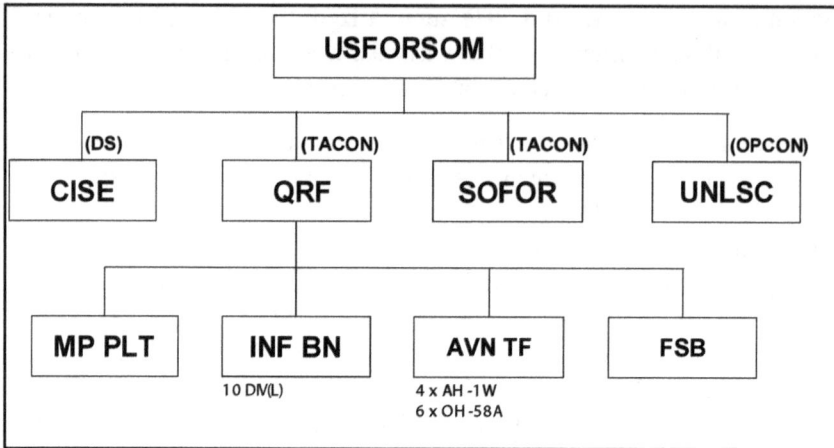

Figure 5. USFORSCOM - Command and Control

to support the expansion of the security zone through central and northern Somalia. Third, it was to provide a reaction force to support contingency operations, particularly in Mogadishu and Kismayo.[20]

However, the need for a muscular QRF to mount numerous tactical operations was yet to present itself. At the assumption of control from UNITAF in May, the environment seemed only mildly threatening. In June it would become abundantly clear that the superficial calm in the capital belied a far more dangerous reality. Montgomery later speculated that Aideed had merely been waiting until the more militarily powerful UNITAF departed to play his hand.[21] Walter Clarke, the deputy chief of the mission, US Embassy, from March through July 1993, concurred: "I think he [Aideed] tended to look at the UNITAF period as a period for putting his force together, restoring some of his units, but certainly in preparation for other events after UNITAF had gone. . . . If he was going to get the UN out of there, which I think was clearly one of his objectives, he was going to have to take some actions."[22]

In contrast, others believed that UN policy departures, coupled with UNOSOM II actions on the ground, provided the prime catalyst for trouble. Cooling argued, "Disregarding the long-established Somali cultural order, the U.N. felt that, in the interest of creating a representative, democratic Somali government, they would be better served by excluding the clan leadership. The policy reeked of arrogance coupled with cultural ignorance."[23] As a result, Aideed may have believed that UN policy makers were giving tacit support to his enemies. Whatever the causes of subsequent clashes, they set events in Somalia on a new course.

According to the official UN After-Action Report (AAR) of UNOSOM II, "the UNOSOM II staff, like that of UNITAF, underrated the intentions of the Aideed-led [United Somali Congress] USC/[Somali National Alliance] SNA. At worst, UNOSOM II expected large-scale street riots."[24] Cognizant that his combat capabilities were far less than those of UNITAF, Montgomery was concerned from the start to strengthen his forces. Among other steps to fortify UNOSOM II's constituent elements, especially the Pakistani brigade, Montgomery obtained 72 M-113 armored personnel carriers (APCs) and a small number of M-48 tanks from NATO stockpiles. Later, in July, he would request far more robust firepower for the QRF as well but would find his own national chain of command less forthcoming.

Within days of UNOSOM II assuming the mission, events gave credence to Montgomery's apprehensions. One indicator was the attempt by elements of Colonel Omar Jess' faction of the SNA to recapture Kismayo on 6 to 7 May 1993. Belgian forces responded quickly and effectively to the developing situation and thwarted Jess' scheme. Further trouble appeared on the horizon with the failed Galcayo Peace Conference in mid-May, during which a contentious Aideed demonstrated his resolve to dominate the political process in Somalia.[25]

Meanwhile, in Mogadishu, UNOSOM II launched a concerted effort to inspect authorized weapons storage sites (AWSSs) in accordance with interfactional agreements dating from February. The plan designated five such sites for inventory on 5 June. One chosen site was collocated with Radio Mogadishu, the source of a seemingly endless stream of anti-UNOSOM vitriol that Aideed sponsored. In fact, there were no weapons at the site—as inspectors would soon discover. Rather, as members of the UNOSOM II staff would later view the matter, Aideed had arranged to have the compound listed as a site under his control to gain access to the radio station. Although the station was not formally an objective of inspection patrols on 5 June, its proximity to the weapons storage facility may have nurtured suspicion among the Somalis about the true purpose of the inspection and contributed to the escalation of tension. To be sure, many among Aideed's rivals, and even some in UNOSOM II, believed that shutting down the radio station would have been entirely appropriate. Still, no such plan was in motion on 5 June, although Aideed's men logically might have anticipated such an act.[26] Indeed, Ambassador Oakley later argued that the UN "showed very bad judgment in doing what they were authorized to do, because without knowing that, they touched off this confrontation."[27]

Right or wrong, that day Pakistani troops arrived to conduct a weapons inspection with instructions to enter forcibly if faced with noncompliance. This should not have been a surprise since UNOSOM II forces had abided by terms of the weapons control agreement and given prior notice of its intended inspection on the preceding day. Yet, the initial reaction of USC and SNA representatives to the letters had not augured well. In fact, the minister of internal affairs became visibly disturbed and warned that the inspections would start a war.[28]

On 5 June, Aideed's forces took a fateful step. They mounted two ambushes against different Pakistani units: one ambush attack came on 21 October Road against a company-size security element in movement between AWSS 3 and the Baluch battalion area at the stadium; the second came against a team of guards at feeding site 20. At the end of the day, Pakistani casualties stood at 23 dead, some horribly mutilated, and 56 wounded. In addition, Aideed's men seized six Pakistani soldiers, one of whom would perish during his imprisonment. Overall, as information streamed in to the UNOSOM II headquarters about a cluster of incidents across the city, a pattern emerged that revealed a coordinated scheme of attack against UN personnel and resources. In other words, there was nothing spontaneous about the events of 5 June. On the contrary, they constituted deliberate acts aimed at derailing the UNOSOM II mission.[29]

The first hint of orchestrated trouble began with a minor confrontation at the radio compound during the inspection. The episode typified the risks attending the conduct of military operations in an urban environment. As a considerable crowd of unfriendly Somalis gathered in the street, trouble erupted and may have resulted in the shooting death of one of the demonstrators. At that time, a soon-to-be-familiar Somali tactic revealed itself, as agitators employed women and children in the crowd as human shields. Despite this turbulence, the overall inspection mission proceeded successfully. By 0930, inspection teams had completed their assigned tasks and began returning to their base areas.

Then, as noted, a Pakistani escort unit ran headlong into an ambush on 21 October Road en route to the stadium. Delayed at hastily erected barricades, UNOSOM vehicles came under intense fire not only from small arms but also machine guns and rocket-propelled grenades (RPGs). Calls went out for reinforcements, but the relief column, in a scenario that foreshadowed the events of 3 and 4 October, immediately came under attack. In the ensuing chaos, Italian helicopters inadvertently sprayed fire at the very personnel they came to aid. At the same time, scattered roadblocks appeared around the city to hinder relief forces' movement, and additional ambushes ensued.[30] Fighting continued into the afternoon. Ultimately, the list of wounded included an Italian and three Americans.

Meanwhile, a second action occurred when a Pakistani platoon guarding a food distribution station at National Street attempted to hold off an angry mob. To their peril, they permitted unarmed civilians to draw close enough to grab at their weapons and otherwise obstruct their ability to defend themselves. Then, according to the official UN account, "From positions behind the women and children in the crowd, weapons were fired at the troops."[31] Three of the 24 Pakistani dead that day fell at this location. A rescue convoy of four APCs attempted to reach the scene from a nearby Pakistani strongpoint, but it could not pierce the obstacles and fire in its path. The same fate awaited a separate rescue force that embarked from a different point in the city. Only at about 1600 did a column of Italian tanks manage to reach the scene. The seemingly late dispatch of tanks later became a source of controversy. Records subsequently indicated that the Italian brigade at Balad only received an order from UNOSOM II headquarters to move out at 1400. An official assessment concluded sadly, "The inadequacy of the military equipment and lack of preparedness of UNOSOM II forces for such armed confrontation was starkly demonstrated."[32]

Almost overlooked in light of the explosion of violence on 5 June were the facts of the weapons site inventories. UNOSOM II inspectors found that the quantity and types of weapons actually present at the storage locations deviated markedly from the official lists UNITAF had passed on. Site 3 contained 12 times the antiarmor rounds previously logged, not to mention an SA-7 surface-to-air missile and 86 TOW missiles. Furthermore, in contrast to existing records, the inspectors found no "technicals." The import of these discoveries was indeed ominous.[33]

The subsequent passage on 6 June 1993 of UN Security Council Resolution 837, authorizing a forceful response against Aideed's SNA faction and the arrest of responsible parties, marked the transformation of the humanitarian mission into something entirely different. A briefing prepared for Secretary of Defense Les Aspin on 16 June 1993 emphasized the significance of a shift to offensive operations implied by the UN directive.[34] From that point forth, US forces on the ground would assume an increasingly prominent role, beginning with a series of missions assigned to the QRF, composed of elements of the 10th Mountain Division, and followed by the arrival of Task Force (TF) Ranger, consisting of US special operations forces. They would encounter dangerous situations regularly, a trend that marked an important new aspect of the mission in Somalia as a whole. In responding to the aggressive new posture of Aideed's forces, the UNOSOM II Force Command (Bir's headquarters) became increasingly preoccupied with the tactical struggle in the capital. This fact of life was readily apparent to some on the scene. According to a former intelligence officer in Somalia, then Captain John Evans, after 5 June, all attention focused squarely on Mogadishu.[35] Similarly, then Lieutenant Chuck Walls, an aviator who served as the executive officer for B Troop, 3-7 Cavalry, later recalled June as marking the beginning of combat operations for pilots serving with the QRF.[36]

UNOSOM II offensive action could not begin immediately. Neither the necessary combat assets nor a comprehensive strategy were in place. At the same time, even as UNOSOM II staffers intensified their planning efforts, Aideed labored furiously to turn events to his political advantage. While conducting psychological operations (PSYOP) of his own to fan the flames of public animosity toward UNOSOM II, Aideed skillfully maintained the public posture of a reasonable and willing peacemaker. Radio Mogadishu proclaimed the firefights a victory for the Somali people in the face of unjustified assaults by UNOSOM II personnel against civilians engaged in peaceful protest. Aideed then made public overtures to the UN to reduce tensions. The command of UNOSOM II, however, was now convinced that its credibility was at stake and that criminal proceedings against the USC and NSA leadership would be appropriate. In short, the respective sides had crossed a political Rubicon of sorts, and compromise—assuming it had ever been possible—now was beyond reach. Equally important, events in Mogadishu increasingly assumed a central position in the struggle to save Somalia, and the UNOSOM II force commander explicitly referred to it as the "center of gravity."[37] Rising tensions would undermine success in Somalia, which largely depended on the ability of nongovernmental and UN agencies to function without fear of attack.

UNOSOM II tactical operations began in earnest on 12 June, although Italian and Pakistani armored patrols began on 6 June. The focal points of this heightened activity included the ambush sites as well as other critical traffic nodes in the city: K-4 circle, the Bakara market, 21 October Road, the cigarette factory, feeding point 20, strong point 50, and checkpoint 89. The execution of such patrols encountered friction within UNOSOM II because of the inevitably complex and ambiguous command relationships between different national contingents. For example, according to the

110

UNOSOM II AAR, "In order to get the operation executed, Italian forces could only be tasked to conduct separate patrols and operations within the Pakistani [area of responsibility] AOR under the control of the Italian forces commander."[38] In turn, the Pakistanis did not want to reenter certain areas of the city without armor support.

On 12 to 14 and 17 June, UNOSOM II forces attempted to regain the tactical initiative with the help of AC-130 gunships authorized by CENTCOM. The additional firepower was reassuring but could not fix inherent UNOSOM II organization problems. Because the diverse UN combat elements could not work together effectively, Bir and Montgomery, by default, assumed responsibility for coordinating tactical operations. Often the problem boiled down to a simple unwillingness of different national contingents to subordinate themselves to a commander of another country. For example, in the aftermath of 5 June, the governments of France and Morocco authorized their armored forces to support the Pakistanis in the city only if they were under the operational control of Deputy Force Commander Major General Montgomery.[39]

Despite such frustrations, once it was ready, UNOSOM II exerted its will with heretofore unseen demonstrations of resolve. This was fully consistent with the overall concept of operations, which stipulated that military operations must reinforce political initiatives. As UNOSOM II Commander Lieutenant General Bir subsequently observed in a confidential UN cable dated 16 July, "it is felt that negotiations without complementary military action would not have the positive effect needed to bring about factional reconciliation and posture the city for future disarmament operations."[40]

Meanwhile, early on 12 June, UN forces struck three weapons storage sites with AC-130 gunships. For good measure, they also knocked Radio Mogadishu out of action with planning and direct support from Special Operations Command and Control Element (SOCCE) 5200. This operation enjoyed the benefit of superb photographic intelligence. Among the participants was First Sergeant John Buckley, A Company, 1-22, 10th Mountain Division. The assault force airlifted in before dawn and scaled the compound walls with aluminum ladders with knotted ropes attached to slide down on the interior side.[41]

The successful raid delivered a powerful message of UN resolve but also foretold what would become increasing reliance on US forces for operations requiring speed and surprise. Even as they curbed Somali broadcast communications, UNOSOM II forces secured an important radio relay site so that it might later support UNOSOM-sponsored Radio Manta. Overall, the reliance on aerial strike platforms gave a clear indication of a change in methodology. Most important, this shift reflected a determination to avoid entrapping ground forces in the city. Aerial operations continued for two more days, focusing on arms and ammunition stores in neighborhoods that Aideed controlled. Although conducted with considerable force, the mission design emphasized limiting casualties and destruction. Thus, the approved modus operandi entailed broadcast warnings to Somalis on the ground to clear the area, after which the gunships would fire precision munitions.[42]

Unfortunately, in raising the level of violence, UNOSOM II drew increased attention from the international community, especially the US government. Planned operations for 17 June, which entailed the further use of AC-130 gunships, received White House scrutiny before approval. Following the mission, authorization for tactical operations using US Army ground or air assets became still more difficult to obtain.[43]

In any case, the follow-on mission of 17 June sought to disrupt Aideed's command and control by dismantling its infrastructure. The target list included Aideed's headquarters compound and the residential compounds of two top lieutenants. The elimination of weapons stores would, in turn, incapacitate his forces to some extent. Operations began in the middle of the night at 0130 with selective strikes by AC-130 gunships against known storage sites. Then, shortly before daylight, French, Moroccan, and Italian troops converged on the area between the Bakara market and the Benedir hospital to permit the Pakistanis to conduct a clearing operation unhindered by crowds or hostile militias rallying to the trouble spot from outside. This scheme of maneuver took accurate account of Somali street tactics, particularly the ability to move crowds so as to harass and impede UNOSOM II forces.[44] Unfortunately, however, the conduct of several mission rehearsals may have tipped off SNA observers about the operation's intent and modus operandi.

Minutes after establishing the outer cordon, Italian and Moroccan soldiers began to encounter angry protesters, while the French received scattered hostile fire near the cigarette factory. Sometime after 0730, the Pakistani 7th Frontier Force and the 6th Punjab finished the initial stage of the clearing operation while US helicopters provided overwatch. Still, within 2 hours, hostile activity around the outer cordon intensified, especially against the Moroccans, who engaged in a firefight that lasted about 4 hours. Because the shooting took place at close quarters, aerial support was too risky to friendly elements. This compelled French troops to force their way along 21 October Road to relieve the pressure. As the battle developed, in a situation that epitomized the surreal unraveling of a humanitarian mission gone haywire, French tanks engaged snipers hiding in the Digfer hospital with main gun rounds. As the fury of the fight intensified, the Pakistani commander, judging his forces to be too small to risk prolonging the effort, suspended clearing operations in the vicinity of Aideed's house. Back at headquarters, the force commander greeted this decision skeptically, believing that the mission objective was still achievable and the risks were within tolerable limits. Nonetheless, events yielded to the appraisal of the commander on the spot, and the Pakistanis withdrew. In their totality, the actions of the day gave yet further indication of the escalating perils of operating in Mogadishu. Among coalition units, the Moroccans suffered by far the most, absorbing four deaths and an additional 41 wounded out of a total of five killed in action and 46 wounded in action. Unverifiable estimates of Somali losses suggested that as many as 150 locals perished.[45]

The UNOSOM II command judged the mission a success, and the operation confirmed that its evolving approach to operations in urban Mogadishu was effective. In material terms, the raid collected more than 2,000 grenades, 50 rockets, 20 82-millimeter (mm) mortar rounds, assorted small-arms ammunition, and more than 100 prisoners. Indeed, for the moment, the UNOSOM II leadership was flush with confidence and planned follow-up operations on Aideed's own turf. Despite the populace's worsening animosity in Aideed-controlled areas of the capital, evidence of public support for UN efforts abounded elsewhere. Even as the firefight transpired on the 17th, a vast pro-UNOSOM demonstration, largely unnoticed by the press corps, drew as many as 30,000 participants in the northern sector of Mogadishu.[46]

Yet, whatever momentum the UNOSOM II command thought it had gained in Mogadishu quickly evaporated. The magnitude of the battle caused the separate national contingents that formed the 17 June coalition to reconsider their participation in future missions. French forces would no longer stray out of their AOR in Baidoa to join such operations without specific approval from the chief of defense in Paris. In turn, the Italians, Moroccans, and Pakistanis concluded that further missions into the so-called Aideed enclave posed unreasonable dangers. As if to follow suit, US President Bill Clinton declared that the success of 17 June obviated further operations in the USC/SNA-dominated sector of the capital.[47] The collective reluctance to challenge Aideed militarily on his own turf

113

avoided major combat in the near term. However, it also weakened the UNOSOM command's leverage to influence Aideed's behavior. Secure within his enclave, Aideed was able to regather his strength.

Another complication resulting from the events of 17 June was the sudden need to deal with large numbers of Somali detainees. The mission to secure more than 100 Somalis fell to the 300th US Army Military Police (MP) Company from Fort Leonard Wood, Missouri, a unit whose tasks already stretched its capabilities. When it had arrived in Somalia in May, the 300th MP Company took the place of a battalion of MPs that had supported UNITAF. To that point, MP operations had gone smoothly. Captain David Kelly, who commanded the 504th MP Company from January to April, believed the populace received his troops very well. He attributed this to the relatively unthreatening posture the MPs assumed, which to some degree, allayed public fears.[48]

Among the tasks the 300th MP Company inherited were operating customs for redeploying UNITAF soldiers, maintaining convoy security, patrolling key main supply routes (MSRs), conducting area security for the logistics command, and handling civilian internees. Faced with the sudden requirement to take care of about 100 prisoners, Captain David Farlow, commander of the 300th, directed one of his platoons to set up a hasty camp. Farlow quickly realized, however, that his legal authority to detain the new Somali wards was at best ambiguous. A prompt visit from a representative of the International Committee of the Red Cross (ICRC), as well as a consultation with UN lawyers, reinforced his misgivings and brought about the abrupt release of all detainees under his control.[49] Fortunately for Farlow and the 300th MP Company, the task of operating a detention facility passed to the Pakistanis. Clarification of the camp's legal status followed shortly as well.

The general situation in the capital remained cloudy, but the overall effect of 17 June was to reshape the political environment in Mogadishu to Aideed's advantage. Weapons raids and other operations occurred elsewhere in the city, but in the absence of direct military pressure, the USC and SNA could begin to turn the tables, especially in their own urban strongholds. Starting on 22 June, harassing fire with small arms and RPGs became nightly fare around UNOSOM II compounds. The material impact was modest, but the message that coalition forces were vulnerable was clear. One response was to increase the level of helicopter overwatch as part of "eyes over Mogadishu." Carried out primarily under the cover of darkness, this operation consisted of route reconnaissance and aerial photography for the dual purpose of protecting UN and US troops and monitoring Somali militias' activities. As hostilities intensified during the summer, road blocks, ambushes, and land mines posed an increasing hazard to ground movement. Aware of regular aerial surveillance, Aideed's forces carried out a constant "shell game" below, frequently relocating barricades and mines to keep coalition forces off balance. Even air travel entailed significant risks, however. Operating at low altitudes and slow speeds, US helicopter pilots well understood their vulnerability to ground fire. This fact also was not lost on the SNA militiamen whose improving proficiency would eventually enable them to strike back at American aviators.[50]

Events in early July revealed that Aideed and UNOSOM forces were in a contest for dominance. On 2 July, Aideed's militia lashed out at Italian forces in the vicinity of the pasta factory following a search operation. Despite the arrival of QRF aviation and Italian armor, Italian forces sustained three deaths and numerous wounded. UNOSOM II intelligence subsequently learned that operations security had been compromised, thereby enabling hostile militias to synchronize their attack along well-planned axes.[51] The dangerous implications of this revelation led to even greater hesitancy among coalition contingents to act assertively or even to comply with the force commander's directives.

The vagaries of coalition politics and tortuously complex chains of command caused UNOSOM II to assume a more reactive stance at a most inopportune moment. At the level of the UN Secretary General, a campaign to marginalize Aideed politically and even seek his capture was well under way. The USC/SNA leader was not about to submit quietly. In early July, UN convoys found themselves subject to harassing fire in broad daylight, and on 7 July, six Somali UN employees died in an ambush. Two days later, Aideed's militias lobbed the first mortar rounds into the Embassy compound that housed the American QRF. To be sure, scattered firing around the perimeter of UNOSOM bases at the university, the port, and the airport had become routine, but such harassment noticeably increased in intensity in July.

Remarkably, a situation assessment contained in fragmentary order 70, published on 7 July, sounded optimistic. The arrival of additional forces placed Force Command "in a position of strength" and made the disarmament of the capital a realistic objective. In more concrete terms, as outlined in the statement of commander's intent, Lieutenant General Bir planned to "retake the streets of Mogadishu with an aggressive presence in the city, keep the USC/SNA militia off balance, and then focus combat power to clear Mogadishu of all unauthorized weapons." The document further indicated Bir's explicit aim "to arrest Mr. Aideed and investigate his complicity in the events of 5 June 1993."[52] To dramatize the point, the UN even announced a $25,000 reward for the so-called warlord's capture.[53] The declaration of a manhunt, in fact, altered the focus of the mission in Somalia and would have far-reaching consequences.

Curiously, even as its planning became increasingly emboldened, UNOSOM II documents reflected an underlying mood of concern. Observations of activity in the streets of the capital led the UNOSOM II staff to begin to sense that its influence was inexorably ebbing. A 9 July assessment of enemy forces aptly summarized the dangers that lay ahead:

> The general population in Mogadishu is slowly losing confidence in the ability of UNOSOM II forces to protect them. Enemy forces are moving freely within the city. . . . Small groups of 10-20 armed militia may conduct ambushes against isolated UNOSOM II forces. Children may be used by USC/SNA forces to approach UNOSOM positions with hand grenades. Aideed has started a guerilla war, utilizing hit and run tactics against UNOSOM II forces.[54]

Major General Montgomery realized that UNOSOM II would have to strengthen its hand in the capital and directed the Pakistanis to concentrate their armor, including well-maintained if outdated M-48 tanks, in that strategic center. The arrival in the capital of the Malaysian contingent, complete with armor, furthered improved the odds. Once again, UNOSOM II patrols became more assertive. Despite its bold posture, the UNOSOM II command privately voiced profound reservations about the evolving course of events. During a July visit, the State Department coordinator for Somalia, David Shinn, led an interagency review of the UN mission. Most important, Bir and Montgomery offered a candid appraisal that there was no military solution to the stalemate in Mogadishu.[55] By the same token, the UNOSOM II command refused to sit by passively and wait for the situation in Mogadishu to develop on its own. Outside of public view, Montgomery sought release of a US Army armored cavalry squadron complete with tanks and Bradley fighting vehicles. Montgomery realized that available forces were not fully equipped to address future contingencies. Yet, concerned about the political signals attending such a step, Secretary of Defense Les Aspin declined the request. Subsequent events would ultimately make this a hotly controversial decision.

Meanwhile, the seminal event during the midsummer phase of the mission in Mogadishu was a raid conducted on 12 July at what was known as the Abdi House. Some members of the press corps at the time viewed this as a watershed event.[56] According to Mark Bowden, whose journalistic history of events, *Black Hawk Down*, appeared several years later, the Abdi raid irrevocably altered the political environment in Mogadishu, effectively extinguishing any lingering hopes of a settlement with Aideed's faction.[57] One veteran of the mission, First Sergeant Buckley of the 1st Battalion, 87th Infantry, 1-87, later reflected, "I guess we created trouble for those who followed."[58] Perhaps he was right. Looking back, however, Montgomery remained convinced that Aideed had already made up his mind to escalate the conflict, a decision amply illustrated by increasing attacks on UNOSOM and UN personnel long before 12 July.[59]

The genesis of the raid on the Abdi House was the accumulation of intelligence at UNOSOM II headquarters that it was the site of regular meetings of USC and SNA leaders at which they planned attacks on coalition soldiers. Consequently, the command regarded the raid as a legitimate defensive action, one that would undermine Aideed's support within the Habr Gidr clan. The UNOSOM II staff also received credible reports suggesting that Italian officials in Mogadishu were engaged in unilateral talks with Aideed. At such a delicate moment, Montgomery's advisers feared that Aideed's prestige within the USC and SNA could only improve if he enjoyed de facto recognition by a member of the coalition.

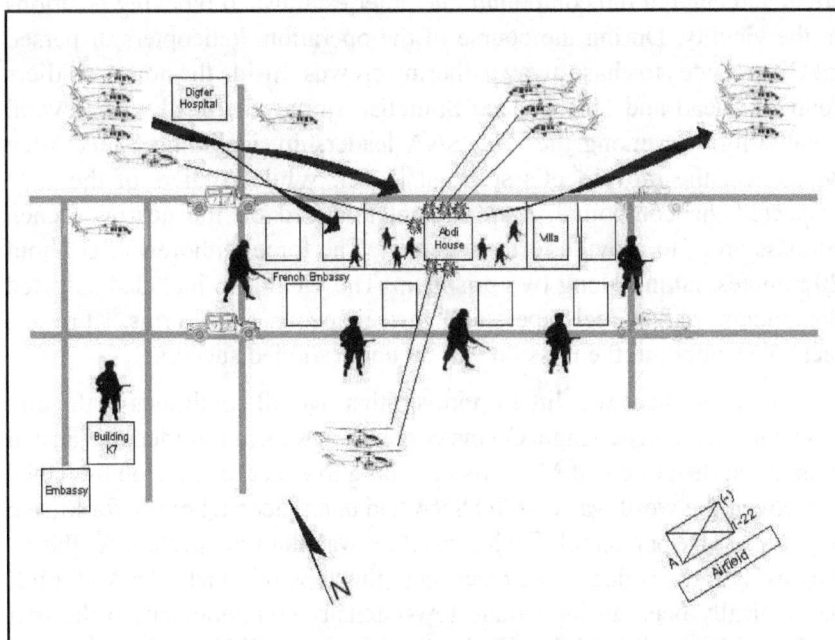

Figure 6. QRF Attack on ABDI House, 12 July 1993

117

Subsequently, an 18 July cable from the special representative of the secretary general in Somalia warned the UN leadership in New York that the Italian forces' passivity was jeopardizing the UNOSOM position.[60]

The takedown of the Abdi House, situated no more than one-half mile from the US compound at the university, benefited from superb intelligence, meticulous planning, and precise rehearsal. Awaiting an execution order for several weeks, the force was prepared to launch on 5 minutes' notice. The chosen force to execute the deliberate attack comprised QRF air (TF Safari) and ground elements (1-22, 10th Mountain). US aviation arrived shortly after 1000. Following a brief broadcast warning, the assault began with a 6-minute preparatory fire by six AH-1 and four OH-58 helicopters employing TOWs and 20mm cannon rounds. Liberalization of the rules of engagement (ROE) mirrored the shift to combat operations. Somalis who did not evacuate the building were "fair game."[61]

Unfortunately, despite careful application, the use of such firepower in the compact environs of Mogadishu resulted in limited but deadly collateral damage when a few 20mm rounds and a single TOW missile struck the nearby French Embassy compound. Minutes later, both air assault and ground troops converged on the scene. While the former, consisting of 53 men arriving in three UH-60s, landed on an adjoining street and entered the compound, the latter established blocking positions in the vicinity. During the course of the operation, helicopters dispersed 22 CS grenades to chase away gathering crowds. Inside the house, soldiers found 17 dead and 10 wounded Somalis. Among the dead were several notable figures among the USC/SNA leadership, including Sheik Aden Mohamed, the movement's spiritual leader. While soldiers of the 1-22 inspected the compound, one helicopter landed on the nearby French Embassy roof to provide further security. The force withdrew after about 20 minutes, taking along two prisoners. The yield also included assorted documents, reel-to-reel tapes, and miscellaneous small arms.[62] From a tactical standpoint, the mission was an unquestioned success.

However, there was little optimism that overall conditions in the city would immediately change. On the contrary, a "source reported that armed men are in the streets of Mogadishu hoping to exact revenge on the UN." Moreover, the word was that the SNA had announced a bounty for killing any US or UN personnel. Such a reaction was not unexpected. As the 12 July assessment added, "The reaction to this type of attack [the Abdi raid] has typically been an immediate low-intensity counterattack on the part of the SNA. . . . it is highly likely that attempts will be made to ambush vehicles and perhaps take hostages." In reaction to the heightened state of alert in the capital, the command kept QRF helicopter support on call at 30-minute notice, directed daily aerial reconnaissance of key facilities, and maintained active coordination with PSYOP broadcast teams.[63]

Increased, sustained pressure produced limited results. According to a staff assessment of 29 July, "Indications are that increased activity by UNOSOM II forces have affected the enemy's capability to conduct operations. We expect attacks (low intensity) on key facilities such as ports, the Force Command HQ, the airfield, Hunter Base and Sword Base."[64] In other words, the apparent reduction of Aideed's strength had not crippled his ability to resist in a variety of ways.

In the meantime, the aftermath of the Abdi House mission aroused considerable controversy from other perspectives. An angry mob murdering four Western journalists in the area of the attack highlighted the continuing instability pervading Somalia's capital city. A particular point of contention, however, arose over allegations concerning the deaths of Somali noncombatants during the raid. The ICRC estimated the total Somali casualties at 54 dead and 161 wounded. In turn, the USC and SNA claimed 73 Somalis perished during the raid, with a number of women and children among them, and put bodies on display to focus media attention.[65] Of course, bullet-riddled corpses were not hard to come by in Somalia, and the UN maintained that the bodies had no connection to the Abdi raid. Montgomery, who had been at the scene, flatly disputed the ICRC and SNA accounts, asserting that Somali deaths ranged from 20 to 25 and that women and children were not present. Indeed, UNOSOM II planners had carefully sifted through available intelligence before the strike to minimize the risk to noncombatants, and combat videotape shot during the event reportedly accorded with official accounts. Consequently, Montgomery termed the USC/SNA claim as "ridiculous" and added, "From a military standpoint, [it was] a very precise, and very decisive operation"[66]

The UNOSOM II report concurred, indicating that all those killed at the compound were adult males. Still, Aideed's backers stirred further controversy by claiming that the gathering at the Abdi House had been a political rather than a military meeting. Among those surviving the meeting was Mohamed Hassan Farah, a clansman of Aideed, who later asserted that the intent of the gathering was to consider the latest UN initiative for a political solution to the multisided conflict that beset the country. In his view, UNOSOM II actions on 12 July united the clan leadership against aggressive, foreign intrusion.[67]

Criticism in the US domestic press corps rose as well. In an editorial column in *The New York Times* on 22 July, Frances Kennedy questioned, "Are the military decision-makers becoming dominant in what is meant to be a humanitarian mission?"[68] Other critics, such as Edward Luttwak, argued that the humanitarian, nation-building mission in Somalia was ill conceived and faced impossible obstacles: "outside intervention would make sense only if it were prolonged indefinitely, in effect turning Somalia into a colony again, this time under U.N. control. Otherwise, all the costs and risks of intervention can achieve only ephemeral results at best."[69]

In this context, late July saw a continuation of aggressive UNOSOM patrolling and weapons searches. Aviation, operating by night as well as by daylight, struck at militia forces and soon proved an effective constraint on their activities. Still, at UN force headquarters there was a perceived lack of initiative among national subordinate commands, which meant that centralized direction of tactical operations remained necessary. Ultimately, Force Command believed that managing the situation in the capital would entail mustering two full brigades, a goal that appeared achievable with the Indian Brigade's scheduled arrival. In the meantime, control of the main routes within the city depended on more effectively employing available resources. One timely development was integrating the Somali police into the network of Pakistani checkpoints.[70]

Nurturing the Somali Police Force and gradually expanding its level of involvement required delicate balancing. The police force plan carefully stipulated that it would not to be used against the clan militias. According to the concept of operation, "The police do not have the equipment, training, confidence, or freedom of action to fight directly against a particular clan militia. Do not risk the collapse of the police with an improper tasking, or by shaping the police into a paramilitary force."[71] Nevertheless, the synchronization of military and humanitarian efforts proved more difficult to accomplish due to divergent operating styles and the variety of agendas among humanitarian relief organizations themselves. Moreover, the entire campaign struggled due to the simple impossibility of disarming a capital city in a war-torn country where weapons abounded.[72] This was especially true since UNOSOM II forces did not range into the central Bakara market area.

In a general sense, the entire mission floundered due to an inadequate understanding of the cultural, social, and political context in which it took place. The normal logic of military operations, and perhaps even more the delicately nuanced intricacies of peace operations, did not apply in Somalia. In particular, there was a failure to appreciate the depth of clan loyalties and the profound repercussions of making Aideed the focal point of the mission. As noted in the UNOSOM II AAR, "Military planners had clearly underestimated the intentions of the Aideed-led USC/SNA militia."[73] A crucial underlying problem was the acute resource deficit that plagued the UNOSOM II intelligence staff. UNOSOM II staffers and the various national contingents had to practice "discovery learning" upon taking over their AORs. In this culturally complex urban environment, intelligence, or "information" as the UN euphemistically referred to it, was at a premium, and at least for a while, it was hard to come by.[74] Still, the overt indicators of trouble were unmistakable.

USC and SNA aggression manifested itself in a variety of ways. In mid-August, during the scheduled rotation of US Army units in Somalia, four MPs died when their vehicle was destroyed by a carefully placed command-detonated mine. The soldiers were members of the 977th and 300th MP companies, which were patrolling together while the 977th was learning the ropes of urban operations in Mogadishu. The attack was indicative not only of mounting Somali aggressiveness but also of a dilemma facing the American contingent. Increasingly frequent skirmishes slowly led to a decreased presence of UNOSOM II forces in the streets. One manifestation of this trend was a decision to curtail round-the-clock patrolling of the key MSRs by the 300th. The intent was to keep US soldiers in their compounds by night, when the risk of ambush was greatest. Avoiding some risks meant exposure to others, however. MP Company Commander Captain Chad McCree, who served in Somalia until the transition to UNOSOM II, later argued that direct control of the terrain and 24-hour operations were crucial to success in Mogadishu.[75]

One who was directly affected by the decision was Captain Farlow, who believed that maintaining MP visibility on the main roads by night constituted a sound doctrinal use of his company. While recognizing the perils confronting his 300th MP Company soldiers during periods of darkness, he feared that their absence would only embolden hostile elements. The sequence of events leading up to the tragic incident lent credence to his argument. Following the cessation of night patrols, Farlow's MPs would conduct an initial reconnaissance of the main routes to begin each day with the benefit of overhead observation by TF Safari aviation. Of course, the command-detonated mine had been planted overnight. With hindsight, it was clear to see that the Somalis had set the stage carefully. Days earlier, US patrols had noticed what appeared to be a minor road repair in progress. Gradually, they became accustomed to seeing signs of routine digging, thereby diminishing the probability that anyone would become alarmed at the sight of any freshly turned ground where the mine had been laid. While in the aftermath it remained uncertain whether night patrols would have prevented the attack, they would, in Farlow's estimation, have made such a scheme harder to carry out.[76]

Broadly speaking, the mine incident had a powerful psychological impact on all concerned. Members of the departing 300th had lost a valued, veteran noncommissioned officer on the eve of departing for home. At the request of the 977th, he had volunteered to accompany a patrol for one final "right-seat ride." The 977th MP Company, in turn, faced the deaths of three soldiers before it had even fully taken over the mission. Indeed, the deaths resonated beyond the units directly involved. Concurrently with the 977th, a number of fresh units arrived from the United States to receive news of the tragedy. For instance, members of B Company, 46th Forward Support Battalion (FSB) who assisted in recovering the wreckage, found the incident sobering to say the least.[77] Ultimately, this episode stood as one more reflection of the transformation of the Somalia mission from a nation-building operation with a humanitarian purpose into a combat operation.

To be sure, Americans were not the only targets of SNA ambushes. On 5 September, Aideed's militia attacked Nigerian forces that were stepping in for the Italians at strong points 19 and 42 in north Mogadishu. Upon arrival at strong point 42 that morning, a Nigerian company commander encountered a clan elder who insisted that there was no agreement to permit new forces to occupy the strong point. The Nigerian commander refused to back down and, within minutes, was under attack. Nigerian reinforcements immediately deployed from strong point 19 in two elements along separate routes. On one of the routes, Balad Road, a Nigerian APC became isolated and absorbed serious casualties. Overall, 17 UNOSOM soldiers were wounded that day. Once again, the implications of a street clash rose above the tactical level.[78]

One source of concern was the Italian contingent's failure to provide support, itself an episode of such seriousness that the UN Security Council called for an investigation. Montgomery acknowledged that a rift developed between the Italian contingent and UNOSOM II. In the general's opinion, "They [the Italians] felt they had a special relationship with the Somalis. . . . And they were rather independent and there were problems between the headquarters, Admiral Howe, and the Italians that resulted in the Italians leaving North Mogadishu and moving to a new location."[79] A second consequence was a delay in turning over other strong points. Direct involvement of the Force Command operations staff in talks with local clan leaders became necessary, but the immediate result was improved cooperation.[80]

Trouble quickly flared elsewhere in the city, however. On 9 September, the QRF responded to an emergency in the Pakistani sector when roughly 100 UNOSOM II soldiers with three tanks and four APCs became embroiled in a raging firefight, in which SNA militia unleashed not only a torrent of small-arms fire but also a barrage of RPGs. The episode began after the 362d Engineer Company, on a routine mission, cleared a roadblock on 21 October Road near the cigarette factory. Scattered hostile fire prompted the company's Pakistani escort to deploy in defense of the position, and a battle ensued. Throngs of Somalis, many with weapons, swirled about in the combat zone. After a protracted shootout and the arrival of US Cobra helicopters, the crowd scattered and the besieged elements on the ground extricated themselves from trouble. During the fight, helicopters from TF Falcon "established 'racetrack' patterns for mutually supporting fires." The Cobras employed 20mm cannons until they exhausted their ammunition and then switched to 2.75-inch rockets and TOW missiles. The TF headquarters authorized use of "whatever means were necessary to suppress hostile fire."[81]

This show of overwhelming strength achieved tactical success, but its strategic implications were unclear. The bitter reality of fighting in Mogadishu was that combatants seldom operated as discrete elements. Indeed, on the contrary, they typically welcomed the presence of noncombatants, seeking protection in the knowledge that American ROE emphasized avoiding casualties. Of course, this Somali tactic was becoming increasingly familiar by September. On this day, to relieve the pressure on the fellow UNOSOM forces, the aircraft opened fire with 2.75mm rockets and 20mm cannons, killing a large but undetermined number of Somalis. The repercussions in the global press cast growing doubt over the common sense of a mission that had begun with lofty humanitarian objectives and had devolved into an apparently senseless, bloody turf battle in Mogadishu. Meanwhile, the TF Raven AAR added this ominous note: "The Somali SNA militia demonstrated a strong will to fight not evident during previous employment of attack aircraft."[82]

On the way to 3 to 4 October, the episode of 9 September was one of five major missions the QRF undertook that entailed significant combat with the USC and SNA militias. The next and most violent such mission occurred on 13 September. At the center of events that day was Captain

Mark Suich, who led Company B, 2-14 Infantry, as part of the QRF the 10th Mountain Division provided to UNOSOM II. Suich had come to Somalia expecting to find combat. Before his deployment, he had seen videotapes from the 1-22 Infantry, 10th Mountain Division, that showed evidence of a more dangerous environment than contemporaneous news coverage on television suggested. In addition, Suich had been a member of the 2-14's advance party before it replaced the 1-22 and saw for himself that the situation in Mogadishu was not benign. The wary captain subsequently told his soldiers in no uncertain terms that they must not hesitate to shoot when confronted with dangerous circumstances. As if to reinforce his point to the soldiers, Company B's arrival at the beginning of August was greeted by mortar fire during the very first night.[83]

Despite this inauspicious omen, Suich's company quickly fell into a sequential pattern with its sister companies of the 2-14, rotating every four days between duty as the QRF company, training for military operations on urban terrain, and maintenance. All the while, Suich's Company B, which was about 20 percent below authorized strength, worked to become familiar with the Somali capital. What it found was that land navigation was extremely difficult, especially due to the inadequacy of available maps that gave only a crude approximation of the layout of blocks and buildings. It also discovered that parts of the city, such as around the Bakara market, were virtually off limits. Mogadishu was awash in weapons. Suich's interpreter advised that he could purchase an RPG at Bakara for about $10.[84]

During his first two missions in the city before 13 September, Suich's intuition told him that hostile elements in the population were increasingly emboldened. Crowds in parts of the city, such as the area north of the K-4 circle, were growing larger and mobilized more quickly. Rock throwing was more common. "I think at this point they were casing us a little bit," he later surmised.[85] Certainly, the general perception that hostile incidents were on the rise is borne out by the official UN chronology for 31 July to 13 August, during which time 13 separate episodes occurred.[86]

Efforts to keep aggressive Somalis back from US vehicles seldom worked for long. At one time, members of the 1-22 tried fixing bayonets on their rifles to intimidate the bolder Somalis and maintain minimal physical separation. At least during the early days of the mission, the real concern of US soldiers on the streets of Mogadishu was not self-defense against a direct attack; rather, they tried to prevent theft by destitute and determined young men in a society in which any piece of American equipment might have significant value on the open market. Unfortunately, the locals soon concluded that the Americans had no intention of actually wielding their bayonets as weapons and became emboldened once again. Afterward, one Somali interpreter recommended using sticks to ward off swarming locals. This approach better conformed to local customs. Furthermore, because sticks, unlike bayonets, could not inflict lethal wounds, they would be perceived as more likely to be employed.[87]

Nonetheless, on numerous occasions, US personnel found themselves in real danger. Most who left the living compounds with any frequency found themselves subjected to occasional hostile fire. Sergeant Buckley began to think of himself as a target in a carnival shooting gallery. He just kept moving, prohibited by the ROE from firing back at enemies he could not positively identify. "When's my day?" he repeatedly asked himself.[88]

The experience of driving around Mogadishu proved equally harrowing to members of Company B, 46th FSB, who arrived in August as violence was spiking. Each convoy outside the base seemed to be an adventure, although gradually a sense of routine developed. Captain Marian Vlasak described a 2-mile trip in August between the university and Sword base as "the longest 10-minute drive of my life." The danger did seem to improve some aspects of soldier performance, though. According to Vlasak, her soldiers took exceptionally good care of their vehicles—nobody wanted to have a breakdown in Mogadishu. Meanwhile, the presence of female soldiers, especially officers, continued to surprise the natives.[89] In fact, UNOSOM II personnel did not even have to get out into the streets to appreciate the changing nature of the environment. Late-night mortar fire directed against the university living compound grew not only more frequent but also more accurate.[90]

As part of the UNOSOM II response, on 13 September Companies B and C departed the university compound on a cordon and search mission to find weapons thought to be stored near an identified SNA enclave. The force included a mounted infantry platoon with 40mm Mark 19s and 7.62mm M-60 machine guns. The objective lay 2½ kilometers away. The aim was to arrive on the objective by 0507 when the search was to begin. The timing would also put US troops on location before the residents arose for early morning call to prayer. Intelligence did not anticipate aggressive resistance, although a worst-case scenario envisaged an organized defense of the area.[91]

On location, the mounted vehicles provided an outer protective cordon. Company B formed an inner cordon made up exclusively of light infantry around its objective, which consisted of six buildings wrapped within an encircling wall. Company C did the same at a virtually collocated objective, a five-building compound just to the north. The plan required Companies B and C, upon establishing their positions, to notify Somali personnel inside the objectives that they were surrounded and that a search would be conducted. Even before the PSYOP message concluded, members of 2d Platoon noticed Somalis inside the main building removing firearms. Unfortunately, the objective was surrounded by concrete walls topped with shards of glass, thus denying Company B unobstructed access. Moreover, having declared its presence and purpose, Suich's Company B was not granted immediate admission to the compound. Unwilling to take no for an answer, Suich decided to cut the gate lock. Prior intelligence indicated that SNA militiamen inhabited the compound, an assessment that was corroborated upon entrance when only able-bodied males were present. Inside, Suich's men seized a modest assortment of weapons and mortar rounds, not to mention a few maps of the university compound that served as home to the QRF. Nearby, Company C uncovered a similar arms stash.[92] The entire process took approximately 2 hours, during which time about 30 to 40 Somalis were detained on the premises.

At some point during the search, Company C received scattered hostile fire from the Benedir Hospital, located about 200 meters to the northeast, and began to return fire.[93] Also in reply, Suich placed M-60 gunners on the roof of the Bravo objective, with the order to return fire if they could confirm a target. Of course, an additional element of complexity in this scenario was that the source of fire was a civilian hospital. The complete willingness of the Somali militias to seek cover behind noncombatants or in a humanitarian facility such as a hospital typified the difficulties of operating in Mogadishu. Gradually it became clear to Suich, as well as his battalion commander, Lieutenant Colonel Bill David, that armed, hostile elements were beginning to apply pressure all along the eastern edge of the two company objectives. Burning road obstacles, a sure indicator of brewing trouble, were visible in the distance. Subsequently, brigade intelligence concluded that Aideed's militias could mass anywhere in his area within 20 to 40 minutes.[94]

According to the plan, Company C was to exit the area, with its detainees on board trucks, by the same route on which it arrived. One platoon of Company B would accompany it on the return to the university compound. As the QRF elements began their departure, "All hell broke loose."[95] RPG explosions now added to the din created by small-arms fire. One blast shattered the western gate of Company B's objective, injuring seven soldiers who were subsequently treated for concussions, including Lieutenant John Reynolds, the company executive officer.[96] Suich concluded that his remaining platoons, as well as the company command group, would be moving directly into an ambush if they were to follow the same route as Company C. Consequently, he decided to blow a hole in the wall along the west side of the of the search objective compound to bound across an adjoining intersection while avoiding prolonged, direct exposure to enemy fire. Suich's intent was to let his force of three platoons slip away by a more westerly route and, if necessary, request aerial support to enable his force to break contact with the SNA militia. Lieutenant Reynolds was in command of the final 3d Platoon as it departed the objective. Reynolds had noticed several men still on the objective and returned with his platoon to retrieve them. The stranded individuals turned out to be from the battalion and brigade tactical command post. No one in the company, it seemed, was responsible for getting them out.

Amid the confusion, Captain Suich was on the radio trying to discover the nature of the delay. To make matters worse, Reynolds' platoon was delayed by hostile fire on the way to link up with the rest of the company near the university where the first two platoons occupied an extended position along a small berm running from east to west. From that location they were receiving considerable hostile fire along a 180-degree arc from the south. Out of concern for inadvertently directing fire toward his own men from 3d Platoon as it was on its way to rally with him, Suich kept a tight reign on return fire against the enemy. General confusion and obstructed visibility within the city brought Suich face to face with the friction of combat. The wait for the rest of his force was not the only problem. Suich later observed, "Really, I was outgunned at this point."[97] The essence of the dilemma was that Suich's company would have to move through the gauntlet and then take an exposed left turn that constituted, for practical intents and purposes, a chokepoint between him and the entrance to the university compound.

Reynolds finally rejoined his company but had little time to savor this success. He later described the scene: "It was so bad you could see the bullet holes hit the embassy wall over our heads." Under pressure, Reynolds had his platoon squad automatic weapon gunner take out a Somali RPG nest and put his force on line, thereby enabling Suich's lead platoon to `engage the enemy freely. During the ensuing action, a soldier in 3d Platoon suffered a serious stomach wound. Luckily, an allied APC

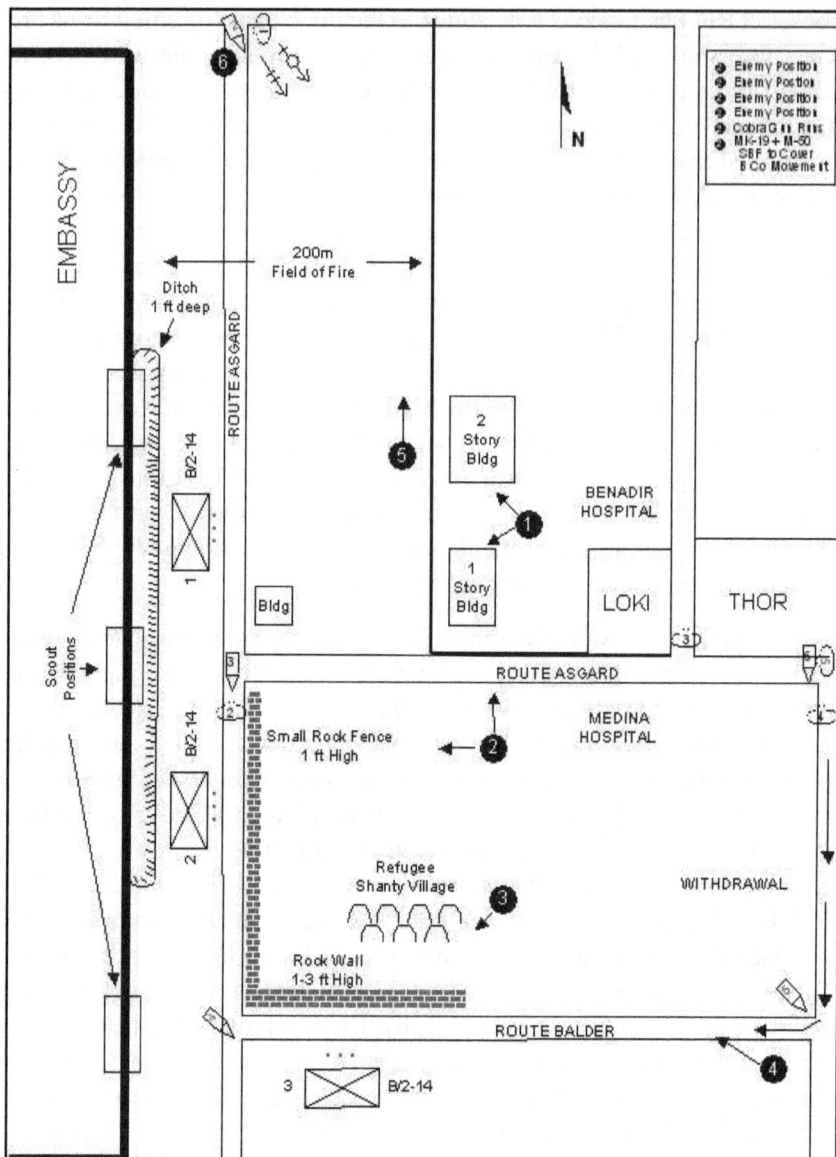

Map 8. Contact Under Fire

happened by. Reynolds dashed over and asked for assistance in evacuating his soldier back into the university. Reynolds placed his injured man inside the vehicle and pointed the way but realized upon closing the vehicle hatch that the driver, instead of following his lead, was moving out smartly in the opposite direction. Meanwhile, the company medic advised by radio that the soldier's condition demanded urgent attention. Reynolds then removed his man from the vehicle and sought a shortcut into the safety of the embassy grounds. He successfully conscripted help from an engineer team to blow a hole in the embassy wall to facilitate this maneuver. Once inside the embassy wall, movement to the UNOSOM compound at the university would be relatively easy because the soldiers could bypass the perilous intersection near the entrance. As usual, however, executing a good idea proved tricky. After some discussion of where to place the blast, the engineers unfortunately chose one of the thickest points in the wall. The explosion produced a hole that was too small to allow the wounded soldier to pass through. By this time, the soldier's survival depended on the timely arrival of the company reserve's antitank (AT) platoon that had been detained at the gate by Tunisian guards who had received no authorization to permit its departure. Thoroughly exasperated, the AT platoon leader opened the gate himself and arrived in time to rush the victim to medical assistance.[98]

At the same time, Suich was deeply concerned that if he could not achieve fire superiority, he would not be able to complete his return without taking serious additional losses. Fortunately, Colonel Mike Dallas, Suich and David's brigade commander, was present at the scene that day and was able to expedite requests for air support. The fact that he was on the ground rather than aloft, however, later became a point of discussion with Major General Montgomery, who had become accustomed to Dallas' predecessor observing from above.

In this instance, it so happened, Dallas was seeking to obtain the ground commander's perspective. To be sure, Dallas' situation was peculiar as the 10th Aviation Brigade functioned as the command and control headquarters for ground and air fire support. Whatever the pros and cons of the situation, having already spent several months in Somalia, Dallas had reached the personal conclusion that "probably the single greatest impact . . . continues to be now both operationally and psychologically" the attack helicopter. He added, "When the Somali warlords started to threaten action and in some cases carried through with threats and moved—or thought they were moving on rival factions or possibly on US forces—the attack helicopters showed up and stopped them dead in their tracks. In many cases, [they] didn't have to fire a shot; all they had to do was show up."[99]

Able to communicate directly with gunships overhead, Suich directed the fire by marking enemy positions with smoke rounds. To provide complementary ground reinforcement, Lieutenant Colonel David called out the QRF AT platoon to help cover Company B's withdrawal into the compound and, in particular, to extract several seriously wounded soldiers.

At about the same time, QRF scout snipers, upon learning from David of the situation just outside the compound, assumed firing positions along the southern wall to reverse the fire equation still further in Suich's favor. Thus supported, Suich's platoons bounded their way to the university's front gate. As Suich later reflected, this near brush with disaster bore striking similarity to the scenario of 3 and 4 October.[100] Above all, he observed, "To this day I still can't figure out why it [the 13 September firefight] did not serve as a catalyst to get more stuff over here." The essence of the problem was that on more than one occasion, Suich's troops on the ground lost fire superiority in addition to facing superior numbers.[101]

How had circumstances in Somalia evolved to the point where the QRF was becoming the force of choice for an assortment of dangerous urban missions? A memorandum for the QRF commander dated 19 October addressed that very question. The essence of the problem, the memo concluded, was that the peacekeeping forces provided to UNOSOM II were not necessarily well suited to what had become a far more violent environment than had been anticipated. In short, the memo argued, UNOSOM II lacked sufficient "quality tactical forces." Conversely, the QRF was a combat force whose inherent advantages were now manifestly clear: "The soldiers are prepared for this environment because they are prepared for warfighting. . . . If we are prepared for war we can make modifications to our tactics, techniques, and procedures based on the environment."[102]

The main difficulty associated with being the premier combat element in Somalia was that the QRF mission gradually grew to include protecting UNOSOM II forces by all means at its disposal. One assessment noted grimly, "Because of the inability, unwillingness, and incompetence of many coalition forces, the role and involvement of the QRF in daily operations expanded." What made this widening of responsibility of its mission more troublesome was the fact that the QRF by definition controlled no territory, meaning that wherever it went it was operating in someone else's area of operations.[103] Equally important, some coalition partners had limited interoperability with US forces, thereby presenting an additional source of friction in what was already an inherently dangerous environment.

Still, such assertions hardly meant that a combat force did not struggle with some aspects of adapting to a peace enforcement mission in an alien urban setting. One notable adaptation was learning to depend on the staff judge advocate (SJA) in the planning and execution of all operations. Interpretation of the ROE and assessing the risks of collateral damage

130

helped keep the QRF on the straight and narrow path to success. The employment of the QRF's substantial combat power in densely populated Mogadishu demanded an acute sensitivity to the presence of noncombatants. Accordingly, among the SJA functions was the maintenance of operational summaries in the unit log to confirm compliance and provide a basis for subsequent adjustments to the ROE.[104]

The ROE in Somalia eventually gave UNOSOM II personnel extensive latitude. The command, with the UN's blessing, declared "open season" on so-called technicals—any vehicle mounting a heavy or crew-served weapon. Snipers from Company B, 1st Battalion, 5th Special Forces Group, facilitated force protection in Mogadishu by placing accurate fire on targets at 1,000 meters or more. Snipers also rode aboard TF Raven helicopters as part of eyes over Mogadishu to provide aerial coverage above 2-14 Infantry.[105]

One clear manifestation of restraint in conducting QRF operations was the principle of graduated response. The execution of cordon and search operations, for example, required the open and peaceful formation of a security cordon around the objective followed by PSYOP announcements conveyed via loudspeaker and in translation to the effect that armed resistance could result in injury or death. If this initial step failed, the first graduated response was to saturate the premises with CS (tear gas). If this measure failed, the second graduated response was to enter the objective forcibly by using a cutting charge to create a hole in a wall. Soldiers would then lob concussion grenades and move in to seize control of the inhabitants with as little violence as possible. In a volatile urban context such as Mogadishu, exercising restraint helped keep a damper on violent public passions. At the same time, however, restraint gave the inhabitants of the objective extra time to formulate a response or to summon outside assistance. This time lapse posed risks for the QRF element, which could be subject to direct attack or could find its chosen exit route blocked.[106] Such was the situation before the 13 September firefight.

Meanwhile, in late August, the United States was quietly reconsidering its role and strategy in Somalia. In part as a result of the Shinn mission, the Americans initiated a search for political solutions even as they moved to bolster their military strength. The former approach manifested itself in the form of intense pressure on the UN to seek a settlement among the factions. The latter, requested by Admiral Howe to carry out an intensified search for Aideed, arrived in the form of an elite combat formation that came to be known as TF Ranger.

Overall, however, it would be easy to overlook the peaceful achievements during the first months of UNOSOM II. Even in Mogadishu, August witnessed a voluntary disarmament initiative and establishing district councils to restore a semblance of real local government. Nevertheless, as on the military front, the key to the UN's strategy was to use its leverage to marginalize Aideed. As one UNOSOM II staff officer later summarized, "Force Command's plan sought to convince clan leaders that continued support of Aideed would result in their exclusion from political and economic processes."[107] Still, the broad UN effort suffered from serious problems of its own. Central to the plan was the attempt to work in concert with nongovernmental organizations (NGOs), including UN agencies that did not answer to the force commander. The NGOs were understandably anxious to maintain a perceived distance between their humanitarian activities and the mounting UNOSOM II military campaign. Even so, the presence of so many independent actors to some degree impaired the common cause. As one Pakistani officer in the UN Department of Peacekeeping Operations put the problem, the NGOs simply could not understand the military dimension of the mission.[108]

The events of summer 1993 in Mogadishu revealed an unmistakable pattern of escalating and better-coordinated resistance to UNOSOM II. At the same time, the mission grew more complex and dangerous. The decision to conduct an overt campaign against Aideed raised the ante in Somalia to a level that strained the military capabilities of UNOSOM II. Coalition members were progressively more reticent to undertake the challenge of controlling the capital. The American QRF, although combat hardened and well trained, was a light infantry force that lacked the mobility, firepower, and protective capabilities of heavier units.

Equally important, UNOSOM II simply did not possess the intelligence capabilities the mission in Mogadishu demanded. Success in the Somali capital and the campaign to capture Aideed required superb local intelligence. In a society that lacked a developed communications infrastructure, this meant that human intelligence was crucial. Unfortunately, from the start, the Americans lacked deep insight into the Somali culture. Capable, unbiased, or politically neutral translators were in short supply. UNOSOM II personnel stood out in Somalia and had no hope of infiltrating the streets even if they had been disposed to do so. Thus, they were unable to sense the rhythm or dynamic that governed local behavior. Even so, UNOSOM II elements were doing a good job of constructing a behavioral profile of their adversary. What they learned was disturbing indeed. Somali militiamen were proving tactically adept and developed a system of night signals with tracers to allow them to mass on an objective. By late September, noted Staff Sergeant Mike Claus, " a force on the ground had 20-30 minutes" before it would be under intense pressure.[109]

The SNA's rapid responses to breaking events were indicative of the other side of the information coin. Ubiquitous observers around US and UNOSOM II bases, not to mention Somali contract employees, were able to pass intelligence to Aideed and his commanders quickly, thereby almost completely denying coalition forces any chance of stealth or surprise within the city. Even more disturbing was a creeping perception within UN and US headquarters that some coalition elements had ensured their own safety by cutting private deals and trading information with the clans. As SSG Mike Horan recalled, "the contingents that stick out most in my mind in regard to these safe passage agreements were the Italians and Saudis. They both drove around Mogadishu without a care in the world."[110] Whatever the truth of the situation, a pervasive suspicion that the coalition was an information sieve threatened to tear the delicate fabric of unity on which UNOSOM II efforts depended.

Finally, UNOSOM II forces had to wrestle with unending ambiguity. This began with the inexorable devolution of the mission from a humanitarian campaign to a manhunt. Foreigners could not discern friend from foe, a fact that immeasurably increased the danger of operating in a complex urban environment. ROE kept pace with the shifting political climate but could never eliminate the need to make quick, subtle judgments. Somalis routinely put noncombatants, even young children, in harm's way, a fact that served as a testament to their own cold-blooded insights into the cultural norms of coalition and especially American soldiers. Members of the 10th Mountain Division never grew comfortable with the presence of noncombatants in a combat zone. If this stood as a credit to their professionalism, it also put them in danger.

Notes

1. UNOSOM II, OPLAN 1, Mogadishu, Somalia, May 1993, 1.

2. Jonathan Howe, "Somalia: Frustration in a Failed Nation," *Soldiers for Peace: Fifty Years of United Nations Peacekeeping*, Barbara Benton, ed. (New York: Facts on File, Inc., 1996), 165.

3. John Hillen, *Blue Helmets: The Strategy of UN Military Operations* (Washington, DC: Brassey's, 1998), 213.

4. UNOSOM II, OPLAN 1, 4.

5. "United Nations Operation in Somalia II, Profile," UN Department of Public Information, 31 August 1996 at <www.un.org.Depts/DPKO/Missions/unosom2p.htm>.

6. UNOSOM II, OPLAN 1, 4.

7. Lieutenant Colonel Thomas Daze, "Centers of Gravity of United Nations Operation Somalia II," unpublished master of military arts and science (MMAS) thesis, US Army Command and General Staff College, Fort Leavenworth, KS, 1995, 48. The author is deeply appreciative for Daze's help in obtaining copies of numerous UNOSOM documents.

8. Norman Cooling, "Operation Restore Hope in Somalia: A Tactical Action Turned Strategic Defeat," *Marine Corps Gazette* (September 2001), 100.

9. Lieutenant General Carl Ernst, e-mailed observations, 19 October 2001.

10. Lieutenant General Thomas Montgomery, US Army, Retired, interview with Dr. Robert Baumann, Colorado Springs, CO, 17 February 2002, hereafter cited as Montgomery interview.

11. Ibid.

12. Tom Daze, e-mail message to the author based on data retired Lieutenant General Thomas Montgomery provided, 10 December 2002.

13. Tom Daze, e-mail to the author, 17 January 2003.

14. Montgomery interview; Thomas Montgomery, PBS FRONTLINE interview, "Ambush in Mogadishu," at <www.pbs.org/wgbh/pages/frontline/shows/ambush/interviews/montgomery.html>, hereafter cited as Montgomery FRONTLINE interview; Tom Daze, e-mail message to the author, 10 December 2002.

15. Ambassador Robert Oakley, PBS FRONTLINE interview, "Ambush in Mogadishu" at <www.pbs.org/wgbh/pages/frontline/shows/ambush/interviews/oakley.html>, hereafter cited as Oakley FRONTLINE interview.

16. Major Khan A. Gulraiz, Pakistan, interview with Dr. Robert Baumann, Fort Leavenworth, KS, 26 September 2001, hereafter cited as Khan A. Gulraiz interview.

17. Lieutenant Colonel Frank Gorski, interview with Dr. Robert Baumann and Major Versalles Washington, Fort Leavenworth, KS, 24 October 2001.

18. Montgomery FRONTLINE interview.

19. Admiral Jonathan Howe, PBS FRONTLINE Interview, "Ambush in Mogadishu" at <www.pbs.org/wgbh/pages/frontline/shows/ambush/interviews/howe.html>.

20. UNOSOM II, OPLAN 1, 12.

21. Montgomery interview.

22. Walter Clarke, PBS FRONTLINE interview, "Ambush in Mogadishu" at <www.pbs.org/wgbh/pages/frontline/shows/ambush/interviews/clarke.html>.

23. Cooling, 95.

24. UNOSOM II AAR, chapter III, "Mission and Operational Concept."

25. Daze, unpublished MMAS thesis, 57-58.

26. Report of the Commission of Inquiry established pursuant to Resolution 885 (1993)

to investigate armed attacks on UNOSOM II personnel, 1 June 1994, as printed in *The United Nations and Somalia, 1992-1996* (New York: United Nations Publications, July 1996), S/1994/653, 375, hereafter cited as Report of the Commission of Inquiry. Some personnel even within UNOSOM suspected the 5 June inspection at the radio station compound was, in reality, a reconnaissance of the station itself in expectation of a future attempt to close it. The observation that the Radio Mogadishu site was not a real storage facility is drawn from US Forces Somalia AAR, chapter IV, "Review and Analysis of UNOSOM II Operations, Reception and Consolidation (4 May-5 June 1993)." This AAR was evidently based on the UNOSOM II AAR but expanded on it substantially in some areas.

27. Oakley FRONTLINE interview.

28. UNOSOM II AAR, chapter IV, "Reception and Consolidation (4 May 1993-5 June 1993)."

29. Ibid.; *The United Nations and Somalia, 1992-1996*, Executive Summary of the report prepared by Professor Tom Farer of American University, Washington, DC, on the 5 June attack on UN forces in Somalia, 298. Farer concluded that the attack was premeditated. He cites as evidence the SNA militia establishing an infantry killing zone and obstacles on 21 October Road as well as tactical flank protection and camouflaged positions.

30. First Sergeant John Buckley, interview with Dr. Robert Baumann, Fort Drum, NY, 28 August 2002, hereafter cited as Buckley interview. Buckley was a member of the QRF that day. As would happen later in October, US troops did not bring night vision goggles on a daylight mission. As it became apparent that US personnel would secure the ambush site past darkness, Buckley was asked to lead a small element back to base to retrieve them. The appearance of roadblocks led to canceling the mission.

31. Report of the Commission of Inquiry in *The United Nations and Somalia, 1992-1996*, S/1994/653, 376. See also Thomas Mockaitis, *Peace Operations and Intrastate Conflict: The Sword or the Olive Branch* (Westport, CT: Praeger Publishers, 1999), 63. The author is highly critical of the UNOSOM II decision to conduct the inspection in the face of explicit warning. Of course, Bir and Montgomery were convinced of the need for firmness to preserve the credibility of UNOSOM II.

32. Report of the Commission of Inquiry in *The United Nations and Somalia, 1992-1996*, S/1994/653, 377.

33. UNOSOM II AAR, chapter IV, "Reception and Consolidation (4 May 1993-5 June 1993)."

34. Somalia AAR, briefing for the Secretary of Defense, 16 June 1993, slide 27.

35. Major John Evans, interview with Dr. Robert Baumann, Fort Leavenworth, KS, 29 September 1999, hereafter cited as Evans interview.

36. Major Chuck Walls, interview with Dr. Robert Baumann, Fort Leavenworth, KS, 7 November 2001.

37. UNOSOM II AAR, chapter IV, "Combat Operations (5 June 1993-29 August 1993)."

38. Ibid.

39. Daze, unpublished MMAS thesis, 75. Here Daze cites his own field notes from Somalia concerning the Pakistani command relationship to Major General Montgomery.

40. Lieutenant General Bir, code cable to Admiral Howe, Subject: Concept of Operations in Mogadishu, 16 July 1993.

41. Colonel Joe Celeski, "A History of SF Operations in Somalia," *Special Warfare* (June 2002), 21; Buckley interview.

42. UNOSOM II AAR, chapter IV, "Combat Operations (5 June-29 August 1993)."

43. Ibid.

44. Report of the Commission of Inquiry in *The United Nations and Somalia, 1992-1996*, S/1994/653, 378.

45. Ibid.

46. Ibid.; UN Operation Log of Events, 17 June 1993, final update as of 1130 C 18 June 1993. Suspicions of passing information to the Somalis fell on the Italian contingent, which ever more seemed to be working according to their own script. There is reason to believe that the Italian government doubted the wisdom of a policy that focused on Aideed as the "bad guy."

47. UNOSOM II AAR, chapter IV, "Combat Operations (5 June 1993-29 August 1993)."

48. Major David Kelly, interview with Dr. Robert Baumann, Fort Leavenworth, KS, 14 February 2000.

49. Major David Farlow, interview with Dr. Robert Baumann and Lieutenant Colonel Walter Kretchik, Fort Leavenworth, KS, 5 May 1999, hereafter cited as Farlow interview.

50. Mike Horan, "Eyes Over Mogadishu," chapters 4 and 9. This as yet unpublished monograph is a personal memoir and was available online as accessed on 6 January 2003 at <http://www.megapass.co.kr/~horanjoh/>. See also AAR, Task Force Mountain Warrior, Operation Restore Hope/Continue Hope, Somalia, 10 April-1 August 1993, 3-25 Aviation Battalion, tab G.

51. UNOSOM II AAR, chapter IV, "Combat Operations."

52. Fragmentary Order (FRAGO) Number 70 to UNOSOM II OPLAN 1, 7 July 1993.

53. Some critics would later contend that the bounty was too small to do any good and merely served as an insult to Aideed.

54. FRAGO Number 73 to UNOSOM II OPLAN 1, 9 July 1993.

55. Tom Daze, e-mail to the author, 12 December 2002.

56. Major David Stockwell, "Press Coverage in Somalia: A Case for Media Relations to be a Principle of Military Operations Other Than War," 18 April 1995. This unpublished master's degree thesis is available online at <http://www.globalsecurity.org/military/library/report/1995/SDB.htm>.

57. Mark Bowden, *Black Hawk Down: A Story of Modern War* (New York: Atlantic Monthly Press, 1999).

58. Master Sergeant John Buckley, conversation with Dr. Robert F. Baumann, Karshi, Uzbekistan, 6 March 2002.

59. Montgomery interview.

60. UNOSOM II AAR, chapter IV, "Combat Operations," and Daze, "Centers of Gravity of United Nations Operation Somalia II," 75, 78-79.

61. Walls interview; Buckley interview; and AAR Task Force Mountain Warrior, Warrior Brigade Unit History in Somalia, tab B, 9.

62. TF Mountain Warrior, Operation Restore Hope/Continue Hope, Somalia, 10 April-7 August 1993, AAR; 3-25 Assault Helicopter Battalion, TF Safari/Operation Continue Hope, briefing slides, 26 August 1993.

63. FRAGO Number 77 to UNOSOM II OPLAN 1, 12 July 1993.

64. FRAGO Number 92 to UNOSOM II OPLAN 1, 29 July 1993.

65. *The United Nations and Somalia, 1992-1996*, "Synopsis of the Attacks on UNOSMOM II Personnel," annex V, 404-5.

66. Montgomery FRONTLINE interview. See also Scott Peterson, *Me Against My Brother: At War in Somalia, Sudan and Rwanda* (New York: Rutledge, 2001) 123-35. Peterson, a reporter for *The Christian Science Monitor*, arrived on the scene just in time to view the conclusion of the raid on the Abdi House (referred to as Qaybdiid house in his book). There, he was confronted by an angry mob and suffered a machete wound to the

head. In the aftermath, Peterson doubted the wisdom of the raid against what his informants asserted was a political gathering and questioned whether it complied with the law of war. Based on the damage he observed, he concluded that UNOSOM II underestimated the number of Somali dead. More important, he concluded that the raid provoked rage among Aideed's clan and only set the stage for escalating violence. Peterson reiterated this assessment in a phone conversation with me on 16 November 2003.

67. Bowden, 70-74.

68. Frances Kennedy, "In Somalia, Machiavelli Vs. Rambo," *The New York Times*, 22 July 1993.

69. Edward Luttwak, "Wrong Place, Wrong Time," *The New York Times*, 22 July 1993.

70. USFORSOM AAR, chapter IV, "Review and Analysis of UNOSOM II Operations, Search for Aideed (31 August 1993-3 October 1993)."

71. Major Mark Inch, Deputy Force Provost Marshal, UNOSOM II, Somali Police Program, briefing notes, 2 November 1993.

72. UNOSOM II AAR, chapter IV, "Combat Operations."

73. Ibid.

74. UNOSOM II AAR, chapter V, "Special Subject Areas: Intelligence."

75. Major Chad McCree, interview with Dr. Robert Baumann, Fort Leavenworth, KS, 1 April 1999.

76. Farlow interview; Dan Bolger, "Down Among the Dead Men," *Savage Peace: Americans at War in the 1990's* (Novato, CA: Presidio Press, 1996), 266-338. In an otherwise fine article, Bolger attributes the mine incident, in part, to mixing troops from two different MP companies and asserts that this reflected a pattern of employment that plagued the mission. In fact, the units in question were not thrown together but engaged in a standard "right-seat ride" in which an experienced unit helps acquaint a replacement unit with its responsibilities. Of course, no one can ever establish whether the 8 August mine incident would have occurred had the MPs maintained 24-hour operations. Certainly, the capabilities of a single company of MPs were limited.

77. Major Marian Vlasak, interview with Dr. Robert Baumann, Fort Leavenworth, KS, 8 August 2002.

78. *The United Nations and Somalia, 1992-1996*, "Synopsis of the Attacks on UNOSMOM II Personnel," annex V, 405-406.

79. Montgomery FRONTLINE interview.

80. UNOSOM II AAR, chapter IV, "Search for Aideed (31 August-3 October)".

81. TF Raven AAR, entry for 9 September 1993.

82. Ibid. TF Raven replaced TF Safari as the principal aviation element in Somalia.

83. Major Mark Suich, interview with Dr. Robert Baumann and Lieutenant Colonel Walter Kretchik, Fort Leavenworth, KS, 3 March 2000.

84. Ibid.

85. Ibid.

86. *The United Nations and Somalia, 1992-1996*, "Military Operations," annex IV, 392-93.

87. Buckley interview.

88. Ibid.

89. CPT Marian Vlasak, Somalia Journal, entries for 10, 15, and 21 August 1993.

90. Evans interview.

91. John Reynolds, The Operation of Company B, 2-14 Infantry, 10 MTN DIV (LI), Battle of 13 September, Mogadishu, Somalia (personal experience of a rifle company executive officer), unpublished paper, 6; Eric Patterson, "Breaking Contact Under Fire,"

Infantry (January-April 1999), 7-8; Major Eric Patterson, Interview with Dr. Robert Baumann, Fort Leavenworth, KS, 17 March 2003. Patterson commanded the 2-14 support platoon that took a position next to the battalion tactical operations center at the objective. The timing of the arrival was intended to precede the Somalis' emergence into the streets after the morning call to prayer.

92. Major Mark Suich, interview with Dr. Robert Baumann, Fort Leavenworth, KS, 1 June 2000, hereafter cited as Suich interview; Reynolds, 9. Suich did not recall the correct date of the operation in the interview, but his account conforms perfectly with official records of the events of 13 September. See also Patterson, "Breaking Contact Under Fire," 7. Patterson's account concurs but describes the open, exposed area along the embassy compound wall differently. When US forces, including Cobras and snipers along the wall, brought their fire to bear on the Somali militia, they were able to prevent the enemy from closing. In other words, with the shift in fire superiority, the open space became an obstacle to the enemy.

93. Patterson, "Breaking Contact Under Fire," 7. Concerning the round directed at US forces from the hospital, Patterson explained that determination of the source of fire was based on the angle of impact.

94. Major John Reynolds, interview with Dr. Robert Baumann, Fort Leavenworth, KS, December 2001.

95. Suich interview, 1 June 2000.

96. Reynolds, 9.

97. Suich interviews, 1 June 2000 and 3 March 2000.

98. Reynolds, 11-12.

99. Colonel Mike Dallas, interview with Lieutenant F.D.G. Williams, Center for Military History Catalog No. RHIT-C-040, 12 July 1993.

100. Suich interview, 1 June 2000.

101. Suich interview, 3 March 2000.

102. Memorandum for Commander, QRF, Mogadishu, Somalia, 19 October 1993.

103. Ibid.

104. Ibid.

105. Colonel Joe Celeski, "A History of SF Operations in Somalia, 1992-1995," *Special Warfare* (June 2002), 20-21.

106. Memorandum for Commander.

107. Daze, unpublished MMAS thesis, 85.

108. Khan A. Gulraiz interview.

109. Staff Sergeant Mike Claus, e-mail to Dr. Robert Baumann, 18 August 2002. In addition, Colonel David Buckley, who commanded the 1-22 as a lieutenant colonel for part of the summer of 1993, later related to the author in a conversation on 24 March 2003 that it was altogether too easy to underestimate the seemingly primitive techniques of the Somalia militias. He noted, for example, that they would mark their mortar firing positions in the streets so that they could return to those spots at any time and know the range to specific targets.

110. Horan, chapter 10.

Chapter 5

UNOSOM II: PART II
The Battle of Mogadishu

Robert F. Baumann

The horrid shock: now storming fury rose,
And clamor such as heard in heav'n till now
Was never, arms on armor clashing brayed
Horrible discord, and the madding wheels
Of brazen chariots raged; dire was the noise
Of conflict; overhead the dismal hiss
Of fiery darts in flaming volleys flew,
And flying vaulted either host with fire.
— *Paradise Lost*, John Milton

Even before the battle of 13 September, a new and critical element had unobtrusively entered the Somali stage. During late August, Task Force (TF) Ranger arrived to as little fanfare as it could manage. Its mission was to break the Somali National Alliance (SNA) leadership and, if possible, to snatch General Mohamed Farah Aideed. This extraordinary venture would require an extraordinary force. To be sure, Secretary of Defense Les Aspin; General Colin Powell, the outgoing chairman, Joint Chiefs of Staff; and General Joseph Hoar at U.S. Central Command (CENTCOM) initially opposed the decision to deploy special operations forces to Somalia because they doubted whether Aideed's capture was possible and were concerned about the unforeseen consequences of such a step. Indeed, an air of skepticism about this new facet of the Somalia mission pervaded the joint staff at the Pentagon.[1] Conversely, Admiral Jonathan T. Howe held to his conviction that a force with increased capabilities was critical to executing the UN Security Council mandate in Somalia and would make possible a more robust campaign to track Aideed.

Without doubt, events took a hand in shaping the US course of action. Washington's decision to deploy TF Ranger, which had been training for weeks, followed the 8 August detonation of a mine that killed four American military police (MPs). As American casualties mounted, high-level thinking changed. Powell recalled, "In late August, I reluctantly yielded to the repeated requests from the field and recommended to Aspin that we dispatch the Rangers and the Delta Force [an elite commando unit]. It was a decision I would later regret."[2] Appropriately, TF Ranger brought a distinctive modus operandi (MO). Consisting of an elite commando unit and elements (a battalion minus) of the 3-75 Ranger Battalion, TF Ranger was under the command of Major General William Garrison, who reported not to the UN force commander (FC) but through a parallel chain back to CENTCOM. This particular fact went unmentioned to the press corps, which cheerfully assumed that TF Ranger worked for Major General Thomas M. Montgomery that along with the quick-reaction force (QRF). The reality was quite different. TF Ranger brought with it a distinct approach as well as a special objective. Viewed another way, there was no unity of command although there was unity of purpose.

TF Ranger appreciably elevated the striking power of US forces in Somalia. Superbly supported and trained to a fine edge, its soldiers were supremely confident. Their mission was to cripple the SNA by grabbing Aideed or taking down his command infrastructure. Focus quickly shifted to the latter in the form of his top lieutenants as it became apparent that Aideed would be difficult to locate. Either way, success would hinge on superior intelligence followed by a rapid, resolute response. Such tactical agility could only come at the expense of any opportunity for detached reflection or second thoughts.

TF Ranger operated under a cloak of complete secrecy because its missions normally resulted from late-breaking intelligence—obtained primarily through its own exclusive and jealously guarded sources—and were extremely time-sensitive in their execution. Meticulous information collection and analysis could at any time give way to a furious burst of activity. Thus, when targets of opportunity appeared, the luxury of patient planning or careful prior coordination with the QRF was unavailable.

TF Ranger wasted little time reaching Somalia before moving aggressively to capture Aideed. Just days into the mission, TF Ranger raided the Legatto House north of K-4 in Mogadishu, believing it to be a command center that assisted in directing mortar fire against the UNOSOM II forces situated at the airfield. Unfortunately, this episode highlighted the difficulty of coordination with UN personnel in the capital. Contrary to the wishes of the security manager of the special representative of the secretary general, a small number of UN personnel were present at the Legatto House and became TF Ranger's temporary detainees.[3] This embarrassing mishap demonstrated the need to notify Major General Montgomery before initiating each operation—a process that was subsequently formalized. Even so, Montgomery would learn of impending TF Ranger operations only minutes before launch. This

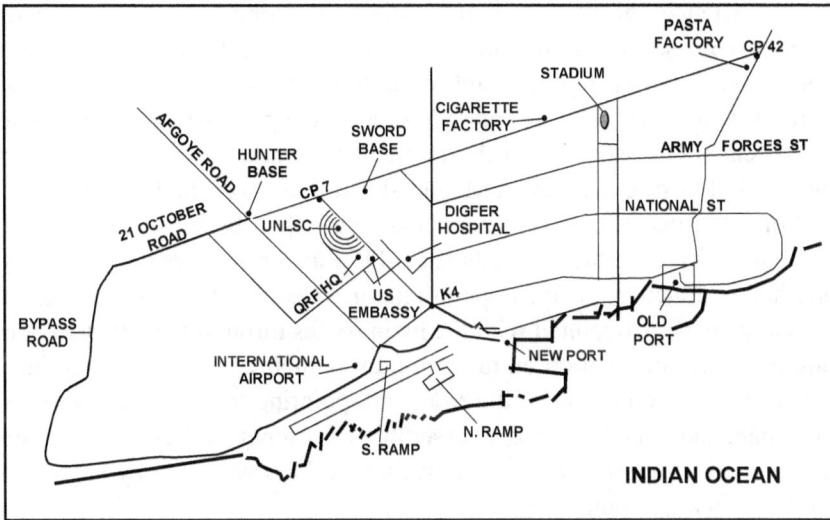

Map 9. Mogadishu - Black Hawk Down

would, however, allow enough time to ensure that no UNOSOM II or UN personnel were in the target area.

In fairness, the tactical execution of the mission at the Legatto House went smoothly, but that fact did not entirely erase the stigma of fiasco associated with the episode. Not surprisingly, the press pounced on the incident. In turn, some of the conventional soldiers in Mogadishu felt the affair was mildly amusing and might even administer a healthy dose of humility to TF Ranger.[4] It would not be the last time that TF Ranger would unintentionally detain the wrong individual. A subsequent operation in mid-September resulted in capturing a former Somali police chief, who was speedily released.

If nothing else, the September TF Ranger missions eloquently demonstrated that accurate, timely information concerning Aideed's whereabouts was a scarce commodity. Among the conventional contingent in Mogadishu, awareness of this reality had already become common currency. The close-knit fabric of Somali society, combined with the formidable concealment offered by a heavily populated urban environment, enabled the Habr Gidr leadership to move invisibly within the capital. In addition, their "low-tech" communications infrastructure neutralized many US means of electronic surveillance. Ironically, the successful capture of a key Aideed adviser, Osman Atto, on 21 September, only compounded the difficulty of locating Aideed, who responded by increasing his personal security measures.[5]

141

Persistence, however, finally yielded the opportunity that Major General Garrison's men had been waiting for. On 3 October, TF Ranger undertook a daring daylight raid to capture top members of the United Somali Congress (USC) and SNA leadership. Based on real-time intelligence, Garrison seized the moment to conduct a lightning raid in the heart of hostile territory in Mogadishu, not far from the Bakara market and the Olympic Hotel. These areas generally had been off-limits to US personnel for months. Nevertheless, TF Ranger had trained carefully and had conducted previous operations in Aideed's area of influence. Its personnel were acquainted with the main routes through the city, which is not to say that orientation on the ground was in any way easy or routine.[6] Garrison was well aware of the risks and, pointing to the Bakara vicinity on a map, had once informed an assembly of company officers, "I will not send you in here unless it is a lucrative target. I know if I send you guys in we'll get in a gunfight."[7]

On this occasion, both the time of day (just after 1530) and the location of the objective elevated the danger. Ordinarily, given their night-vision capabilities, US soldiers enjoyed a huge combat advantage after dark. The cover of night afforded the chance to achieve stealth and surprise against forces that lacked comparable capabilities. Still, TF Ranger had no control over where and when opportunities to strike at Aideed might occur. Knowing it was taking a calculated risk, TF Ranger tried to seize the moment in broad daylight on 3 October. This meant that the enemy would be able to mass on the target area within minutes, leaving TF Ranger almost no margin for error or delay. Making a decision they would later rue, TF Ranger soldiers left their night-vision goggles behind to minimize their already substantial loads in the intense Somali heat. On one level, this choice made sense. By reducing their individual loads, TF Ranger personnel were maximizing their chances of success based on the mission plan. Striking in midday on a mission designed to take under an hour, no one expected to need specialized night gear. On the contrary, operational requirements placed a premium on quickness and agility. Unfortunately, once Clausewitzian "friction"—an amalgam of bad luck, accident, and other unforeseeable factors—took over, initial assumptions went out the window.[8]

The plan was elementary in concept but exquisitely difficult in execution. Based largely on well-rehearsed battle drills, the scheme came together quickly on 3 October. Lieutenant Larry Perino, then a platoon leader in Company B, later recalled that the time elapsed from briefing

142

to mission launch was only about 40 minutes to 1 hour.[9] Junior officers, as well as some noncommissioned officers who would carry out the operation, had a hand in the planning. AH-6 Little Birds would first drop specially trained commandos on the target. Then, even as they landed, Black Hawk helicopters were to fly TF Ranger to the objective where its personnel would "rope" down to the street. This was trickier than it may at first seem. As noted in a TF Mountain Warrior after-action review (AAR) for the preceding rotation ending on 7 August, "There are very few [landing zones] LZ/[pickup zones] PZs in a [military operations in urbanized terrain] MOUT environment."[10] Wires and blowing debris posed a constant hazard. Once on the ground, the commandos would seize and clear the objective while Company B, 3-75 Ranger Battalion, organized into four "chalks," would secure the approaches along adjoining streets. Then, within minutes, a well-synchronized truck convoy would arrive to remove both detainees and TF Ranger personnel. In all, the scheduled mission involved about 160 men, 19 aircraft, and 12 vehicles.[11]

Friction was to visit the TF early and often. One Ranger on his first mission suffered serious injury while descending from a helicopter. He missed the rope and to this day does not know why.[12] His fellow Rangers responded swiftly, but this mishap added a further element of complexity to the situation, as did the fact that the same helicopter had made its drop-off a block or more from the intended spot. This was probably a result of brownout as aircraft rotors produced thick dust clouds. Subsequently, perhaps ½ hour later when the mission was all but complete, a second event created a tragic cascade of first- and second-order consequences. A Somali rocket-propelled grenade (RPG) struck one of the Black Hawks providing cover for operations on the ground. The crash of the Super 61, as it was known, made the helicopter an objective in itself. TF Ranger would not return without all of its personnel or without securing and, if necessary, destroying the downed aircraft.

Although not expected, such a contingency was not unimagined. Colonel Lawrence Casper, who had recently assumed command of the QRF, had asked his predecessor, Colonel Mike Dallas, what would constitute a worst-case scenario in Somalia. The answer was a downed aircraft on Aideed's turf.[13] Apparently, the enemy had reached the same conclusion. Just a week earlier, a Somali militiaman had downed a Black Hawk helicopter participating in "Eyes Over Mogadishu" with an RPG in what most observers at the time judged to be a lucky shot. Traveling at an altitude of about 100 feet and a speed of 110 knots, the Black Hawk went down at around 0200.[14] On that occasion, the Black Hawk belonged to US conventional forces in Somalia, a fact of modest note except that it seemed to create an artificial psychological distance between the event and TF Ranger personnel. Although everyone was well aware of the incident, TF Ranger's aura of invincibility remained unaffected.

In any case, organizational reactions differed. The aviation brigade suspended all Black Hawk flights over the so-called Black Sea area in central Mogadishu. The decision reflected not only a frank appraisal of aircraft vulnerabilities but also a grim understanding of the terrible risks associated with any extraction attempt. Some perceived this decision to be a mistake. SSG Mike Horan later contended that the Somalis quickly drew their own conclusions and assumed US forces would "be less aggressive in their search for Aideed."[15] If Horan's assessment was correct, it might well also have occurred to the SNA leaders that by inflicting casualties they could rapidly influence American behavior. Ominously, even before this incident, the QRF began to suspect that the SNA would try to lure low-flying helicopters into an ambush.

Meanwhile, perhaps because of their extraordinary experience and rigorous training, there was little sense among the special operators that they were as vulnerable as their conventional brethren.[16] Major General Montgomery later recalled his concern: "They routinely flew in low circles above the ground force at about 500 feet—well below the burnout elevation of an RPG. . . . It was almost as if they thought they could not be hit."[17] This is not to say that they were contemptuous of SNA capabilities, but their unalloyed faith in their own skills meant that they did not measure themselves by conventional standards. In reality, TF Ranger, and above all the elite commandos at its core, were the Army's very best; difficult or perilous missions were their stock in trade. Still, to at least a few observers in the conventional forces, TF Ranger behaved with a swagger that was irksome at best and reckless at worst. Of course, what was not fully known to any of the US forces at that time was the great number of RPGs the Somalis had or their increasing tactical proficiency in firing them. Experts would later recognize that former Mujahideen fighters from the Soviet-Afghan war played a significant role in passing on the lessons of that unconventional struggle against a technologically advanced opponent.[18] Although the TF Ranger command knew it faced a dangerous foe, it had experienced rather little misfortune on previous missions.

Years later, the former battalion assistant S3, then Captain James Klingaman, realized that he would have benefited from a more detailed knowledge of the harsher experiences of 2-14, 10th Mountain Division, in August and September. It was fate's decree that in 2001-2002 he would serve as the battalion commander of 2-14. Only then did he have the opportunity to examine carefully the unit's historical record. The signs were there, he concluded, not only that the SNA militia posed a real danger but that its ferocity was intensifying.[19] Similarly, Jeff Struecker, a sergeant in the 3-75 in 1993, subsequently observed, "We didn't have time for a formal review of 10th Mountain's mission." Informal channels to some extent compensated, however. Shortly before TF Ranger's deployment, the battalion received a new staff sergeant fresh from service with the 10th Mountain Division in Somalia. Small-unit leaders in the 3-75 "picked his brain" extensively.[20] In addition, Struecker remembered carefully reviewing the details of the command-detonated mine incident that killed the MPs as well as the routine sniping at troop convoys. "What caught me off guard on 3-4 October," he added, "was how intense the enemy fire was. It was a shower of bullets almost all night long."[21]

With the deaths of three crew members, the 25 September crash was certainly a tragedy. Only a series of fortuitous circumstances prevented greater losses. On that occasion, the crippled Black Hawk had hit the ground much closer to a less hostile area that coalition forces routinely patrolled. Even then, a QRF company arriving at the scene had a relatively modest but extended firefight on its hands. Fortunately, the surviving crew members, armed only with 9-millimeter (mm) pistols, managed, with a friendly civilian's assistance, to find their way to UNOSOM II forces. In contrast, on 3 October, the Habr Gidr clan militias enjoyed all the advantages of a perfect scenario. Organized by neighborhood and able to act promptly according to prearranged signals, they began to flood the area where TF Ranger remained on the ground. As the situation was beginning to develop, the trucks arrived and Sergeant Struecker led a small caravan with the injured private back to base. The caravan was to return to nearby National Street, a wide road facilitating easy movement, and then back via K-4 circle to their seaside compound.

For Struecker and others, the return trip marked the start of a nightmarish journey. Swarming crowds, burning tires and other obstacles, and above all, ambushes at seemingly every turn marked his route. Suddenly, the full spectrum of the perils of urban operations appeared with blazing clarity. Fire came from every direction, high and low. Struecker, noticing that his high-mobility, multipurpose wheeled vehicle (HMMWV) gunners were spraying return fire, hastily improvised a more rational order. To provide general but more accurate fire suppression, he had one fire ahead, one to the right, and one to the left. Struecker's small force suffered numerous casualties, including the mission's first confirmed soldier killed in action. Upon his return, one sage veteran of previous combat advised him to clean the blood out of the rear of his HMMWV. Otherwise, over the course of the day it would affect the men who would go back out in the vehicle. It turned out that Struecker, fighting fear and the logic of the situation, would be one of those going back out.[22] In fact, *because* he had just come from the scene of trouble, he was directed to guide the rescue force back to TF Ranger's location.

Struecker knew orientation in the city would be difficult as he tried to evade hostile strong points. Fortunately, a Black Hawk overhead would guide him. What the pilot above apparently could not discern was that, upon exiting the airfield, Struecker's vehicles were driving headlong into an ambush. Backing away from the firing, Struecker received guidance to leave the compound in the opposite direction. Eventually, he opted for a circuitous route to the besieged TF that took him virtually around the city.

In the meantime, two helicopters, an MH-6 assault aircraft and an MH-60 ferrying a 15-man combat search and rescue (CSAR) team, flew to the crash site. The MH-6 immediately airlifted two wounded Rangers back to a field hospital.[23] On the ground, as well, Rangers began to move rapidly from the mission objective to the Super 61 Black Hawk crash site. Ranger chalk 2 held the northeastern perimeter. Knowing the crash site was close by and that a crowd would form, Ranger Specialist Shawn Nelson wanted to move out right away. His platoon leader, who shared that assessment, simply informed his chain of command over the radio that the chalk would advance to secure the site several blocks away. Before they could depart, the company commander, Captain Mike Steele, insisted that some men remain behind to hold the intersection.[24]

Eventually, what would be known as the first, or northern, crash site would lie at the edge of a hastily formed defensive perimeter as TF Ranger rallied to a common location. It would hold that position for the duration of the fight. Special operations helicopters provided unrelenting fire support under a furious enemy barrage in addition to dropping much-needed ammunition and medical supplies. As the toll of damaged aircraft mounted, further evacuations became impossible. As for all likely contingencies, TF Ranger had rehearsed a CSAR exercise in the event of a downed aircraft but in a relatively open area. Here, the constricted environs and withering fire posed a tougher dilemma.

Even before the first helicopter crash, Lieutenant Perino's men had already begun to encounter Somali urban tactics. Four or five young Somali boys cautiously but steadily approached his position near the target building, giving directions to unseen persons behind them. Recognizing that the youths were acting as spotters and hoping to chase them off before real fire started, Perino fired a few rounds into the dirt not far away. The ploy succeeded in scattering the unwelcome observers and also provided a defining moment for a young lieutenant with 3½ years of experience. "That was a big moment for me," he remembered. "I had to pull the trigger." Soon, Perino's M-60 gunner fired on an armed man who was creeping forward while concealing himself behind a woman.[25] Matters escalated abruptly.

With the completion of the mission at the objective, from which the sound of nearby shooting was audible, Perino's Rangers began moving toward the crash site. In their approach, they suffered one casualty and then came over a gentle rise as they closed in on the crippled Black Hawk. There, upon making a left turn, "All hell broke loose." Perino remembered flying concrete fragments and bullets dancing between his legs, and realized the situation was turning bad. One soldier suffered a mortal wound as the shocked lieutenant stood next to him with his hand on his shoulder. As best they could manage, Perino's men scrambled into an adjoining courtyard, but soon only three members of his chalk remained unwounded.[26] Beleaguered on all sides, the Rangers hunkered down to survive the night. AH-6 Little Bird helicopters provided life-saving fire support, breaking up advancing militia groups and attacking hostile firing positions. Brilliantly piloted, the Little Birds demonstrated an extraordinary capacity to maneuver in tight spaces and place fire accurately. During the engagement, OH-58 Scouts and Cobra attack helicopters from the QRF offered to assist but received guidance from Major General Garrison to "back off." The concern was primarily one of air space management.[27] The sky directly over the battle area could only accommodate a small number of aircraft at any one time.

Still another piece of the puzzle that day was the ground convoy transporting Somali detainees from the objective. Unable to work its way to the first crash site, this element returned to base. On the way, it encountered another convoy that had set out from the airfield in an ill-fated attempt to locate the second downed Black Hawk. The two forces returned to base together.

All the while, observers back at the various coalition headquarters in Mogadishu were trying feverishly to grasp the dimensions of the breaking crisis. Colonel Casper, the QRF commander, had just returned to the capital from travel elsewhere in Somalia. Once at the tactical operations center, he learned that a mission was under way but little else. "I was astounded by the lack of information," he recalled later in his book, *Falcon Brigade*. "We were the reinforcements for every US and UN force in theater, and we didn't know what was occurring in our backyard."[28] To be sure, the QRF had a TF Ranger liaison officer on the staff, but due to the secrecy surrounding the operation, he knew only the operation's general location. Immediately before launching any assault operation, TF Ranger routinely passed this information to the QRF, as well as to Major General Montgomery. A principal reason for withholding detail was concern over leaks from within the UN headquarters.

As the crisis unfolded, Casper received word from Brigadier General Greg Gile, the assistant division commander, 10th Mountain Division, that Major General Garrison wanted the quick reaction company on standby for immediate departure under his control. In this instance, Company C, under Captain Mike Whetstone, was the ready force. As commander of the 2-14 Battalion, Lieutenant Colonel Bill David faced a difficult decision concerning moving the force to the airport, home to TF Ranger. In a moment of extreme urgency, he had to choose between the fastest, and almost certainly most dangerous, route and a much longer but more certain one. To select the former would not only mean increased danger to his men but also a much higher risk of being stopped. Therefore, he opted for the latter course of action after receiving assurances that the TF Ranger perimeter, although under pressure, was not in danger of imminent collapse. Of course, the men inside the perimeter anxiously awaited the arrival of reinforcements, even though most believed they could hold the position.[29] Meanwhile, even as the relief operation was getting under way, a second Black Hawk, piloted by Michael Durant, went down as a result of enemy fire about 1 mile from the first.

Many would later question how matters could have gone so far wrong. One much-discussed point was whether trouble was inevitable as TF Ranger's MO became more familiar to the USC/SNA military leaders. Certainly, Colonel Casper was among those who suspected that TF Ranger was slowly losing the element of surprise. He explained:

> The complexity of the mission, the congestion and diversity of urban terrain, and the heavy reliance on near-real-time intelligence drove

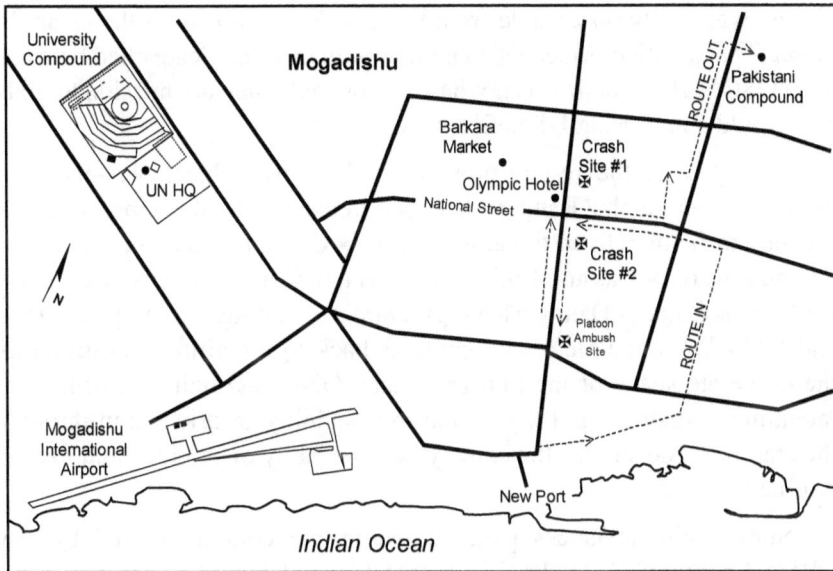

Map 10. Battle, Mogadishu, 3-4 October 1993

TF Ranger to a templated approach for the accomplishment of its task. . . . Garrison and his task force attempted variations to mask their procedures, but repetition and consistency had unintentionally telegraphed their mode of operation to those who were interested.[30]

Ultimately, given that TF Ranger's purpose was widely known, strategic surprise was impossible. Aideed did not have to conduct exhaustive analysis to deduce that any Ranger mission could turn out to be an attempt to seize him. In addition, the airfield from which TF Ranger helicopters departed was itself visible to observers on rooftops outside the perimeter not more than 1 kilometer (km) away. Operating in a small city and highly dependent on rapid aerial insertion, TF Ranger could conceal only the timing and specific location of its operations—and even then only briefly.

Still, as seen through Lieutenant Perino's eyes, everything possible was done to remain unpredictable. Several times daily, at irregular hours and along varying routes, TF Ranger helicopters left the airfield and toured the Mogadishu environs. Sometimes they landed on an objective. The intent was that the frequency of activity would make it appear routine, thereby to some extent "desensitizing" Aideed's militias to TF Ranger's movements around the city. Furthermore, to avoid establishing a pattern, the Rangers would at times depart the objective by air, at other times by land.[31] Despite everything, however, certain facts were inescapable. The airfield was easily observable from the city. Moreover, from the enemy's "threat" perspective, Aideed's men knew well that their leader had become a UNOSOM II target. It was not hard to conclude that any mission to grab him would entail using US helicopters.

In any case, the rescue now focused on two objectives—the first crash site where the Rangers had congregated and the more isolated second crash site. Given the extraordinarily difficult situation, the rescue attempts were not assured of success. Major General Garrison directed Lieutenant Colonel Danny McKnight, already leading a convoy of trucks and HMMWVs complete with captives back to the airfield, to divert to the desperate scene of the first crash site. Given the hail of hostile fire, mounting casualties, and the virtual impossibility of orientation through the cramped side streets, the convoy became badly disoriented and finally returned to base.

Similar circumstances plagued the rescue column headed by the QRF's Company C. Under Lieutenant Colonel David's command, the relief force assembled at 1747, about 2 hours after the first alert. The aim was to travel via the K-4 traffic circle to the objective. David asked for and received air cover from TF 2-25. Unfortunately, the overhead support did not arrive before Company C approached K-4 and came under fire. Undeterred, the convoy returned suppressing fire and made its way to National Street. Yet, a short distance farther along, David's force became mired in a major fight until Colonel Casper ordered it to break contact and return to the airfield.[32]

With frustration mounting, Casper moved by air with his staff and coalition liaison officers to the airfield to plan a new reaction effort. Company A, under Captain Drew Meyerowich, would spearhead the new reaction force. While Casper labored over the plan, UNOSOM II Deputy Force Commander Major General Montgomery worked on fortifying Lieutenant Colonel David's column. Montgomery wanted to use the Italian mechanized battalion, but its commander could not oblige without first consulting Rome for authorization. A comparable request for support from Indian T-72s met a similar fate.[33] Instead, critical assistance came from the Pakistanis and Malaysians, who readily agreed to provide tanks and armored personnel carriers (APCs), respectively. In fact, due to a rare piece of good luck that day, four Pakistani tanks were already poised to go at the airfield.

By 2130, Lieutenant Colonel David had his varied forces at hand at the new port up the road from the Ranger base and presented the operation plan. In all, he had at his disposal two Malaysian companies, comprising

32 wheeled APCs; one Pakistani tank company; three US Army light infantry companies from the 2-14 Battalion; four HMMWVs; a Ranger platoon; and a few dozen volunteers who wanted to help their stranded comrades. Potentially contentious issues were inescapable with such an eclectic force. After consulting with Brigadier General Gile, David wanted the Malaysian APCs to transport his men, not theirs. Malaysian infantry was not part of his tactical vision. Only soldiers trained in the tactics he planned to employ would fit in. David's proposed solution was not particularly diplomatic, but it met his intent and addressed the urgency of the situation. Even then, however, there was the language barrier. Some, but by no means most, of the Malaysians and Pakistanis spoke English. It was a given that the Americans did not speak Urdu or Malay. Furthermore, as light infantrymen, 10th Mountain Division soldiers had little experience with armored vehicles.

Perhaps the greatest challenge confronting all of the coalition personnel in the rescue column was psychological. All were aware, in at least broad terms, of the dire predicament at the northern crash site. On top of that, they knew that there was no chance they would enjoy the advantage of stealth or surprise. Their coming would be expected, and they would be driving through obstacles and ambushes, exposed to withering small-arms fire, mines, and explosives.

The convoy departed at 2323 but encountered its first obstacle about 1 km away. Concerned that a key intersection might be mined—not an outrageous assumption—the Pakistani tank commander declined to cross until a US lieutenant sprayed fire into the barricade. The column then proceeded as far as the last Pakistani checkpoint, but the Pakistani tanks were not authorized to lead past that point. Several Malaysian APCs moved to the front but quickly strayed off the planned route, taking one US infantry squad and a platoon leader with them. Somali RPGs subsequently disabled the APCs. Captain Meyerowich's efforts to communicate by radio with his accidentally detached element were to no avail. They would not make contact again until the next day as Meyerowich kept the main column oriented on the crash site. In the interim, the US squad took shelter in an adjacent building and held out until Company C arrived hours later.

With tanks in the lead once again, the column's main body proceeded along the designated path toward National Street. Meyerowich decided that he had to deal with the situation at the objective first and then attempt to locate his missing men. On the way, however, the lead Pakistani tank paused in an intersection where it came under attack by RPG fire. By stopping to engage instead of forcing its way through the gauntlet, the tank driver responded in a manner that was out of step with US doctrine, which regards stopping in a "kill zone" as tantamount to suicide. Over the radio, both Lieutenant Colonel David and Captain Meyerowich urged the driver to push forward, but excruciating minutes elapsed before he did so.[34]

This episode was a perfect example in microcosm of the problems encountered when mixing forces with different training, doctrine, and standing operating procedures in a combat scenario. Meyerowich later surmised that many of the coalition soldiers did not have the same level of combat training as his own men and therefore tended to "freeze" under fire. Scared soldiers, he believed, would revert to whatever their training told them to do.[35] This was a reasonable supposition since only the QRF had prepared explicitly for a combat mission instead of peace keeping. Members of the 2-14 Infantry had ample reason to respect their adversaries. As Company A's executive officer, Lieutenant Chuck Ferry, summarized, previous operations had shown the Somalis "were capable of operating in fire team and squad-size elements and of coordinating the movement and actions of larger elements. They seemed to know when we were coming, and on which routes, and built hasty obstacles to try to slow our mounted movement." It just so happened that Company A had spent the preceding three days carrying out close-quarters, live-fire drills at a training base just outside the capital. In addition, only days before that the company had withstood a brief firefight following a successful raid on a militia mortar site.[36]

Toughened and confident by virtue of training and experience, Meyerowich's Company A had already gone out as a QRF on six occasions and twice had come under fire.[37] Dubbed the "terminator element" on 3 October, the company's past experiences would pale in comparison with the mission now under way. According to the plan, Company A and the QRF worked their way north to National Street near the Olympic Hotel. Squads bounded forward by teams, alternately moving and providing covering fire. Meyerowich's company proceeded to the northern crash site while another diverted toward the southern one. They would make the journey with overhead cover from TF Raven aviators.

Along the way, Meyerowich and some of his soldiers had to exit the Malaysian vehicles to dismantle a roadblock on the Hawaldig Road. Like the Pakistani tank driver before him, the Malaysian driver of the lead APC feared that the roadblock concealed mines. Even before the obstacle was cleared, Meyerowich decided that they were already close enough—not more than a few hundred meters—to the trapped TF Ranger element to go the rest of the way on foot. As the company advanced, Lieutenant Ferry ran from vehicle to vehicle in a vain attempt to get the drivers to push forward. Finally, he rushed to rejoin the company. As he reached his unit, Ferry hollered, "XO coming through!" It was an act of prudence to avoid being shot at by fellow soldiers.[38] Ahead, Meyerowich and 1st Platoon were stuck in an enemy crossfire between the Olympic Hotel and other nearby structures. The maps were confusing and by now the unit had suffered casualties. There was no immediate chance of aerial medical evacuation.

As the convoy with Meyerowich's soldiers on board neared the first crash site, members of TF Ranger were unable to see their rescuers but could monitor their approach by tracking the intensifying roar of gunfire and explosions. Not surprisingly, members of both combat elements shared the same concerns about the impending linkup, which actually occurred at 0155 on 4 October. Lieutenant Perino wondered whether there was a plan and who was leading the convoy. He could well imagine the frame of mind of members of the 2-14 who had waged a fierce, running gun battle all the way into the middle of the city. Moreover, they were in near total darkness. He noticed that QRF soldiers (or so he assumed) were firing flares to light their way, a technique that helped them but tended at times to create "whiteout, " thus blinding the Little Bird pilots who were wearing night-vision goggles.[39]

From Company A's point of view, the prospect of approaching the lines of besieged TF Ranger posed yet another a source of apprehension. Although, in fact, there had been several linkup rehearsals with the Rangers, these had largely been "communications exercises" conducted during the light of day within the relatively benign context of such scenarios as turning over prisoners from one unit to the next.[40] Fortunately, for orientation purposes, TF Ranger had infrared (IR) strobe lights to help guide the QRF to its position. Moreover, there were Rangers with the QRF to facilitate coordination. Still, Meyerowich did not anticipate the relative quiet as his men drew near the objective. The way matters turned out, he was able to walk to the Rangers' defensive perimeter, where he met Captain Steele. There, in large measure due to the lack of opportunity for prior coordination, a momentary disagreement ensued over who was in control of what. More-senior officers of TF Ranger who came in with the convoy soon clarified the issue.[41] Having joined forces, Company A and TF Ranger waited almost 3 additional hours to extract a body from the downed aircraft, crumpled and wedged between two buildings, before departing.

Meyerowich also found that the crash scene was not as he had mentally pictured it. Normally a besieged force would form a 360-degree perimeter, presumably with the downed aircraft in the middle. Because a defensive circle is hard to form in an urban environment consisting of rectangular grids, somehow the defense would adjust its shape to the terrain, perhaps by holding four city blocks and controlling the approaches. In this instance, because of the way the street fight had evolved, the stricken Black Hawk was actually along the edge of the defensive perimeter, making the work of extraction appreciably more dangerous and difficult.[42]

Meanwhile, Pakistani observers passed word that hostile forces were beginning to clog the expected route of egress. As Little Birds and Cobras pulverized the sources of enemy fire, Meyerowich made certain that all personnel were accounted for. The Rangers and Company A finally left the northern crash site at 0537 with 40 to 50 wounded in tow. In the mad scramble under fire to get on board the Malaysian APCs, many soldiers ended up riding on top of the vehicles. Others, Lieutenant Perino among them, were supposed to jog alongside, using the vehicles for cover. This method, never rehearsed, broke down quickly as frightened drivers left those on foot behind. Perino, a small group of astonished fellow Rangers, and a few soldiers from Company A's 2d Platoon made the best of a bad situation and exited at a brisk trot. Along the way, one of the men grabbed a water bottle from inside the hulk of a smoking HMMWV. The thirsty soldiers passed the bottle around as they ran. Eventually, they overtook and stopped a Pakistani M-113—though not before one soldier threatened to shoot at the driver—and managed to jam inside with more than 20 other exhausted soldiers. The door would not even close, and Perino had to hold on to one of the men to keep him from falling out. Finally, they rolled into friendly territory, where they met smiling, waving crowds of Somalis who were not affiliated with the Habr Gidr clan and proceeded to the Pakistani base at the stadium.[43]

In the meantime, Whetstone's Company C (Tiger element), which had split off earlier to investigate the southern crash site, had a tough trip as well. Although receiving machine gun and RPG fire, they found neither Rangers nor helicopter pilot Michael Durant, the only survivor of the crash. Not yet known, of course, was that Durant had been taken captive. There, shortly after the Black Hawk hit the ground, two special operations Army snipers, Sergeant First Class Randy Shughart and Master Sergeant Gary Gordon, had bravely requested permission to be dropped on the ground to hold the site as armed Somalis began to overrun it. Both gave their lives in the attempt but probably deserve credit for Durant's survival.[44] In any case, Lieutenant Colonel David directed Whetstone to find the Malaysian platoon and "to ensure that we did not leave anyone on the battlefield. "[45] This order applied to Malaysians as well as Americans.

Overall, soldiers of TF Ranger and the QRF from 10th Mountain Division acquitted themselves admirably on 3 to 4 October. Yet, in the aftermath, 18 American deaths far overshadowed every other aspect of the event. Especially disturbing were televised images of jubilant Somalis dragging the corpse of an American soldier through the street. Meanwhile, hundreds of Somali dead, not to mention Malaysian and Pakistani casualties from the battle, went virtually unnoticed by the press corps. A policy reversal, entailing the scheduled withdrawal of US personnel and followed by Secretary of Defense Les Aspin's resignation, marked the politicization of the public review process. One contentious question concerned the refusal of Major General Montgomery's July request for armored reinforcement, including a full mechanized battalion and an air cavalry squadron. In fact, the scenario of 3 to 4 October was the very sort of which Montgomery was thinking when he had asked for help. As the general later explained, "It was increasing concerned over my inability to get to US or UN forces in extremis that led to my request for armor/mech reinforcements earlier in July and August. The Pakistanis had the only armor in the city and it was old and inadequate."[46]

Without doubt, US M-1 tanks could have plowed through roadblocks with ease. Yet, as Meyerowich later pointed out, American tanks and Bradleys would have been vulnerable to some extent in the narrow alleys where much of the urban fighting took place.[47] Nor, because of their enormous potential to cause collateral damage, was using deadly AC-130 aircraft permissible under the rules of engagement in place on 3 to 4 October. Upon assuming the mission with TF Ranger, Garrison had sought AC-130 support but did not receive it. Still, Garrison later declined to fault the refusal, expressing doubt as to whether AC-130s could have operated effectively during the battle in the same constricted airspace the more maneuverable Little Birds and Cobras already occupied.[48] In any case, it was evident that it was not Meyerowich's or Garrison's concerns that led to denial of combat assets but the perception in Washington that these tools were ill suited to a peacekeeping mission and would send the wrong message by their presence.

Accordingly, the principal fire support role fell to Army combat helicopters. In fact, the extensive use of rotary-wing aviation over urban terrain was something new for many pilots. Early in UNOSOM II, 10th

Mountain TF Safari aviators experimented with various combinations of OH-58D Kiowa Warriors and AH-1F Cobras for security and observation. During attacks, orientation and aiming proved tricky, especially after dark. But, working together, the OH-58D and Cobra crews developed effective night targeting procedures. The OH-58D crew would use its laser to help the Cobras identify a target. The Cobras then would put their IR laser on the target for verification and await clearance to engage.[49]

IR spotlights and hand-held lasers also proved their value under darkened conditions. By day, ground elements used M203 or M79 grenade launchers to mark targets. This was no small matter on 3 to 4 October when TF Raven rotated 14 aircrews for 7 hours to provide cover and support for the QRF. At the same time, TF Ranger Little Birds defended the northern crash site throughout the night. As noted in the TF Raven after-action review, "This operation, conducted at night exclusively over densely populated urban terrain, is the first of its type in the history of Army aviation."[50] Still, despite the excellent performance of Army aviators, challenges arose not only with regard to air-ground coordination but air-to-air as well. During the combat of 3 October, Major General Garrison's headquarters directed the QRF scout and attack helicopters to stay out of the compact airspace over the TF Ranger perimeter because of the complexity of integrating forces in combat that employed different procedures and had not previously trained together.[51]

Notwithstanding the enormous services Army aviation provided in Mogadishu, vast collateral damage and civilian casualties were virtually unavoidable. Still, some allowance could be made to minimize likely errors with most types of ordnance. Bad missiles, for example, tended to fall short, while errant 2.75-inch rockets overshot the target. Moreover, experience showed that it was best to begin attacking a series of targets by starting with those that were downwind. This limited obfuscation by dust and smoke. Overall, the AH-1 Cobra proved in Mogadishu that it could be effective during periods of limited visibility, and 20mm fire had the greatest utility because of its superior accuracy.[52]

For all the lessons uncovered about conducting military operations in urban terrain, attention after the fact focused heavily on higher-level questions such as the complex command structure that prevailed under UNOSOM II. Although Major General Montgomery was Turkish Lieutenant General Cevik Bir's deputy as UNOSOM II FC, he was also the commander of U.S. Forces Somalia. Because of political sensitivities at home about placing American personnel under UN command, a separate chain of accountability existed. The absence of a U.S. Forces Somalia headquarters meant relying on the UN headquarters for coordination. Then, with the arrival of a joint special operations TF, TF Ranger, in August, there were essentially three parallel chains of command. The TF Ranger commander, Major General Garrison, reported to CENTCOM separately and was obliged only to consult with Montgomery.

Despite excellent liaison and daily meetings between the two US commands, neither would enjoy full and timely knowledge of what the other was doing because of their separation. Further, at least hypothetically, integrated training would have been simpler to plan and coordinate within a unified command. Overall, in practice, mutual understanding between organizations was probably stronger at the command level than down at the unit level. Many officers in the QRF felt completely ignorant of TF Ranger operations. To some degree, the unique status of special operations forces—and the extreme secrecy in which they operated—created a psychological distance between the two elements.[53] Of course, to some degree, such cultural gaps, based on different standards, procedures, and terminology, often exist between similar conventional units as well. Working relationships under such conditions are routinely discontinued and new ones begun.[54] Therefore, were it not for the extreme security attending all TF Ranger activities, the regular rotation of conventional units in Somalia could be said to have produced a similar degree of friction.

A much greater source of command friction was embedded in the structure of the UNOSOM II coalition. As one scholar put it, "The loose interpretation of command necessarily used by a voluntary organization such as the United Nations could not be effective in complex and controversial missions."[55] Different national agendas and institutional cultures translated directly into varying interpretations of the mission and definitions of operational readiness. In practice, UNOSOM II could not consistently depend on compliance, at least in a timely manner, with its directives. Assembling the rescue convoy on 3 October, although handled professionally by all parties, entailed precious time for coordination and authorization.

Finally, as if the complexity were not great enough, the arrival after 4 October of a new joint task force (JTF) under Major General Carl F. Ernst created a situation that was almost without precedent. The new command became yet another distinct player with its own perspective on the mission. One possible solution would have been to place the JTF under Montgomery's operational control. As the situation stood, however, the

United States did not speak with a single voice in Somalia. To be sure, the arrival of robust new forces served momentarily to overawe Aideed's clan, which was still in turmoil after heavy losses sustained in the bitter fight of 3 to 4 October. The new leverage also quickly procured the release of pilot Michael Durant. One key to the impact of JTF *Somalia* was a full headquarters and joint combined arms formations.[56]

A lesson less often discussed but equally fundamental was the importance of cultural-historical insight into the operational environment. Certainly, US forces across the board knew little about Somali society and behavior.[57] This ignorance, combined with the limited utility of conventional intelligence-collection methods, plagued US and UN decision making from the strategic to the tactical level. Those in Somalia learned their way around in the unforgiving school of trial and error. Under the best of circumstances, understanding the Somalis did not come easily. Yet, for at least some, the experiences that most gave meaning and a sense of purpose to their presence were those such as visits to schools that put them in direct personal contact with the natives they had ostensibly come to assist. It is worth remembering that even as conditions in Mogadishu deteriorated, the mission in most of the country went well, and the UN enjoyed genuine popularity.

From this point, although US forces would remain in Somalia until early in the new year, debate focused on what went wrong. Much concern centered on the more aggressive policy toward Aideed following the start of UNOSOM II. US Marine Corps Brigadier General Anthony Zinni believed that this shift made the Somali operational environment far more hostile and cost the coalition staff critical sources of information. Overall, he believed a poor grasp of the local culture and politics "maybe led to things like not understanding where a particular individual was, or who he was, or what his relationship was, and maybe caused mistargeting in some cases by those that were after Aideed or his lieutenants."[58]

Ultimately, however, the lessons of Somalia would not be applied there. This was a source of disappointment to Force Command, which "was placed in a position of accepting a unilateral cease-fire during a period when Aideed was arguably at his weakest."[59] An impressive show of force aside, the military mission in Somalia drew to a quiet, if slightly prolonged, close. Reflecting the change, UNOSOM II ceased assertive disarmament operations and resorted to the expedient of a voluntary program among the factions. Above all, US policy changed irreversibly after 3 to 4 October, proving once again that a major tactical event can have profound strategic consequences. Lacking an active US presence, UNOSOM II attempted to limp forward but no longer possessed the muscle or political backing to sustain an ambitious nation-building program.

Map unavailable for online viewing
per copyright holder.

Map 11. Map of Mogadishu

1. Courage 53 struck by RPG, crashes trying to reach the New Port. (25 September)
2. TF Ranger capture 24 Somali prisoners at Olympic Hotel. (3-4 October)
3. Super 61 shot down. Rangers secure crash site. A Co, 2-14th Infantry join Rangers, retrieve Wolcott's body at first light. Relocate to Pakistani stadium.
4. Super 64 shot down. MSG Gordon & SFC Shughart reach crash site. C Co., 2-14th Infantry arrive crash site reach soldiers from two lost APCs.
5. LTC David & Charlie Co. QRC head for airport.
6. LTC David and soldiers arrive Ranger headquarters. Remainder 2-14th Infantry head to airport fromuniversity complex.

Map unavailable for online viewing
per copyright holder.

Map 11 cont. Map of Mogadishu

7. LTC David and force ambushed enroute to Super 64 crash site.
8. Four Pakistani M48 tanks relocate, link up with 2-14th Infantry and Malaysian APCs at the New Port.
9. LTC David and force pass Checkpoint 69.
10. Two Malaysian APCs make wrong turn, become separated from LTC David's force. TF Raven's AH-1 Cobra hit Malaysian APCs..
11. The rescue force and TF Ranger pass Checkpoint 207.
12. LTC David and convoy reach Pakistani stadium.

Notes

1. Dr. (Colonel, USAR, retired) Bruce Menning, conversation with Dr. Robert Baumann, 19 August 2002. Menning served on the Joint Staff in summer 1993.

2. Colin L. Powell and Joseph E. Persico, *My American Journey* (New York: Ballantine Books, 1996), 569.

3. Report of the Commission of Inquiry in *The United Nations and Somalia, 1992-1996*, S/1994/653, 380.

4. Based on author's conversations with participants in the Somalia mission.

5. USFORSOM AAR, chapter IV, "Review and Analysis of UNOSOM II Operations, Search for Aideed (31 August-3 October 1996)."

6. Major Larry Moores, interview with Dr. Robert Baumann, Fort Leavenworth, KS, 20 August 2002.

7. Major Larry Perino, interview with Dr. Robert Baumann, Fort Leavenworth, KS, 21 March 2002 hereafter cited as Perino interview.

8. Lawrence E. Casper, *Falcon Brigade: Combat and Command in Somalia and Haiti* (Boulder, CO: Lynne Rienner Publishers, 2001), 33; Mark Bowden, *Black Hawk Down: A Story of Modern War* (New York: Atlantic Monthly Press, 1999), 21. For another account of the events of 3-4 October based on personal recollections, see Kent DeLong and Steven Tuckey, *Mogadishu Heroism and Tragedy* (Westport, CT: Praeger, 1994).

9. Perino interview.

10. Task Force (TF) Mountain Warrior AAR, Operation RESTORE HOPE/ CONTINUE HOPE, Somalia, 10 April-7 August 1993; TF 3-25 Aviation (TF Safari) AAR, 10th Mountain Division (LI), Mogadishu, Somalia, 8 September 1993.

11. Bowden, 5.

12. Captain Jeff Struecker, address to Men of the Chapel, Fort Leavenworth, KS, 18 April 2002.

13. Casper, 25; Colonel Michael Dallas, interview with Lieutenant Colonel F.D.G. Williams, Center of Military History Catalog No. RHIT-C-040, 12 July 1993, 39.

14. TF Raven After-Action Report, Operation CONTINUE HOPE, Somalia, 27 August 1993 to 9 July 1993, Incident Report of 25 September 1993; Casper, 275.

15. Mike Horan, "Eyes Over Mogadishu," chapter 10. This as yet unpublished monograph is a personal memoir and was available at <http://www.megapass.co.kr/ ~horanjoh/>, accessed by the author 6 January 2003.

16. Mark Whitaker, interview with Dr. Robert Baumann, Fort Bragg, NC, 31 July 2002 hereafter cited as Whitaker interview; Colonel Jim Oeser, interview with Dr. Robert Baumann, Fort Bragg, NC, 31 July 2002 hereafter cited as Oeser interview. Retired Colonel David Hackworth concluded that US forces in Somalia had forgotten the experience of Vietnam, which exposed repeatedly the vulnerability of helicopters to small-arms and other fire. See David H. Hackworth and Tom Mathews, *Hazardous Duty: One of America's Most Decorated Soldiers Reports From the Front With the Truth About the U.S. Military Today* (New York: Avon Books, 1996), 181.

17. Lieutenant General Thomas M. Montgomery, US Army, Retired, observations on 3 to 4 October faxed to the author, 24 October 2001, hereafter cited as Montgomery faxed observations to the author. The author also wishes to acknowledge insights on the 3-4 October mission offered by Major General William Boykin.

18. Norman Cooling, "Operation RESTORE HOPE in Somalia: A Tactical Action Turned Strategic Defeat," *Marine Corps Gazette* (September 2001), 97; Yossef Bodansky, *Bin Laden: The Man Who Declared War on America* (Rocklin, CA: Forum, 2001), 78-79.

19. Lieutenant Colonel James Klingaman, interview with Dr. Robert Baumann, Fort Leavenworth, KS, 17 August 2002.

20. Captain Jeff Struecker, e-mail to Dr. Robert Baumann, 23 April 2002.

21. Ibid.

22. Captain Jeff Struecker, talk to men of the Chapel, Fort Leavenworth, KS, 18 April 2002.

23. *U.S. Special Operations Command History* (MacDill Air Force Base, FL: U.S. Southern Command, 1998), 46.

24. Perino interview; Bowden, 84-85.

25. Perino interview.

26. Ibid.

27. Casper, 77.

28. Ibid., 24.

29. One of those inside the perimeter, Mark Whitaker, acknowledged moments of doubt but recalled feeling that their position was relatively secure, especially with the benefit of at least some night-vision capability and aerial support. See Whitaker interview.

30. Casper, 37.

31. Perino interview.

32. Quick Reaction Force (QRF), Falcon Brigade, 10th Mountain Division, "U.S. Army Support to UN Operations in Somalia (UNOSOM II)," Summary of Combat Operations, 3-4 October 1993, Mogadishu, Somalia.

33. Lieutenant General Thomas M. Montgomery, US Army, Retired, interview with Dr. Robert Baumann, Colorado Springs, CO, 17 February 2002.

34. First Lieutenant Chris Hornbarger, "TF Raven's Role on 3 October," unpublished paper dated 27 December 1993, 10.

35. Major Drew Meyerowich, interview with Dr. Robert Baumann, Fort Leavenworth, KS, 19 March 1999, hereafter cited as Meyerowich interview.

36. Captain Charles P. Ferry, "Mogadishu, October 1993, Personal Account of a Rifle Company XO," *Infantry* (September-October 1994), 4-6; Major Charles Ferry, interview with Dr. Robert Baumann, Fort Leavenworth, KS, 9 November 2000, hereafter cited as Ferry interview.

37. Ferry interview.

38. Ferry, "Mogadishu, October 1993, A Personal Account of a Rifle Company XO," 8.

39. Perino interview.

40. Ferry interview. There was, however, at least one linkup rehearsal under simulated combat conditions according to a former TF Ranger officer.

41. Meyerowich interview.

42. Ibid.

43. Perino interview.

44. For a detailed account, see Bowden, 164-65, 189-95.

45. Major Robert Biller, battalion S5, Untitled Summary of 3 to 4 October.

46. Montgomery faxed observations to the author.

47. Meyerowich interview.

48. Major General William F. Garrison, US Army, Retired, e-mail correspondence concerning lessons learned from Somalia, September 2001.

49. Major Chuck Walls, interview with Dr. Robert Baumann, Fort Leavenworth, KS, 7 November 2001.

50   TF Raven After-Action Report, Operation CONTINUE HOPE, Somalia, 27 August 1993-9 January 1994, Summary for 3 to 4 October 1993.

51. Casper, 77; Whitaker interview; Oeser interview.

52. TF Raven After-Action Report, Operation CONTINUE HOPE, Somalia, 27 August 1993-9 January 1994, 3-9, 3-11.

53. There was also much discussion in Mark Bowden's *Black Hawk Down* over perceived friction with TF Ranger. Many of the individuals I consulted, such as Major General William Boykin, felt that such tension never reached the level of creating any real dysfunction. Most of the commandos were former Rangers. To be sure, differences in uniform standards and demeanor were a genuine source of consternation to some in the Ranger command chain. Because the Rangers were younger and more impressionable, there was a very human tendency to emulate their more veteran comrades, even when it meant deviating from their own regiment's standards. The most serious problems, however, appear to have been isolated to a few individuals and did not pervade the relationship between the two units.

54. This point was raised in particular by Dr. Chuck Briscoe in a conversation with the author during a research trip to Fort Bragg in July 2002. Indeed, because each arriving unit must learn the ropes of operating in the mission environment, the Army tends to have a process of "discovery learning" over and over again. To some degree, this problem is mitigated by the right-seat ride process and efforts by the Center for Army Lessons Learned to disseminate the latest wisdom from the field.

55. John Hillen, *Blue Helmets: The Strategy of UN Military Operations* (Washington, DC: Brassey's, 1998), 208; C. Kenneth Allard, *Somalia Operations: Lessons Learned* (Washington, DC: National Defense University Press, 1995), 32.

56. Lieutenant General Carl Ernst, US Army, Retired, e-mail observations, 18 October 2001.

57. Lieutenant Colonel Thomas Odom, US Army, Retired, conversation with Dr. Robert Baumann, Fort Polk, LA, 22 July 2002.

58. Cooling, 102-3.

59. Lieutenant Colonel Thomas Daze, "Centers of Gravity of United Nations Operation Somalia II," unpublished master of military art and science degree thesis, US Army Command and General Staff College, Fort Leavenworth, KS, 1995. LTC Mark Inch, who served as a captain in Mogadishu working with the local police and was therefore unusually well connected, contended that Aideed's support within the Habr Gidr clan reached a low point after 4 October. In short, a sustained effort might well have brought about Aideed's downfall.

Chapter 6

Buildup and Withdrawal
October 1993 – March 1994

Lawrence A. Yates

On 4 October, just hours after Task Force *Ranger*'s ordeal in the streets of Mogadishu ended, the UNOSOM II force commander, Turkish Lieutenant General Cevik Bir, sent a message to retired US Admiral Jonathan Howe, the special representative of the UN Secretary General in Somalia, reiterating the widely held conviction that Mogadishu was the political and military "center of gravity" in Somalia and that future UNOSOM II military operations would focus on "stabilizing the security situation" in the capital. Bir's staff continued to work on plans for "offensive action" against USC-SNA targets in Mogadishu, believing that such operations, by "enhancing the local environment for reconciliation," would still be supported within the coalition, despite the months of fighting to date and the casualties suffered on 3-4 October. Task Force *Ranger,* under the separate command of US Army Major General William Garrison, certainly echoed Bir's assessment, as members voiced their eagerness for a rematch with Aideed's militia. In essence, then, few if any UN or US officers in Mogadishu during the immediate aftermath of the 3-4 October battle perceived the engagement as an event that would reverse existing policy and strategy.[1]

The decision on what course of action to take, however, would not be made by UNOSOM II officials on the scene or even by the United Nations in New York, but by President Bill Clinton in Washington. And it would be a decision based as much on political considerations as on the correlation of forces in Mogadishu. Well before 3 October, opinion polls in the United States were showing diminishing public support for American involvement in Somalia,[2] even as the Clinton administration was considering increasing US military commitments abroad by sending troops to Bosnia and Haiti. The opinion polls themselves did not connote any organized pressure on the government to disengage from Somalia, but they did indicate that should something in that country go wrong, it would be extremely difficult for the White House to justify a policy of continued involvement on the basis of national interest. As details of the battle between Task Force *Ranger* and Aideed's militia surfaced, complete with film footage of the body of a US soldier being dragged through the streets of Mogadishu, the American public soon concluded that something, in fact, had gone wrong in Somalia.

This conclusion took a few days to develop. The first reports reaching Washington Sunday night, 4 October, indicated that the fighting had been limited, with only a handful of US casualties in what had otherwise been a successful mission. On the basis of that initial information, the president issued a statement regretting the loss of life but applauding the operation. By the next day, perceptions had changed, as word spread that the engagement had been much worse than originally described. When the full extent of the battle became known, a barrage of public criticism, some reasoned, some shrill and clearly partisan, rained down on the administration. Republican senators and congressmen literally lined up to denounce the new president's policy—or, as they would have it, the lack thereof—and to demand that US troops in Somalia be withdrawn. Several Democrats, including senior leaders such as Senator Robert Byrd of Virginia, joined the hue and cry. How had Somalia turned into such a disaster, the critics wanted to know. Who had changed the mission? To Major General Thomas M. Montgomery, the US Forces commander in Mogadishu, the question seemed disingenuous. "You've got 25,000 staffers on the congressional staff, and you didn't know that there was a UN mandate that the United States authored in the Security Council in May that clearly set out the expanded mission? . . . Give me a break. They were playing politics with this finger pointing. It was infuriating."[3]

While others, too, deplored the partisan nature of the ensuing debate, many supporters of the president were even more distressed by the administration's seeming ineptitude in countering its critics. When Secretary of State Warren Christopher and Secretary of Defense Les Aspin appeared on Capitol Hill to explain US policy, the latter incurred the wrath of his interlocutors by inviting their views on what the president should do (thus conveying the impression that Clinton and his advisers did not themselves know what course to chart). Nor did it help the White House when word circulated in the press that, since late September, administration officials had been putting pressure on UN Secretary General Boutros Boutros-Ghali to deemphasize the military hunt for Aideed in favor of a more political approach to resolving Somalia's woes. If this was the direction in which American strategy was moving, some asked, why was Task Force *Ranger* conducting a raid against Aideed's lieutenants on 3 October? Had US commanders in Mogadishu been left in the dark about this shift, and if so, why? As one US officer on the UNOSOM II staff later observed, "We now know that a political settlement was being pursued at the same time that US and UN forces were increasing the level of hostility. The different efforts could have worked wonderfully had they been coordinated—they were not." As the questions and criticism mounted, more bad news came out of Mogadishu: just two days after the firefight, a mortar round landed in the TF Ranger living area at the airfield, wounding 13 US soldiers (one of whom later died from his wounds). The retaliatory rounds of a Cobra attack helicopter firing its 20mm machine gun at the offending mortar crew could be heard on a CNN broadcast then in progress.[4]

As the administration weighed its options under increasing pressure, Secretary of State Christopher lamented, "We are really the victims in many ways of instant communications, instant polling. That has its purpose, but we need to be steadier, and have a longer view of American interests." Having thus articulated the predicament diplomats in a democratic society habitually face in a high-speed electronic world, Christopher bowed to the reality that US policy in Somalia was about to change because of a tactical military engagement, the immediate and largely visceral reaction to its coverage in the news media, and the consequent political fallout in Washington. On Tuesday, 6 October, Clinton met at the White House with his national security advisers. Robert Oakley, President Bush's special envoy to Somalia during UNITAF, was also present. Over the course of many hours, the participants hammered out a new policy. US troops would leave Somalia, but only over the course of the next six months. The deadline for withdrawal—attributed by some sources to the lobbying of General Joseph P. Hoar, the CENTCOM commander—would be 31 March 1994, a date administration officials admitted was arbitrary, but which recognized that the United States could not "cut and run" without undermining its credibility in international affairs.[5] As additional insurance against such a spectacle, the president, as a prelude to the withdrawal, decided to increase the US military presence in Somalia. If Aideed or any other warlord lashed out again at American troops on the scale of 3-4 October, he would be met with overwhelming and decisive force. Meanwhile, on the diplomatic front, the United States would undertake immediate initiatives to reverse UNOSOM II's policy of coercive disarmament and seek a political settlement that would include Aideed's SNA. This, in turn, entailed renewing official and frequent contacts with the faction leader and his close advisers.

After deciding on this course of action, Clinton met with congressional leaders, and, then, on 7 October, announced his new policy to the nation. His statement made no explicit reference to Task Force *Ranger* or its mission but focused on the humanitarian aspects of the US military commitment. In emphatic terms, he explained why the United States could not leave Somalia immediately: the Somali people would be denied the chance to rebuild their society, the country itself would return to anarchy, and "Somali children would again be dying in the streets." Moreover,

> Our own credibility with friends and allies would be severely damaged. Our leadership in world affairs would be undermined at the very time when people are looking to America to help promote peace and freedom in the post-Cold War world. And all around the world, aggressors, thugs and terrorists will conclude that the best way to get us to change our policies is to kill our people. It would be open season on Americans.

Having made the case against a precipitous pullout, he announced the 31 March departure date for US forces, revealed that civilian contractors would replace US military logistics personnel, and proclaimed that "the solution to Somalia's problems is not a military one, it is political." As for the reinforcements he intended to deploy, he briefly discussed their missions and assured his audience, "These forces will be under American command."[6]

Many of the president's critics welcomed the new policy. Others continued to question his judgment in foreign affairs. Former Secretary of State Henry Kissinger, for one, condemned Clinton's pledge that the United States had "no interest in denying anybody access to playing a political role in Somalia's political future." To reward Aideed instead of punishing him for his "brutal" action against US forces, Kissinger argued, sent the wrong message to troublemakers around the world. Others took this position as well, but the dye was cast. As Oakley later observed, if Clinton had sought to maintain the status quo in US policy or to adopt a more aggressive posture in Somalia, Congress would have immediately passed a resolution undercutting him.[7]

The Political Track. As a symbolic gesture of his commitment to revive the "political track" initiated during UNITAF, Clinton designated Oakley as his special envoy to Somalia.[8] When Oakley arrived in Mogadishu on 9 October, he was accompanied by another UNITAF veteran, Major General Anthony Zinni, USMC. UNOSOM II officers and officials extended the two men a cordial welcome, even though for many in the UN operation, Clinton's policy reversal had come as an unpleasant surprise. To begin with, the timing seemed all wrong. As Bir's memorandum to Admiral Howe on 4 October indicated, several senior UNOSOM II personnel believed that an unparalleled opportunity existed for exploiting the *military* situation,

168

and subsequent intelligence reinforced their view. The 3-4 October firefight, according to Somali sources, had cost Aideed dearly, in that many families aligned with the warlord had suffered casualties. Aideed's position within the Habr Gidr/USC/SNA ranks seemed to be weakening. "He was on the ropes," one US general stated. Given this vulnerability, decisive UN military moves, it seemed to many on the scene, would result in his downfall. A few weeks of turbulence might follow, Montgomery predicted, but then things would quiet down. Instead, in Montgomery's opinion, "We wound up . . . giving a victory to Aideed that Aideed did not win on the third of October."[9]

To Montgomery, the decision to withdraw US forces startled the commanders in Mogadishu and had a negative impact on the morale of the troops. Besides being ill timed and poorly conceived, the decision was also "an embarrassment." During the course of UNOSOM II, Montgomery and Howe had found it necessary to prod often-reluctant coalition partners into performing a variety of risky tasks. Complicating the process was the fact that the commanders of many foreign units had to receive approval from their national governments before accepting any assignment. As Montgomery put it later, "Everybody's calling home." At least one of the coalition units that he and Bir had found it necessary to goad into action on occasion was the Pakistani contingent responsible for Mogadishu, a unit that had seen over 40 of its members killed by Aideed's militia. Now, US troops, after suffering significant casualties themselves, received word from Washington that they would be pulled out. To many within UNOSOM II, President Clinton's decision broke faith with those coalition units that had taken casualties but stayed the course. Prior to 7 October, Montgomery had often found aggravating the degree to which foreign governments directed the activities of their military forces in Somalia. Now, to his chagrin, his own government had become a source of that aggravation, to be weighed in with "the almost daily decisions of coalition partners to revisit their national commitments to the mission" in light of Washington's shift in policy.[10]

Adding to the consternation of Montgomery and other UNOSOM II officials in Mogadishu was Clinton's choice of Oakley and Zinni to get political negotiations back on track. Both men were critical of the UN's strategy at almost every step, beginning with what they regarded as a regrettable decision to curtail the daily contacts UNITAF military personnel had established with Aideed and his key lieutenants back in December 1992. UNOSOM II, in Oakley's opinion, "didn't really understand the need to maintain the dialogue, to maintain communications." Thus, he argued, the UN's inspection of the AWSS at the radio station on 5 June, having been only cursorily coordinated with Aideed's people, had resulted in tragedy. In a similar vein, he considered the Abdi house raid of 12 July a "disaster" that served mainly to radicalize Somalis throughout the country and increase support for Aideed. Since Zinni shared this negative assessment, both men professed to be shocked by how dramatically the situation had deteriorated since the end of Operation RESTORE HOPE.[11]

Montgomery and others on the scene regarded the Oakley-Zinni critique as inaccurate and unfair. To the charge that UNOSOM II had allowed the dialogue with Aideed to lapse, Montgomery countered that, even before the UN took over from UNITAF, Admiral Howe was already talking with several Somali groups and leaders. In the month between the beginning of UNOSOM II and the 5 June attack on the Pakistanis, "the UN political side," Montgomery later stated, "was in contact as much as was possible with Aideed," who was often out of the country. As for UN military contacts with the Somalis, Montgomery noted that he and Lieutenant General Bir worked under a different setup than Zinni and his boss, Lieutenant General Robert Johnston, the UNITAF commander, and also had a different set of responsibilities. Even so, military officers in UNOSOM II met with Somali leaders in such appropriate venues as the disarmament committee. As for the 5 June inspection of the AWSS, the operation had been well coordinated in advance with Aideed and his people.

Thus, Montgomery argued, it was not a lack of communication that had triggered the crisis but the lashing out of a warlord who realized, as did all the involved parties, that UNITAF and UNOSOM II had related but very different missions: that of the first was to secure humanitarian relief; that of the latter was nation building, a long-term and much more complex— and, to Aideed, a much more threatening—endeavor. Whereas UNITAF engaged in "weapons control" in an attempt to create and maintain just enough security to let the humanitarian effort succeed, UN nation building included the specified task of countrywide disarmament that warlords such as Aideed were certain to resist. Understanding clearly that the UN's plan necessitated a weakening of his military power and political status, Aideed calculated that his ambitions to lead Somalia could best be furthered by striking out violently against the peacekeepers. Ironically, as Montgomery told Zinni, the sense of personal threat and insecurity that drove Aideed to take armed action had been aggravated by what UNITAF itself had started at the local level—the political "empowering" of village councils and the reliance on traditional leaders in many villages and towns, often at

170

the expense of Aideed's followers, who, given their military muscle, had previously dominated local politics in many areas of the south. UNOSOM II's policy may have been to "marginalize" Aideed, but UNITAF, too, had taken the initial steps in that direction. Add to all this Aideed's hatred for Boutros-Ghali and his contempt for the UN, and the fact that UNOSOM II had a larger mission but fewer resources and a smaller force than UNITAF, it was highly probable from the outset that Aideed would mount a deliberate and desperate attempt to disrupt the nation-building process. After the 5 June incident, any effort to accommodate Aideed would have constituted appeasement, the very term that Montgomery later employed to characterize the purpose of Oakley's new mission in Mogadishu.[12]

The day Oakley arrived in the capital, Aideed held a press conference in which he proclaimed a unilateral cease-fire with the UN forces. Bir and Montgomery rejected the arrangement out of hand: they did not need Aideed to provide them a respite, but vice-versa; furthermore, neither general trusted the SNA to abide by its own offer. Still, the gratuitous gesture set the stage for Oakley's first meeting with Aideed's top representatives, during which the special envoy achieved his two principal goals. First, after recalling the dialogue that existed under UNITAF, he reassured the SNA of President Clinton's decision "to depersonalize Somalia policy." Then, after warning the Somali participants that the arriving US forces had the power to lay waste to any part of Mogadishu that attempted armed resistance, he demanded of Aideed's people the unconditional release of the American helicopter pilot captured during the 3-4 October fighting, together with a Nigerian peacekeeper who had been held for over a month. After a reportedly heated debate within the SNA, Aideed acceded to Oakley's demand on 14 October.[13]

Subsequent talks followed, reaffirming that the renewed US policy of inclusive dialogue had in fact superseded UNOSOM II's more confrontational approach. Among other indications of the shift, the UN Security Council on 6 November adopted Resolution 885, which suspended the hunt for Aideed while an international commission investigated the 5 June incident. Two months later, as the result of increasing political pressure on Boutros-Ghali, the Secretary General ordered the release of the eight people, including Osman Atto, Aideed's deputy, still being detained by UN forces for being SNA members or suspected sympathizers. In short, by the end of 1993, the UN had accepted the inevitable: "political reconciliation would continue to be the primary focus of UNOSOM to achieve security goals."[14]

Military Adjustments. Together with Washington's decision to revive the "political track" in Somalia, President Clinton's announcement that US forces would be out of that country by 31 March 1994 had immediate and far-reaching ramifications for the UNOSOM II Force Command, USFORSOM, and all the coalition partners. The plans of Admiral Howe, Lieutenant General Bir, Major General Montgomery, and others for realigning units in several sectors, for expanding operations into the central region of the country, for employing incoming coalition forces, for arbitrating command and control arrangements, for executing "offensive action" against USC/SNA strongholds, and for continuing to implement UNOSOM II's policy of countrywide disarmament all had to be reevaluated. Meanwhile, coalition units in the capital found their movement restricted to neighborhoods that openly supported—or at least were impartial toward—the UN effort. To reduce risks to UN troops even further, UNOSOM II let the population and the warlords know that coalition forces would remain neutral "in any inter-clan conflicts that erupted in the city," a position that left Ali Mahdi's Abgal clan feeling abandoned by the people it had "vocally and consistently supported." Complicating matters for the force commander was the decision by other governments—mainly Germany, Italy, and Turkey—to withdraw their forces in conjunction with the American pullout. In a briefing to UN officials in November, Bir recommended that UNOSOM II operations revert to a Chapter VI peacekeeping mode. After the departure of US and other forces, he maintained, the coalition "would not be capable of coercive disarmament" under Chapter VII peace enforcement guidelines, and it would be "severely constrained logistically." Further, the shift in political strategy "did not allow for the aggressive type of action needed to contain increasing incidents of limited militia activity and banditry." At the time Bir was making these points, UN troops in Mogadishu were already experiencing a degree of "military paralysis," in part as a result of the numerous "garrison activities" to which they had reverted once Washington assumed "leadership in the political arena," leaving Force Command with "no firm political guidance to anchor itself to."[15]

As UNOSOM II headquarters adjusted to the disruptive impact that changing policies and troop commitments had upon the coalition, Bir and Montgomery had to direct their attention as well to accommodating the additional US forces being deployed. The first units arrived on 8 October, the day after the president announced the shift in US policy, and consisted of a mechanized company from the 24th Infantry Division that CINCCENT, early on 4 October, had authorized to deploy via strategic airlift. As part of a battalion task force, designated TF 1-64, the company included two platoons with Bradley fighting vehicles and one platoon with Abrams tanks. The remainder of the task force began arriving a few days later, accompanied by the 43rd Combat Engineer Battalion (Heavy). In between, a battalion—the 2nd of the 22nd—from the 10th Mountain Division (Light) and four AC-130 gunships made their appearance in Mogadishu, as did various Marine and naval units off the coast, including the carrier battle group of the USS *Abraham Lincoln*. The arriving forces made their presence felt immediately. On 10 October, an AC-130 demonstrated a sample of its firepower by destroying weapons in a former SNA storage area north of the capital. The next day, planes from the *Lincoln* began air reconnaissance and other sorties throughout UNOSOM II's area of responsibility.[16]

Once the US buildup reached its peak, American forces inside Somalia had doubled to over 4,300, with an additional 9,100 positioned offshore. In line with these dramatic increases, the Quick Reaction Force (QRF), commanded by Colonel Lawrence Casper of the 10th Mountain's 10th Aviation Brigade, adopted the name "Falcon Brigade," with over 3,500 troops in six battalions attached to it. It was an arrangement that, to Casper's frustration, generated no small degree of controversy.

Even before 3-4 October, when the QRF constituted "a hybrid organization of one light infantry battalion, one mixed attack-lift aviation battalion, one forward support battalion and numerous small platoons and detachments," the use of an aviation brigade as the command element for ground maneuver units had been questioned by officers who argued that such a headquarters was "not ideally suited to the task by organization or Mission-Essential Task List." The debate over this issue intensified with the buildup of US forces, as the Falcon Brigade assumed control over additional light infantry battalions, an engineer battalion, and the heavy maneuver TF 1-64 with its Abrams tanks. Critics of the arrangement argued that the intelligence requirements of aviators and infantrymen were considerably different; that an aviation brigade was not familiar with the organization, weapons, and tactics of an infantry fighting force; and that an aviation brigade had neither the fully functional fire support element nor the "dedicated divisional engineer assets" of an infantry brigade. All this meant, according to the critics, that the Falcon Brigade would have difficulty "conducting the complex missions assigned to the U.S. Quick Reaction Force" and that its staff would have to master "functions that they are not normally required to perform." Casper himself admitted that he had to be educated on the "maintenance nuances" of heavy firepower, but he defended the QRF command and control setup as doctrinally sound. Regarding the acknowledged deficiencies of an aviation brigade operating as a maneuver headquarters, he recounted how with staff augmentation and the help of others, he and his team managed to overcome the challenges posed by an organization that "has thin resources, possesses little depth, and lacks some essential staff functions." Although Casper's outfit learned to manage the extensive combined arms capability that had accumulated under it, the various adjustments it had to make to do so ensured that the debate over the use of an aviation brigade as a headquarters for ground maneuver units would find its way into after-action and lessons-learned reports geared to future operations.[17]

The transformation of the QRF into the Falcon Brigade was not the only organizational change to follow President Clinton's policy statement of 7 October. Driving home his pledge that deploying units would be under American command was the activation of Joint Task Force *Somalia,* a headquarters under CENTCOM that would exercise operational control (OPCON) or tactical control (TACON) over most of the incoming US forces, as well as over some already in Somalia.[18] Picked to command the JTF was Major General Carl Ernst, who was then making the transition from his assignment as the assistant division commander for support, 82nd Airborne Division, to new duties with the US Army Training and Doctrine Command at Fort Monroe, Virginia. When Ernst received word on the day after the president's speech that he was to become the JTF *Somalia* commander, he flew immediately to CENTCOM headquarters at MacDill Air Force Base, Florida, where he was later joined by Brigadier General Peter Pace, USMC, slated to be the JTF's deputy commander. Following briefings from the CENTCOM staff, Ernst and Pace met with General Hoar to obtain guidance regarding their mission and a plethora of related issues.[19]

As the talks got under way, Hoar let both men know that, once the JTF deployed, its "basic mission" would be force protection; there was to be no recurrence of the 3-4 October episode. How Ernst was to accomplish this mission raised a series of complex, at times subtle issues. On one point, however, Hoar was blunt: Ernst was not to allow UN forces to provide security for US troops; that was the task of the JTF. Referring to a security survey CENTCOM had taken in Somalia, the CINC indicated that UN forces and bases were vulnerable in many respects. Effective force protection would thus require JTF *Somalia* to develop a comprehensive plan that would emphasize active as well as passive measures. Ernst would be expected to increase patrols, conduct surveillance, set up

174

outposts, engage in interdiction and ambushes, and find ways to remove Americans from exposed positions within Mogadishu proper. He also needed to enforce the rules of engagement (ROE) as they applied to various weapons the Somali factions were permitted or forbidden to employ. On a related issue, the CINC reminded Ernst that the Somali militia possessed antiarmor weapons and possibly Stinger and SA-7 surface-to-air missiles that could be used against US and UN aircraft. Despite this threat, it was not JTF *Somalia*'s mission to go hunting for Aideed. On that point Hoar was emphatic. If, however, the JTF was forced into a fight, Ernst was to do what was necessary to accomplish his mission while trying to minimize collateral damage, especially civilian casualties.

To the JTF's principal mission of force protection, Hoar added two others. One entailed support of UN forces in Somalia. Guidance for this mission prohibited JTF *Somalia* from taking the lead in UNOSOM II operations but did permit the headquarters to assist UN planning efforts when appropriate. The third mission addressed the perceived need to keep the lines of communication (LOCs) in Mogadishu open and to reopen those that the factions had shut down with roadblocks, strongpoints, and hostile fire. Of the LOCs and strongpoints that needed to be reopened or dismantled, Hoar specifically named the 21 October Road, the cigarette factory, and the pasta factory. He also indicated that the mechanized forces Ernst would control were ideally suited to this mission.[20]

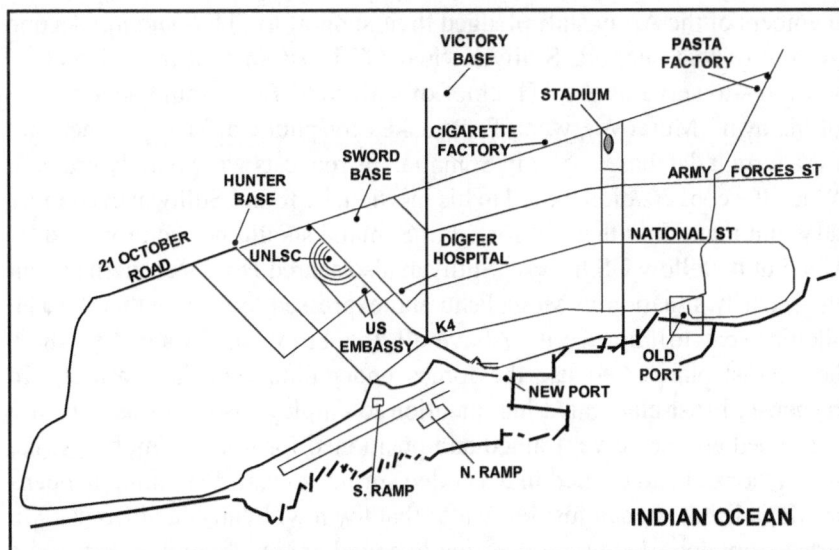

Map 12. Mogadishu - JTF Somalia

175

As the talks with CINCCENT concluded, Ernst believed that he had been given three specified missions—protecting US forces, supporting the UN, and keeping the LOCs open—and one implied mission based on President Clinton's speech—planning and executing the withdrawal of US forces from Somalia. JTF *Somalia,* Ernst understood, would take control of the expanded QRF, whose activities Hoar saw as critical to accomplishing the JTF missions. The QRF, in Hoar's phrasing, held everything together by supporting the UN. But the CINC wanted the QRF returned to its original status as a reserve force, a role from which it had strayed, he believed, when it began conducting operations, such as search and clear, that should have been left exclusively to the UN. As for how far Ernst could go in employing the QRF and the other US forces under his control, the guidance he received was general but straightforward enough. He was to take no unnecessary risks and was not to be unnecessarily provocative. But, in what Ernst regarded as a major caveat to this cautionary guidance, Hoar assured him that he had the authority to determine if a situation required action and, if in his view it did, to use the full combat capability of his heavy force to resolve the problem. When Ernst took the point further by asking if, in the event of another firefight along the lines of 3-4 October where US and UN forces were *in extremis,* he could blow down an SNA enclave if he thought it necessary, Hoar answered in the affirmative.

From CENTCOM, Ernst flew to Washington where, in meetings at the Pentagon, Chief of Staff of the Army General Gordon Sullivan and members of the Army staff pledged their support to JTF *Somalia.* As one gesture of that support, Sullivan "loaned" Ernst an officer—a UNITAF veteran—to serve as the JTF chief of staff until Ernst could acquire one of his own. Moreover, when Ernst asked for public affairs guidance and for a terrain database to use in Somalia, his requests were readily granted. When the conversation turned to his mission, he found Sullivan even more adamant than Hoar that US forces in Somalia should not be protected by UN, but by fellow US troops. Sullivan also shared Hoar's concerns about the security situation in Mogadishu and expressed the desire that the JTF should work to improve it. Above all, the Army chief wanted to know how Ernst planned to use the forces under him, especially armor. In response, Ernst elaborated his intention to employ his armor as part of a combined arms reserve, trained and positioned for use as a mobile strike force, "locked and cocked like a coiled spring, so that if anything happens in Mogadishu, we can just blow into that town with tanks and Brads." In Ernst's opinion, this was a doctrinally sound approach, unlike that of the "reaction" force, in that the former allowed for "positioning, rehearsals based on anticipated commitments (branches), reconstitution," and so forth.[21] Sullivan's response, according to Ernst's notes of the meeting, was an enthusiastic, "Exactly!"

Another issue Ernst raised with Sullivan was whether or not there would be an Army Forces, or ARFOR, component under JTF *Somalia*. CENTCOM plans did not call for one, and Ernst felt this to be a glaring omission. The JTF would have a Marine Forces (MARFOR) component and a Navy Forces (NAVFOR) component. Ernst believed that it was essential for him to have an ARFOR that could deal with the other service components on the same level. Also, as the operational commander, he wanted to be able to give mission-orders to his component commanders and let them determine the best means of tactical execution. Not having an ARFOR in control of all Army combat units in the country would preclude, or at least complicate, this approach. Finally, whether Ernst considered it or not at this point, having a general officer as the ARFOR would allow for the establishment of a ground maneuver brigade alongside the aviation brigade, thus resolving the aforementioned problems that many professed to see in having the aviation brigade headquarters control ground maneuver elements. Ernst wanted to name the assistant 10th Mountain Division commander as the ARFOR commander, but CENTCOM did not approve the request. After Ernst arrived in Somalia, organizational arrangements evolved, but he would not get the ARFOR he wanted. Instead, he initially assumed the role himself, delegating the various functions of a component headquarters to his chief of staff and, when appropriate, certain subordinate units.[22]

From Washington, Ernst traveled to Fort Drum, New York, home of the 10th Mountain Division (Light). There, together with Pace and the designated J3 for JTF *Somalia*, Colonel Buck Bedard, he met with the division's commander, Major General David C. Meade, and others. The talks focused largely on staff issues, since 10th Mountain had been tasked to prepare for CENTCOM, without any guidance from that headquarters, the manning document for JTF *Somalia*. Meade had received the tasking because his division was to provide the nucleus of Ernst's 145-man staff. Initially, Meade offered Ernst the division's tactical command post (TACCP), consisting of 30-some soldiers. The problem with this, as reported later, was that many of these soldiers lacked experience in the joint arena, as was also the case with most of the individuals picked from other units and services to round out the staff. In another issue reminiscent of the UNITAF phase of the US military's involvement in Somalia, the assignment of a significant number of 10th Mountain's headquarters personnel to Ernst's JTF *Somalia* left the division without a functioning staff. It would have been better, in the view of the Army's Center for Lessons Learned, for an operational-level JTF staff to be taken from a corps headquarters, a more "robust" echelon that could absorb the personnel loss better than a tactical-level division and that, theoretically, would have more officers with joint experience.[23] At the time, however, CENTCOM approved 10th Mountain's manning document without change.

For Ernst, however, the manning document contained a number of shortfalls, the most critical of which was that it provided him no planning capability, something he regarded as essential if he hoped to plan, prepare, and execute operations in support of his missions. To fill this gap, he talked to the US Third Army commander, Lieutenant General Larry Ellis, and strongly requested that the JTF be assigned five planners from Army resources. The criteria Ernst laid out included the following: all five should be graduates of the School of Advanced Military Studies (SAMS) at Fort Leavenworth, Kansas; all should have had some practical planning experience; and the group should be able to cover specific operating systems—namely, maneuver, intelligence, special operations, engineering, and logistics. Ernst hoped to get four of the five. To his surprise, he was authorized all five. (He was also pleased to learn that other SAMS graduates would be among the officers sent by 10th Mountain to serve on the JTF staff.)

Besides a plans shop, Ernst also needed a fire support element that he could make into a joint targeting board within the JTF. He especially wanted an expert on digitized firing networks, radars, and laser positioning for the precision-guided weapons that would be so critical if he hoped to limit unnecessary damage and casualties during any fight in an urban environment. Meade took the expert Ernst wanted out of the 10th Mountain. Finally, from XVIII Airborne Corps at Fort Bragg, North Carolina, Ernst received the strategic and tactical communications he would require.

JTF Somalia. Elements of the JTF staff began arriving in Somalia on 13 October. The remainder, including individual augmentees from all the services, filtered in over the next few weeks. Major General Ernst landed in Mogadishu on 15 October and immediately immersed himself in the process of getting JTF *Somalia* stood up and running. One of the many tasks facing him in this respect concerned the physical location and security of his headquarters and of the units under JTF control. In that the old US Embassy compound housed the UNOSOM II Force Command, USFORSOM, the QRF, and US diplomatic personnel, it was the logical place for the general and his staff to set up shop. In Ernst's judgment, however, the whole compound was vulnerable to hostile fire, so he arranged for the building housing the JTF headquarters to have a countermortar roof, a surrounding wall capable of stopping RPGs, and guards from the10th Mountain Division posted 24 hours a day. He also ensured that the units OPCON to him had adequate protection. In the case of the JTF's armored task force, for example, he called on US military engineers, assisted by hired Somali workers, to build Victory Base, a camp located north of Mogadishu beyond the direct and indirect firing range of SNA weapons.[24]

In keeping with the guidance he received from CINCCENT, Ernst also assessed the security of UNOSOM II troops who had established their positions in and around Mogadishu before 3-4 October. As was the case with the embassy compound, he concluded that several of these positions were vulnerable. The location of the UN Logistics Support Command's two principal bases, Sword and Hunter, particularly concerned him. Sword base, he observed, sat on the edge of an SNA enclave in the capital; Hunter base was only slightly less exposed to hostile action. Both bases had been built during UNITAF and inherited by UNOSOM II, which did not have the money or resources to relocate them. Concerned as well about their vulnerability, Montgomery told Ernst to focus on force protection and to do contingency planning that would allow the JTF to "react" to any threat to Sword, Hunter, and logistics convoys.[25]

Besides dealing with issues of force protection and security, Ernst also spent his first days in Somalia getting his headquarters organized. As an ad hoc element, it lacked SOPs and methodology, and those who would man it were people Ernst in most cases was meeting for the first time. The staff he had acquired before deploying was small but efficient and had at its core personnel from the 10th Mountain Division. To augment this group, he enlisted the services of liaison officers (LNOs) sent to his headquarters by those components over which he had operational control: the Falcon Brigade, a joint special operations task force (JSOTF), and a psychological operations task force (POTF) composed of one company (-). As for the Marine and Navy units offshore over which he exercised only tactical control, he could not formally task them to assist the JTF staff. But in what became a series of informal "gentlemen's agreements" or "handshakes," the Marine and Navy component commanders readily provided liaison teams to the JTF headquarters that, in Ernst's words, "not

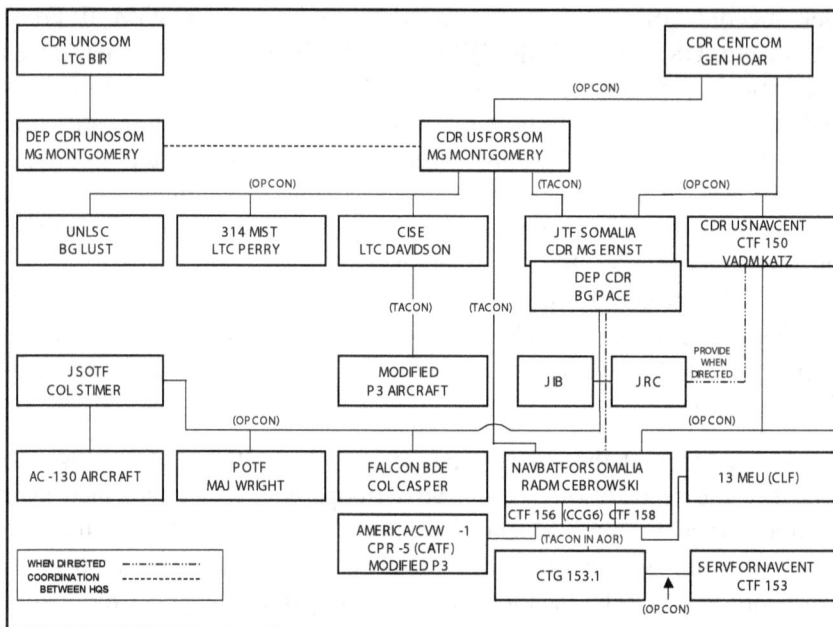

Figure 7. USFORSOM/JTF Somalia - Command and Control
(After 20 October 1993)

only augmented our capabilities but also provided the vital immediate access to their headquarters essential when orders had to be transmitted rapidly and clearly and a response of equal quality had to be received in turn."[26] When Ernst's staff was fully constituted, the Army provided about 80 percent of the personnel, with the Marines providing another 10 percent.

As would be expected, Ernst's initial activities in Somalia also entailed a round of meetings and briefings with key US and UN personnel. Over the ensuing weeks, he would work closely with several of them, and all had something to contribute to his in-country orientation. One man to whom he wanted to talk right away was Major General Garrison, TF Ranger's commander and an old friend. In the course of a lengthy presentation, Garrison gave Ernst a detailed account of his unit's operations, including the 3-4 October firefight. Present for the discussion was a CIA team leader with whom Ernst struck up a conversation. Later, Ernst described the encounter as fortuitous. The CIA official informed him that the human intelligence (HUMINT) system in Mogadishu lacked synchronization. Ernst responded by saying, "I've got an offer for you." The outcome was another "gentleman's agreement" in which the CIA official agreed to have

180

his people set up and run for Ernst's use a Intelligence Support Element (ISE) to handle HUMINT in a more systematic way. In return, Ernst would "cut" some of his intelligence officers to the ISE. That deal, together with the spy aircraft made available to JTF *Somalia,* bolstered the headquarters intelligence capability. So, too, did the ongoing presence of CENTCOM's Intelligence Support Element (CISE), which had "downlinks" to national intelligence systems. In his headquarters, Ernst had other intelligence downlinks as well.[27]

Besides Garrison, Ernst also met with Oakley and Zinni and received their take on the situation. Ernst was particularly impressed with Oakley's desire to learn as much as possible about the combat capabilities of the forces under JTF *Somalia.* The reason for the special envoy's curiosity was clear enough. In meeting with Aideed, Oakley sought to promote reconciliation, explaining that the United States once again considered the faction leader to be a "player" in Somali politics. In return, the Clinton administration expected Aideed to meet certain conditions, one being that he should start working again with Ali Mahdi toward a comprehensive resolution of Somalia's problems. To both warlords Oakley was also to "stress the need to adhere to certain UN guidelines by removing roadblocks and technicals and permitting free movement of UN convoys." If either leader "failed to agree to this minimum requirement then the additional U.S. deployed forces (JTFSOM) would be used to ensure the LOCs were opened and safe." In Ernst's opinion, the answers he gave to Oakley's questions about JTF *Somalia*'s combat power were intended to be conveyed directly to Aideed and Ali Mahdi in a blunt warning of what they could expect if they ignored US demands.[28]

Ernst met with Oakley whenever possible, and the special envoy briefed the JTF after each of his meetings with faction leaders. At one point, Ernst received Oakley's permission to have an officer from the JTF's J5 shop attend meetings held by the US negotiating team with the various subclans and factions. The extent to which Ernst became involved in the political process, however, did not approach the level attained by Lieutenant General Johnston during the UNITAF experience. Ernst's man on the negotiating team was there mainly to keep the JTF commander abreast of developments and, on occasion, to deliver messages from Ernst to SNA representatives. In a similar vein, JTF *Somalia* did not interact closely with humanitarian organizations as UNITAF had. Ernst's principal mission was not to beef up security for relief efforts but to provide force protection for US forces.[29]

```
FALCON BDE                          CTF 156 (COMNAVBATFORSCOM) (COMCARGRU SIX)
TF 2-14 INFANTRY                    (When Directed, TACON)
TF 2-22 INFANTRY
TF 1-64 ARMOR
TF 2-25 AVIATION                    CTG 156.1                    CTG 156.3
C/1-41 FIELD ARTILLERY                 TG 156.1                    TG 156.3
43D ENGINEER BATTALION
46TH FIRE SUPPORT BATTERY              USS America (CV-66)          USS New Orleans (LPH-11)
TACTICAL AIR DEFENSE                   CVW-1                        USS Denver (LPD-9)
                                       USS Simpson (FFG-56)         USS Comstock (LSD-45)
                                       VP DET MOMBASA               USS Cayuga (LST-1186)
JOINT SPECIAL OPERATIONS
    TASK FORCE                       CTG 158 (COMCARGRU SIX) (When Directed, TACOM)
OPERATIONAL DETACHMENT B (-)
4 AC-130
2 KC-135                               TG 158.1(13th MEU [SOC])
4 C-130                                GCE-BLT 1/9
                                       ACE-HMM-268 (REIN)
PSYCHOLOGICAL OPERATIONS               CSSE-MSSG-13
    TASK FORCE
PSYCHOLOGICAL OPERATIONS CO (-)
                                                   NAVY FORCES     7,084
                                                   MARINE FORCES   1,996
TOTAL: 4,360                                       TOTAL:          9,080
```

Figure 8. JTF Somalia Troop List

Perhaps the most important meetings Ernst held at the time of his arrival were with the UNOSOM II military commanders, particularly Major General Montgomery in his role as commander of US Forces Somalia. Since all of JTF *Somalia*'s missions, specified and implied, in some way affected or involved the US and coalition troops under UNOSOM II, there would be a high degree of interaction between Ernst's headquarters and Montgomery's. On the surface, there was little reason to believe that this interaction would not be harmonious. Montgomery and Lieutenant General Bir both wanted the US reinforcements and supported JTF *Somalia*'s missions, especially force protection, which CINCCENT had also made a primary mission for USFORSOM. Montgomery, whose "pocket staff" worked mainly within the UN Logistics Support Command under his operational control, also welcomed the more robust staff that Ernst brought with him. In assessing the situation confronting them, the two US generals acknowledged the "military paralysis" and "bunker mentality" that permeated UNOSOM II contingents, and both shared the view that, should Aideed or any other faction leader reopen hostilities with coalition forces, the full combat power of JTF *Somalia* would be brought to bear decisively against the offender.[30]

Despite agreement on these important points, the personal and professional relationship between Ernst and Montgomery was fractious almost from the outset.[31] The friction derived from several causes. While both men were Vietnam veterans, the same could not be said with respect to Somalia. Since 5 June 1993, Montgomery had dealt firsthand with the bloody effects of Aideed's hostile actions and regarded the UN's strong response to them as fully justified. Ernst, on the other hand, was a newcomer who, in the course of the meetings and briefings he attended before and after deploying, embraced the highly critical view Oakley, Zinni, and others he consulted were voicing about UNOSOM II. This did not sit well with Montgomery, any more than did what Ernst himself conceded must have appeared to USFORSOM as an attempt by JTF *Somalia,* with its larger and multifaceted headquarters, to come in and start running things. There was also the force protection issue: both generals might have had the same mission, but they did not always see eye to eye on how to execute it. When, for example, Montgomery told Ernst to be ready to "react" against any hostile move against the UN logistics bases and convoys, Ernst became angry. He later wrote that he objected to the word itself when used in a military context and favored, instead, the creation of mobile reserves that "acted," not "reacted." Ernst also disagreed with how the UN Logistics Support Command wanted him to disperse his armor in order to guard the fixed log bases. In a heated exchange with the US logistics commander, he rejected the dispersal scheme in favor of keeping his heavy forces in reserve, an argument that reinforced Ernst's negative impressions about UNOSOM II, even though Montgomery did not disagree with the reserve concept. Montgomery, however, did come to suspect—as did other officers on "the US side of the UN staff"—that, on certain critical issues, Ernst was deliberately trying to isolate, circumvent, or ignore USFORSOM and the UN Forces Command and to "marginalize" their staffs. The USFORSOM commander, to cite one minor example, did not know that JTF *Somalia* had asked for and received Oakley's permission to have a staff officer attend talks between US diplomats and Somali leaders.

Besides these annoyances, there were major and substantive disagreements between the two commanders. The most divisive was a difference of opinion over JTF *Somalia*'s mission—not over its wording but over the tenacity with which it should be executed, especially, as will be seen, with respect to keeping the LOCs in Mogadishu open. On the basis of his conversation with General Hoar, Ernst clearly believed that he was supposed to reopen supply routes in Mogadishu. More than that, he believed he had the authority to determine when hostile activity warranted the employment of the forces under him in combat. To Montgomery, all of this exceeded and even contradicted the more cautious guidance CINCCENT had conveyed to him in their daily telephone conversations.

The friction between the two commanders and many officers in their respective headquarters could have been reduced by a set of precise command and control arrangements in which either Montgomery or Ernst was clearly subordinate to the other. Such unity of command, however, did not exist. While Montgomery as commander, US Forces Somalia, remained under the operational control of CINCCENT, he exercised only tactical control over JTF *Somalia*, which meant that he could provide Ernst specific, local direction on tactical operations and that Ernst was responsible to him for the planning and execution of tactical operations in Somalia. Montgomery, however, could not formally issue Ernst orders except under certain specific circumstances. This arrangement notwithstanding, Montgomery understood from conversations with CINCCENT that JTF *Somalia* was established with its robust staff in order "to relieve COMUSFORSOM and U.S. members of the UNOSOM II staff of the burden of tactical command and control of U.S. combat forces." This, in turn, would free Montgomery and his pocket staff "to focus on the operational level and UN force employment." Thus, to USFORSOM and its commander, General Hoar's intent seemed clear: he would "continue to exercise OPCON of all U.S. forces through COMUSFORSOM." The only problem was that Ernst, according to the USFORSOM AAR, "came with a different view of the command relationships with COMUSFORSOM." Ernst, like Montgomery, was formally OPCON to CINCCENT, and except on those matters where he was required to answer to Montgomery, he intended to use his direct channel to CENTCOM whenever he considered it necessary. As all this played out, according to one source, the "actual relationship between USFORSOM and JTF-Somalia was more than TACON but less than OPCON," particularly since CENTCOM directed that JTF *Somalia* contingency plans be "routed through USFORSOM." Still, to most of the staff officers on the scene, the "appearance of parallel lines of command and control especially at the staff level" lent itself to no small amount of confusion and friction.[32]

During Ernst's first hectic days in Mogadishu, there was only a dim perception of the impact the command and control problem would have on upcoming US operations. The more pressing issue at the time was simply getting JTF *Somalia* stood up and running. On 17 October, CENTCOM issued the execute order for the JTF, in the process also revising "the mission, task organization, and command relations" of USFORSOM. Under the order, Montgomery, in the words of the USFORSOM AAR, continued "to control all U.S. military operations in the Somalia Theater in support of UNOSOM II." Furthermore, the logistics command remained under the UNOSOM II chain of command, answerable directly to Montgomery. For its part, JTF *Somalia* assumed OPCON of the QRF, which put under its control all tactical US forces on the ground in Somalia. Working out the details of a few issues not addressed in the order delayed formal activation of the JTF until 20 October. Once activated, the new organization immediately published its first operations order (OPORD) incorporating the four specified and implied tasks that Ernst had acquired in his talks with General Hoar (and that, with slightly different wording, were reiterated in the CENTCOM execute order). Ernst would later say about the JTF OPORD, "We never replaced this original; we instead 'fragged' off this plan with the basic plan remaining constant."[33]

In the days and weeks that followed the activation of JTF *Somalia,* planning and operations became, in Ernst's term, the "hallmark" of the JTF staff. "We never stopped planning." Contingency plans fell to the J3 shop, while long-term planning, including the withdrawal plan, went to the J5. Ernst used this continuous planning as a mechanism for synchronization and team-building. Once a plan had been written and all the identified branches had been run, the field commanders joined the staff in going over the details, conducting map exercises, and engaging in further discussion. The forces involved then prepared and trained for execution, often rehearsing the plan in detail. Consequently, joint exercises became daily occurrences, to include when possible those using live fires.[34]

The first major operation mounted by JTF *Somalia,* Operation SHOW CARE, occurred at the end of October. Billed as a humanitarian operation in Marka and the surrounding area, the undertaking had a political-military purpose as well. The town sat astride a major north-south coastal highway from Mogadishu to Kismayo, and factional strife in the latter city was almost always boiling over. Consequently, the SNA was putting pressure on Marka in order to control the key highway and, by doing so, assist its allies in Kismayo. To intercept this initiative and, in the process, send a signal to Aideed, JTF *Somalia* employed marines from the 13th Marine Expeditionary Unit (Special Operations Capable) [MEU (SOC)] to conduct amphibious and helicopter landings into the town. There, by prearrangement, the marines linked up with the Royal Moroccan Task Force, the UNOSOM II unit in control of Marka. Once the combined force had established secure areas there and in the nearby town of Qoryooley, the medics who accompanied the troops set up shop, providing the local population—which had been informed in advance by US PSYOP handbills—food and medical and dental treatment. Meanwhile, JTF forces and the Moroccan troops "conducted a link up, combined tactical road march, helicopter borne landings, show-of-force operations, security operations, and civic action projects," thus reminding Aideed "about the mobility and capabilities of U.S. forces."[35]

Operation SHOW CARE also served as a model for how operations conducted by JTF *Somalia* could be planned and coordinated with other headquarters. After Ernst's staff planned the venture and the JTF had discussed it with the US units and the Moroccan task force involved, the plan was presented to Montgomery for his approval. (As commander, USFORSOM, Montgomery had the authority to reject or approve most JTF operations. If, however, a proposed undertaking entailed a risk of combat, or if it exceeded standing CINCCENT guidance, he was obliged to forward the plan to CENTCOM for a decision.) This process, which worked very efficiently in the case of SHOW CARE (and other operations), demonstrated that, despite the difficulties caused by the CENTCOM-directed command and control arrangements, USFORSOM and JTF *Somalia* could and would cooperate on a variety of activities. Daily briefings and planning meetings, weekly updates, and several other mechanisms facilitated this cooperation and coordination.

After SHOW CARE, JTF *Somalia* focused its attention on Mogadishu. The biggest operation it would launch—a joint amphibious operation— came in early November and employed "every piece of the Joint Task Force." Given the command and control relationships between JTF *Somalia* and the combat units OPCON or TACON to it, arranging for this massive event was no mean feat. Ernst only had TACON of Marine and Navy units offshore, which meant that he could not employ them or provide them with planning guidance until they were released to him by CENTCOM on a case-by-case basis. What kept this arrangement from hindering JTF operations was the willingness of those commanders involved to work around it. As Ernst put it, "everybody came with the attitude that, 'We've got a problem. Forget about the command arrangements—let's just figure it out on the ground.'" As staff, in organizing the JTF, the key commanders entered into informal agreements to ensure that planning, preparation, and execution would go as smoothly as possible and that units required for an operation would be available with as little red tape as possible. (One means among others of circumventing the cumbersome command and control requirements associated with "real" operations was simply to label certain undertakings "training" events, a convenient "subterfuge," according to Ernst).[36]

Years later, Ernst would summarize the JTF's joint amphibious operation in Mogadishu as follows:

We brought one MEU ashore and then embarked an Army mech/tank company team on LCACs that came in on the second wave. A Marine battalion landing team came into the old port area. They established a presence there and operated in the vicinity for three or four days. The Army task force brought in two mech company teams, leaving one at the airport and the other at the new port, then established a reserve force ashore. We positioned artillery throughout the area to provide fire support if needed. That gave us the Copperhead capture angles we needed to shoot into Mogadishu if it became necessary. The artillery fired out to sea for precise registration that night and it was a max sortie day over Mogadishu for carrier and other aircraft, including the AC-130s. We conducted synchronized target engagement employing A-6s, FA-18s, and AC-130s, not over the horizon, but in sight so that everybody could see them. It was just a big firepower demonstration.[37]

In addition to this, US warships sailed within view of the shore in "a parade of ships," and special reconnaissance and special snipers began "active work that day." As a result of all this maneuver and activity, JTF *Somalia* forces, with the help of some UN contingents already on the scene, established "a big ring around Mogadishu." The purpose was to demonstrate to the warlords, particularly Aideed, the overwhelming force the United States had deployed since early October and the serious intent to use that combat power if necessary. The demonstration seemed to have had the desired effect. Aideed's command net "lit up," Ernst later recalled, as the faction leader's confused lieutenants tried to assess for him what was happening. Several subordinates apparently saw the operation as an attempt to pressure Aideed into attending a new round of national reconciliation talks in Addis Ababa and recommended that he accept the invitation. (Whether the operation or other factors compelled Aideed to take this advice is not clear, but he soon announced that he would go to the conference. To make sure Aideed followed through on this pledge, Ambassador Oakley offered him the use of the airplane Montgomery had placed at the special envoy's disposal. When the day came for Aideed to depart, US marines escorted him to the plane in full view of American troops in the area of the airport and embassy. The morale of those onlookers, by all accounts, plummeted.)[38]

Besides sending Aideed and Ali Mahdi a strong message, the operation in Mogadishu proved to JTF *Somalia* that it could plan, prepare, rehearse, and execute a military demonstration of this magnitude. The operation also helped the commanders and staff to understand better the "geometry" of urban operations and to test air-space command and control. For Ernst, there was another critical lesson. In the course of working on the specifics of the operation, he concluded that it did not fit into any broader context, "an unfortunate reflection of the lack of both U.S. and UN campaign planning." To fill what he regarded as a serious void, he directed his staff to develop a JTF *Somalia* campaign plan.[39]

Having developed an IPB for the joint task force but lacking guidance from higher headquarters regarding the "desired end state" that would obtain once JTF *Somalia* had accomplished its mission, Ernst's staff assumed one: the JTF would leave the country after it had overseen the withdrawal of US forces from Somalia with minimum casualties and with American honor intact. Thus, a critical question driving the campaign planning was, What if the troops have to withdraw under fire? Or, put another way, What needs to be done to defeat any attempt by hostile forces to challenge the withdrawal militarily? The answer came in a four-phased campaign plan, completed around the end of October. In Phase I, JTF *Somalia* would attack hostile elements in Mogadishu while maintaining a posture of operational defense in other areas of the country. Once hostilities in Mogadishu were concluded, Phase II would begin, with UN forces being entrusted with the tactical defense of the capital, while JTF *Somalia* went on the operational offense in other sections of the country, possibly achieving its objectives by establishing a presence rather than through combat operations. Phase III consisted of being on the tactical and operational defense in the capital and countryside while conducting routine operations and setting the conditions and configuring the force for a phased withdrawal. Phase IV would be the withdrawal.[40]

Ernst believed that Phase I, combat operations in Mogadishu, was the key to the success of the plan but would also be the hardest part to accomplish. Like other UN and US officers, he saw the capital as the center of gravity: "If you crack that nut," he told Oakley, one of the first US officials to be briefed on the plan, "you'll send a very powerful message to the rest of the country." Oakley's response: "Exactly right!" The problem, of course, was how to subdue hostile elements in an urban environment. To Ernst, the answer was not in close, hand-to-hand street fighting. "If we were going to get into a fight," he later said, "we didn't want it to be rifle against rifle. We made that decision early on. . . . We would use maximum, overwhelming force. We would engage using standoff and precise overwhelming combat power whenever we could. . . . The best way to clear a room was precision-guided munitions."[41]

And, he added, there was "a whole menu" of these that he could call upon: ground, air, direct, and indirect. Beginning with specially trained snipers and their assortment of deadly, long-range rifles, the list of "precision fire support assets" escalated quickly to AC-130 gunships, US Army laser-guided Copperhead artillery rounds and wire-guided TOW missiles, US Marine laser-guided Hellfires, and laser-guided bombs from marine and naval aircraft. In that most of these were highly complex systems and ones that could be used effectively only through interservice cooperation (for example, Army OH-58D helicopters setting the laser markings for Marine Hellfires), it was essential that the units involved train and rehearse daily to synchronize the operating systems and to prepare for the variety of contingencies in which they might be used.[42]

The best way to deter hostile action, Ernst and others believed, was to develop the appropriate plans, prepare the troops to execute them, and, in the process, conduct exercises and operations that were highly visible and intimidating. In this context, Ernst held that his campaign plan was an "internal document," not meant to drive a real campaign but to be used as a reference for determining where the JTF should devote its attention over time, and how the JTF should conduct its mission in an orderly way, prioritizing and planning for sequential actions. These reassurances notwithstanding, many outside JTF *Somalia* found the plan cause for concern, if not alarm. Ernst himself conceded that the document caused some consternation at CENTCOM, and that consternation was transmitted to USFORSOM by the CINC himself. According to Colonel Casper, the Falcon Brigade commander who now worked for JTF *Somalia*, the impression Ernst imparted when he arrived in Mogadishu was of a general "focused entirely on warfighting," an officer who "lived and breathed maneuver warfare and had rarely served away from troops." Furthermore, Casper later wrote, the belief persisted that "General Ernst had arrived ready to fight, and championed the notion that it was time to 'retake the city.'" Montgomery may or may not have shared this impression, but he also found the campaign plan—about which he was briefed only at the last moment and only after, unbeknownst to him, it had been sent to CENTCOM—cause for consternation. The first two phases, in his opinion, seemed to contradict the spirit of CINCCENT's expressed guidance that US forces were to minimize US, UN, and Somali casualties and were not to expand or engage in offensive military operations unless provoked or unless they "contributed directly to political solution."[43]

The disagreement over the campaign plan added to the friction between USFORSOM and JTF *Somalia*. While the two headquarters continued to cooperate and coordinate on a daily basis, the relationship was, in the words of one commander, "testy." In short time, that strained relationship was exacerbated by another disagreement, this one over what to do about reopening 21 October Road, a principal east-west thoroughfare in northern Mogadishu. The issue arose from the fact that, during the conflict between Aideed and UNOSOM II, the SNA had constructed blockades, conducted ambushes, and taken over strategically located buildings along this key route used by the UN to supply its troops throughout the city. Traversing portions of 21 October Road unscathed was virtually impossible.

General Hoar had given Ernst the mission of reopening several key LOCs, and Oakley, when he met with Aideed, warned him of grave consequences if the warlord did not voluntarily stop trying to impede the flow of traffic. When the blockades did not come down, Ernst began planning an operation that would reopen a 2-mile stretch of 21 October Road. UNOSOM II had already built a road bypassing the disputed segment of this main supply route (MSR), but in Ernst's opinion, that did not obviate the military action he contemplated. Without such action, he believed, Oakley's not so subtle threat would be perceived by the SNA as hollow, the result being a blow to US credibility and possibly an inducement to Aideed to ignore future US warnings and even to resume hostile actions.

The plan JTF *Somalia* developed was elaborate ("a lot of moving parts") and called for a week of rehearsals, with emphasis on the synchronization of precision fires. Summarized, the operation would have a Pakistani infantry battalion, using their US-made armored personnel carriers and M48 tanks and accompanied by American military engineers, move east along 21 October Road toward the pasta factory. If the unit were engaged by the SNA, JTF *Somalia* would "take over" and put a "wall of fire" around the Pakistanis. US forces would then end remaining resistance using precision-guided weapons, Army-Navy-Air Force-Marine aviation assets, two US Army battalions (with another in reserve), and elements from the 22nd Marine Expeditionary Unit, which would conduct an amphibious landing and then link up with Army forces. Ernst personally did not believe Aideed would challenge the Pakistanis. Since the arrival of the JTF, the warlord had refrained from any large-scale violence against the vast force arrayed against him. Occasionally, he mounted a test or probe, but on the whole, he seemed content to sit back and wait for the Americans to leave. Thus, while JTF *Somalia* viewed the proposed operation as risky, the risk appeared worth taking.[44]

When Montgomery learned of the plan, he objected strongly. "Why would I do that?" he asked. To begin with, the bypass route had rendered

190

21 October Road's value as an MSR irrelevant. Reopening it would be largely symbolic, but not just in terms of US policy. The road itself carried a symbolic meaning for Aideed's supporters: it had been named for the date the faction leader had defeated Siad Barre's forces in the Somali civil war. With honor on both sides at stake, Montgomery viewed the proposed operation as a very risky venture, one that could provoke hostilities and incur casualties. In light of General Hoar's guidance to him to avoid combat unless attacked, and given that US troops would soon withdraw from the country, the USFORSOM commander saw nothing that would justify an offensive operation that could trigger another major battle in Mogadishu. If Montgomery needed further reason to oppose the operation, there was also the issue of the Pakistanis to consider. He was not about to send a force that had already taken significant casualties into harm's way again, not unless it was absolutely necessary. "I won't do that," he said. Finally, according to the USFORSOM after-action report, "UN and U.S. political will to use force waned as the chances of a Somali political reconciliation appeared to decline. Virtually no one wanted to undertake operations to open roads today that might be closed tomorrow because of renewed civil war."[45]

Montgomery conveyed his objections to the plan to Lieutenant General Bir, who as UN force commander would have to approve the Pakistani and any other coalition involvement. Meanwhile, Ernst, believing he would receive authorization to execute the plan, had coordinated it with the UN and JTF *Somalia* elements involved, had conducted daily rehearsals, including live-fire exercises, and had positioned his forces to begin the operation. It thus came as "a shock to everybody" at the JTF headquarters, Ernst later recalled, when Bir told him that the plan would not be executed. Ernst lamented the lack of will on the part of UNOSOM II and what he perceived as a failure to follow through on statements both Clinton and Oakley had made about the need to reopen the LOCs in Mogadishu. But he also accepted the verdict and turned his attention to other activities demanding the attention of JTF *Somalia*.[46]

Withdrawal. The controversy over the plan to reopen 21 October Road did not interfere with JTF *Somalia's* other missions, as Ernst's organization continued to support UN operations and provide the "strong, visible presence" that discouraged faction leaders from attacking coalition troops. JTF forces continued to train, conduct joint exercises, and execute a variety of operations that included providing humanitarian assistance (as in Operation MORE CARE), escorting convoys, patrolling, and securing fixed sites. Meanwhile, planning efforts focused more and more on

191

two missions: noncombatant evacuation operations, in case the crisis in Somalia took a turn for the worse, and the redeployment of US forces.

To Montgomery, the projected troop withdrawal involved him in the most complex planning of his career. On 24 October, he formally "assigned Commander, JTF Somalia the specified task to 'be prepared to redeploy U.S. forces,'" thus turning what Ernst originally had regarded as an implied task into a specified one. The withdrawal planning team worked directly for Montgomery, and while planning began soon after JTF *Somalia* was formed, it accelerated only in early December. Even then, the team's efforts were complicated by the "political uncertainties surrounding the future of the UN in Somalia." (Throughout November and into December, the UN in New York and the UN Force Command under Lieutenant General Bir grappled with the issue of what strategy the UN would adopt once the United States and some other nations had pulled their troops out of Somalia. That debate was still in progress when planning for the US withdrawal "accelerated" in December.)[47] Based on Montgomery's guidance to plan a tactical redeployment that would ensure continuous force protection, JTF *Somalia* planners drew up a series of options. In early December, the headquarters also sent representatives to a planning conference at Amphibious Ready Group Three headquarters in San Diego, California, to determine the approximate composition of the naval force that would be needed for the redeployment and to coordinate the relief in place between remaining Army ground forces and the Marine elements that would come ashore to cover their withdrawal.[48]

As the planning progressed, Montgomery and Ernst again found themselves at loggerheads. In general terms, Montgomery wanted to keep a robust US force in Somalia through the last stages of the redeployment in late March. The last thing to leave, he said to emphasize his point, should be an Abrams tank with its gun tube pointing toward Mogadishu. Ernst understood the need to keep a "full combat capability" in Somalia up to the last day, but he voiced objections to moving US forces on the ground into a redeployment support area next to the airport and port facilities. The resulting congestion of troops, he maintained, would make them vulnerable to hostile fire. He also advocated pulling out more troops and the heavier units sooner than Montgomery desired. Montgomery overruled Ernst, and in December, as the Malaysian battalion in Somalia assumed the QRF role from US forces, the American withdrawal began along the lines directed by USFORSOM. Thus ended what Ernst later referred to as "the last major disagreement" between JTF *Somalia* and USFORSOM.[49]

There would not be much opportunity for another. On 17 January 1994, Major General Ernst redeployed to the United States, and Major General Montgomery became the commander of JTF *Somalia*. With the American pullout in progress, USFORSOM was rolled into the JTF and, in Colonel Casper's words, "General Montgomery traded in his blue beret." At about this time, the Somali leaders vying with one another agreed to peace terms, although most observers doubted that the tentative settlement would provide the basis for reconciliation and a lasting peace.[50]

When he left Somalia in mid-January, Major General Ernst could look back on his tenure as commander of JTF *Somalia* with a sense of accomplishment. Beginning with his arrival in the country in mid-October, he had established a JTF headquarters from scratch, assembled and directed an energetic and highly productive staff, and employed a variety of unconventional and informal means to forge a truly joint force capable of training, rehearsing, and conducting highly complex and technically sophisticated operations in varying terrain, including the built-up area of a city. And when he departed, he left behind a situation in which major violence leveled at US and coalition forces had virtually ceased. Under his command, JTF *Somalia* had, in fact, provided force protection and security for US and other troops in Somalia, had supported the UN in a variety of operations, and had helped set the stage for an orderly, phased, and safe redeployment of American forces.

The phased redeployment continued through February and into March. On 4 March, a Marine ground combat unit came ashore to conduct a relief in place with the remaining Army task force. By the 25th, "all U.S. forces, including the JTF headquarters and amphibious forces, had withdrawn from Somalia in good order."[51] For Montgomery and his staff, leaving Somalia evoked a wide range of emotions as they reflected on their experience. Montgomery personally had been involved with the UN effort for over a year, from the frustrating attempts to arrange a seamless transition between UNITAF and UNOSOM II, through the dark days of the 5 June massacre of Pakistani troops and the subsequent hunt for Aideed that culminated with the fierce battle on 3-4 October in the streets of Mogadishu, to the withdrawal of US forces. As Deputy Commander, UN Forces Command, and Commander, US Forces Somalia, he had helped hold the UN effort together during adversity, despite the disparity between missions and resources. In the process, he had taken pride in the US staff officers who, from scratch, had been instrumental in organizing, training and leading the multinational headquarters, and with the US soldiers, marines, airmen and sailors and their coalition partners who had engaged in a myriad of activities, including combat, to accomplish the mission. Now, as Commander, JTF *Somalia*, he was executing an operational-level withdrawal that he had been given the responsibility for planning. In this final phase of the American military's involvement in Somalia, he later observed with satisfaction, US and UN soldiers suffered no additional casualties.

Because of the US and UN intervention in Somalia, hundreds of thousands of Somalis had received the humanitarian assistance that enabled them to survive the combined ravages of drought, famine, and civil strife. What would happen to the country and its people in the coming weeks, months, and years, however, remained unclear. Progress in resolving the political crisis had been marginal, and what gains had been made were generally dismissed by commentators as transitory. In part for this reason, Montgomery regretted the Clinton administration's decision not to stay the course. TF Ranger along with 10th Mountain Division and UN rescuers had taken heavy casualties during 3-4 October, but other US troops had also been killed in Somalia, together with many more soldiers from coalition units. Now the Americans were pulling out in what was, in Montgomery's opinion, an embarrassing breach of faith with those coalition forces that remained behind, reduced to a "hunker down" posture during the UN's remaining year in Somalia, and also with the Somali people in general, who now awaited an uncertain fate. Within a global context, he believed, the message this spectacle sent to America's friends and foes alike was that the will power of the world's strongest nation was vulnerable to adversity. Finally, in reflecting ten years' later on the US involvement in Somalia, Montgomery voiced the conviction that the experience had provided the United States with "a rich, if painful, introduction to the realities of the new strategic environment after the Cold War that remain valid today."

Ironically, within months of the redeployment, U.S. forces—many of whom had served in Somalia—would be intervening in Haiti to effect a change of regime. Soon after that, American troops would be deployed to Bosnia, part of a complex operation to maintain a shaky peace agreement in that volatile area. The experience in Somalia would influence each of these commitments, as government spokespersons, both civilian and military, went to great lengths to assure the American people that the deployments affected US national security, that force protection would be a principal concern, and that the forces sent would not engage in nation building. As for events in Somalia, the American public quickly lost interest in the political and military struggle or the welfare of the Somali people. When the UN ended operations in the country in 1995, the sparse news coverage of the event reached or mattered to few Americans.

Notes

1. *United States Forces, Somalia, After Action Report* [hereafter, *USFORSOM AAR*] (Washington, DC: US Army Center of Military History, 2003), 108-9; Television documentary, "The True Story of Black Hawk Down" (A&E Television Networks: The History Channel, 2002); Oral history interview with Lieutenant General Thomas M. Montgomery, USA (Ret.), 17 February 2002, interviewed by Robert F. Baumann. The first document cited is an unclassified and nearly complete version of a SECRET after-action report written soon after the US military withdrawal from Somalia.

In the immediate aftermath of the 3-4 October firefight, the Force Command staff continued "to finalize plans that would initiate offensive action against USC/SNA targets in Villa Somalia, the Digfer Hospital/SNA Enclave (Digfer Triangle) and 21 October Road (stadium area)." While Force Command was confident that support still existed within the coalition for these operations, the USFORSOM AAR raises the point that the casualties incurred during the TF Ranger firefight and the consequent rescue mission did in fact call into question "the political will of the coalition to remain committed to the mission . . . ." *USFORSOM AAR*, 108-9.

2. *Time*, October 4, 1993, 40. The poll cited was taken in September 1993 by *Time*/CNN.

3. Montgomery interview, 17 February 2002.

4. *Time*, October 18, 1993, 40+; Letter, Boutros Boutros-Ghali to Warren Christopher, 25 September 1993; David Halberstam, *War in a Time of Peace: Bush, Clinton, and the Generals* (New York: Scribner, 2001), 260, 263-64; Email message, Edward Ward to Thomas Montgomery, 3 November 2003; Lawrence E. Casper, *Falcon Brigade: Combat and Command in Somalia and Haiti* (Boulder, CO: Lynne Rienner Publishers, 2001), 95-97.

5. Halberstam, 264.

6. The White House, Office of the Press Secretary, Press Release, "Remarks by the President to the Nation," 7 October 1993.

7. Senator Byrd unsuccessfully proposed a resolution that would have pushed the deadline forward to 1 February 1994; Senator John McCain, a Republican from Arizona, called for an immediate withdrawal, but to no avail. *Time*, 18 October 1993, 75; "The True Story of Black Hawk Down" television documentary.

8. A more ignominious fate awaited Les Aspin, who, blamed for rejecting the requests for armor made by US commanders in Mogadishu prior to October, became the administration's scapegoat for much of the debacle and ended up resigning as secretary of defense in January 1994. Ironically, according to one source, Aspin had been the one key official in the new administration that had from the outset expressed reservations about US policy in Somalia. Halberstam, 254, 260.

Another casualty of the administration's change in policy was the State Department's Robert Gosende, whom Clinton removed as the head of the US Liaison Office in Mogadishu. Gosende had strongly supported the hunt for Aideed and UNOSOM II's policy of refusing to negotiate with the warlord.

9. *USFORSOM AAR*, 108-9, 111; Montgomery interview, 17 February 2002. In the account of the crisis Oakley coauthored, he noted that Howe and other UNOSOM II officials were "upset" with the US reversal of policy and by the fact that they were hearing about it firsthand from Oakley, not the UN secretary general. John L. Hirsch and Robert B. Oakley, *Somalia and Operation Restore Hope: Reflections on Peacemaking and Peacekeeping* (Washington, DC: United States Institute of Peace Press, 1995), 130; Telephone interview, Lieutenant General Thomas M. Montgomery, USA (Ret.), 11 July 2003, interviewed by Lawrence A. Yates.

10. Montgomery interview, 17 February 2002; Montgomery telephone interview, 11 July 2003.

11. Interview with Robert Oakley and Interview with Anthony Zinni, *Frontline* website for program, "Ambush in Mogadishu, " http://www.pbs.org/wgbh/pages/frontline/shows/ambush/interviews/; Hirsch and Oakley, 58; Interview with Robert Oakley on videotape, *Somalia: Good Intentions, Deadly Results*, Knight Ridder Co., 1997.

12. Interview with Thomas Montgomery, *Frontline* website for program, "Ambush in Mogadishu"; Montgomery telephone interview, 11 July 2003.

13. Hirsch and Oakley, 130-31. Oakley and Zinni did not meet immediately with either Aideed or Ali Mahdi, but rather with their representatives.

According to Hirsch and Oakley, Representative John Murtha, a Democrat from Pennsylvania, while visiting Mogadishu on 14 October, "explained forcefully to Howe, other UNOSOM leaders, and the US military commanders the importance of supporting the new policy direction." Ibid., 131 note 37.

14. Ibid., 133-34, 133 note 41; *USFORSOM AAR*, 115.

15. The military ramifications for UNOSOM II forces of the shift in US policy are discussed in *USFORSOM AAR*, 108-14. See also, Casper, 127.

16. *USFORSOM AAR*, Chapter 4, Strategic Reset; Casper, 93, 99-102. In a telephone interview with the author, Montgomery related that Oakley asked that the AC-130 demonstrations be stopped; they were making the SNA nervous. Montgomery indicated that this was his intent but acceded to Oakley's request. Montgomery telephone interview, 11 July 2003.

17. Casper, 100, 102-3; U.S. Army Center for Army Lessons Learned (CALL), *U.S. Army Operations in Support of UNOSOM II: 4 May 93–31 March 94* (Fort. Leavenworth, KS: CALL, no date), I-3-2-3.

18. As several observers have noted, US troops in Somalia had always been "firmly" under US control: under Lieutenant General Johnston during UNITAF, and under Major General Montgomery during UNOSOM II.

19. The following account of Ernst's discussion with General Hoar (CINCCENT), Major General Meade, Lieutenant General Ellis, and General Sullivan is based on two interviews the author conducted with Major General Ernst on 13 April and 20 May 1994 at Fort Leavenworth, KS, and two telephone interviews with Major General Ernst, USA, (Ret.), on 13 February and 20 February 2003. In the interview on 20 May 1994, the one in which Ernst went into the most detail concerning his predeployment activities, the general read from notes he had taken during the course of visits to CENTCOM, Fort Drum, and the Pentagon.

On CINCCENT's decision to set up JTF Somalia, it might be noted that joint doctrine at the time stated that a JTF could be established for "an operation that has limited objectives; does not require centralized control of logistics; and is to be executed by two or more services." These criteria were largely met by the situation that required attention in Somalia.

20. The next day, a front-page story in the *New York Times* informed readers that US commanders in Somalia would use armor and infantry to "evict" the armed Somali militia surrounding coalition bases and located along main roads in downtown Mogadishu. *New York Times*, October 10, 1993, 1.

21. In addition to the interviews cited in note 19, Ernst's views on the need for a combined arms and mobile reserve are contained in comments he made on an Information Paper, 17 October 2001, Subject: Select Lessons from US Operations in Somalia, 1992-1994, Combat Studies Institute, Fort Leavenworth, KS.

22. For additional considerations concerning the need for an ARFOR, see CALL, *U.S. Army Operations in Support of UNOSOM II*, I-2-5. Ernst's elaboration on ARFOR arrangements is contained in his 13 February 2003 telephone interview with the author.

23. CALL, *U.S. Army Operations in Support of UNOSOM II*, I-2-6-7.

24. Carl F. Ernst, "The Urban Area During Support Missions Case Study: Mogadishu— The Operational Level," in Russell W. Glenn, ed., *Capital Preservation: Preparing for Urban Operations in the Twenty-First Century* (Santa Monica, CA: RAND, 2001), 367; Ernst interview, 13 April 1994; Ernst telephone interview, 13 February 2003.

25. Ernst telephone interview, 13 February 2003; Email, Lieutenant General Thomas Montgomery, USA (Ret.), to Lawrence A. Yates, 3 November 2003.

26. Ernst interview, 13 April 1994; Ernst, "Mogadishu," 362. The JSOTF under JTF *Somalia* did not include the SOF elements of Task Force *Ranger*, which redeployed to the United States on 17 October.

27. Ernst interview, 13 April 1994.

28. Ernst telephone interview, 13 February 2003; *USFORSOM AAR,* 110.

29. In contrast to keeping NGOs, other humanitarian organizations, and the Somalian factions at arm's length, JTF *Somalia*, when it proved advantageous, did work with the subclans and elders. During the construction of Victory Base, for example, Ernst's civil affairs and PYSOP people explained what was going on to the locals and hired many of them to help with the project. Ernst interview, 13 April 1994.

30. Montgomery telephone interview, 11 July 2003; *USFORSOM AAR*, 140-41; Ernst interviews, 13 April and 20 May 1994; Ernst telephone interviews, 13 February and 20 February 2003.

Ten years later, Edward Ward, who had been the U3 on Bir's staff, made the following observation about the arrival of the JTF and its more robust staff. "I spent countless hours with counterparts on the US staff of Ernst's JTF. No one welcomed them more than the UN staff and specifically the US members of that staff. Below his level we worked through countless challenges on a daily basis. We welcomed the contingency planning." Email message, Ward to Montgomery, 3 November 2003.

31. On the friction between Montgomery and Ernst, see the interviews cited in the previous note, as well as Montgomery email to Yates, 3 November 2003; Ernst, "Mogadishu," 405; Email message, Ward to Montgomery, 3 November 2003.

32. *USFORSOM AAR*, 122, 242; CALL, *U.S. Army Operations in Support of UNOSOM II*, I-2-1, I-2-3. For additional observations on command and control problems between USFORSOM and JTF *Somalia*, see Kenneth Allard, *Somalia Operations: Lessons Learned* (Fort. McNair, Washington, DC: National Defense University Press, 1995), 54-61; Ernst interviews, 13 April and 20 May 1994; Ernst telephone interviews, 13 February and 20 February 2003; Montgomery telephone interview, 11 July 2003.

33. *USFORSOM AAR,* 140; Ernst, "Mogadishu," 360. On 24 October, JTF *Somalia* issued a message also containing its mission statement: "Joint Task Force Somalia provides force protection for U.S. Forces in Somalia and facilitates continued U.S. support of UN operations. As required, conduct operations to secure lines of communication to ensure the continued flow of supplies. Be prepared to redeploy U.S. forces." *USFORSOM AAR,* 141.

34. Ernst interviews, 13 April and 20 May 1994; Casper, Chapter 11.

35. Ernst telephone interview, 20 February 2003; Ernst, "Mogadishu," 371; *USFORSOM AAR*, 142-43.

36. Ernst telephone interview, 20 February 2003; Ernst, "Mogadishu," 365, 384.

37. Ernst, "Mogadishu," 384.

38. Ibid., 385; Ernst telephone interview, 20 February 2003; Montgomery telephone interview, 11 July 2003.

39. Ernst telephone interviews, 13 February and 20 February 2003.

40. Ernst telephone interview, 13 February; Ernst interview, 20 May 1994.

41. Ernst telephone interview, 13 February 2003; Ernst interview, 20 May 1994; Ernst, "Mogadishu," 359, 361, 369-70.

42. Ernst, "Mogadishu," 361, 381-82. That the training and rehearsals conducted by JTF *Somalia* could be valuable for a variety of contingencies was brought out in an example that Ernst often cited. "I mentioned to you that we chopped the SEALs to the Joint Special Operations Task Force and they did a marvelous job. The first day the SEALs went to downtown Mogadishu they got into a firefight. They did what they were supposed to do; the snipers dropped some guys and a SNA swarm started. But we just happened to be on the USS *New Orleans* in a commander's huddle . . . . I was asked, 'What are we going to do?' 'Execute the CONPLAN,' I replied, and it happened. The joint operations center (JOC) announced REDCON One, the radios lit up, and everybody responded. The petty officer on the roof of the building with the sniper could trigger employment of the assets dedicated to the CONPLAN. He had two AC-130s, four Hellfire-equipped Cobras, and OH-58 Deltas backing him up. They could've put a Copperhead ring around the building if they'd needed to as well as calling on everything else the JTF owned. At that point the armored task force would have been put on REDCON One, standing by for commitment. Everything was on a 15-minute string. A deck alert pair of aircraft immediately appeared overhead with 500-pound laser-guided bombs. We had prepared CONPLANs for events that could happen, those that had happened, and had trained down to the point that execution was like a drill for all of them, including what actions might the JOC officer be able to order without any general involvement." Ibid., 382-83.

43. Ernst interview, 20 May 1994; Casper, 116; Montgomery telephone interview, 11 July 2003; Telephone interviews, Lieutenant General Thomas M. Montgomery, USA (Ret.), 29 October and 3 November 2003, interviewed by Lawrence A. Yates; *USFORSOM AAR*, 140.

44. For further details of JTF *Somalia*'s plan to reopen 21 October Road, see Casper, 117-19; Ernst, "Mogadishu," 386-87; Ernst interview, 20 May 1994; Ernst telephone interview, 20 February 2003. The JTF commander's intent, according to the USFORSOM after-action report, included the following: "(1) Use standoff and precision fires before maneuvering, if engaged; (2) Integrate combined arms; (3) Generate and demonstrate overwhelming combat power, but use it only if necessary; (4) Seize and maintain the imitative; (5) Destroy key buildings, if engaged from them, but clear them only if necessary; and (6) Secure key terrain, including key buildings." *USFORSOM AAR*, 143.

45. Montgomery's response to the 21 October Road plan can be found in Montgomery telephone interviews, 11 July and 29 October 2003; Casper, 119; *USFORSOM AAR*, 143-44.

46. Ernst interview, 20 May 1994.

47. For an overview of the debate over future UN strategy in Somalia, see *USFORSOM AAR*, 112-16.

48. Montgomery telephone interview, 11 July 2003; *USFORSOM AAR*, 145.

49. Montgomery telephone interview, 11 July 2003; *USFORSOM AAR*, 145-46; Ernst telephone interview, 20 February 2003.

50. Casper, 123, 131.

51. *USFORSOM AAR*, 146.

Conclusion

Lawrence A. Yates and Robert F. Baumann

"Somalia: Fights Break Out at Peace Talks."[1] This front-page headline ran in the New York *Times* 10 years after the US-led coalition under Operation RESTORE HOPE set up its headquarters in Somalia, and almost nine years after the United States withdrew its military support for the UN's ambitious effort at nation building in that country. The headline, an evocation of the turmoil plaguing Somalia since the mid-1990s, suggests that the American military presence there from December 1992 through March 1994 had little positive effect in transforming what the fashionable jargon of the day labeled a "failed state" into a peaceful, stable, and functioning nation.

Certainly, most Americans recalling their nation's involvement in Somalia regard the mission as a failure. For many, this judgment requires no further evidence than that produced by one traumatic event: the firefight on 3-4 October 1993 in which Somali militiamen killed 18 US soldiers and wounded over 70 others. *Black Hawk Down*, the name of a best-selling book and motion picture based on the firefight, has become a popularized term whose significance goes well beyond the event to which it refers.[2] It has, in a brief time, become a catchword for all those things that critics of the American intervention in Somalia claim were misguided or wrong with the venture: vague political guidance and the lack of an attainable "end state," "mission creep," political considerations overriding military necessity, a multilateral collaboration that conceded to the United Nations too much influence over American armed forces, and the subordination of genuine national security interests to idealistic humanitarian impulses. Of the numerous prescriptions derived from the experience, the most frequently voiced are couched in normative generalizations to the effect that American troops should not be put in harm's way unless vital national interests are at stake; the US military should not engage in nation building; American forces should not answer to non-American authority, whether national or supranational, military or civilian; and once committed to an operation, US troops should have the wherewithal to protect themselves, to prevail over hostile parties, and to accomplish their mission.

Stated in these terms, several of the so-called lessons of Somalia sound very much like those derived from another US military setback, Vietnam. The "Vietnam syndrome," part of which was manifested as an aversion to sending US troops into life-threatening combat operations for fear that America lacked the political and popular will to stay the course, was pronounced dead after quick and decisive military action in Operation JUST CAUSE in Panama (1989) and the first Gulf War (1991). Somalia, however, demonstrated that the syndrome was only moribund. After the battle of 3-4 October, emotions aroused by the loss of American soldiers in Mogadishu meshed with memories of the "lessons" of Vietnam as encapsulated in the restrictive Weinberger/Powell doctrine of the 1980s to produce what diplomat Richard Holbrooke dubbed the "Vietmalia syndrome." In retrospect, this new synthesis had a significant but selective impact. It complicated high-level national security debates in Washington, but it did not prevent President Bill Clinton from sending American forces into Haiti less than a year after they had left Somalia; nor did it deter him from committing US troops to Bosnia as a condition of a tenuous peace accord designed to replace genocide with stability in that volatile part of the Balkans. In both cases, as US troops deployed, the syndrome asserted itself in Pentagon statements that seemed to emphasize force protection—someone coined the term "zero casualties"—as much as mission accomplishment. Similarly, in both deployments, utterances from high-ranking civilians and military officers sought to reassure the American people that US troops would not fall victim to mission creep, would be under US command, and would steer well clear of nation building. Some of those pledges, however, proved difficult to honor once American forces on the ground confronted the complexities of their mission and the shifting demands of the highly fluid and dynamic situation confronting them.

In January 2001, George W. Bush succeeded Clinton in the White House. When, following the terrorist attacks in the United States on 11 September 2001, the president committed US forces to combat in Afghanistan, he heard few dissenting voices among the American public, even though many of the troops in Operation ENDURING FREEDOM would operate as part of a coalition over which Washington exerted only limited control and even though many would discover that some degree of nation building was inherent in the tasks they were being directed to perform.

Although the Vietmalia syndrome did not prevent President Clinton or President George W. Bush from ordering US armed forces into ambiguous, complex, unorthodox, and highly dangerous situations, the perceived lessons from Somalia associated with the syndrome have not lost all currency within government circles and with the American public. Unfortunately, some of these lessons have been proclaimed with little regard for the context from which they were extracted. In coming to view *Black Hawk Down* as a metaphor for the overall experience of the

202

US military in Somalia, many Americans have unwittingly distorted what actually occurred between December 1992 and March 1994.

This book has sought to provide a lens through which some of the distortion can be corrected. To begin with, the chapter titles themselves serve as a reminder that American military involvement in Somalia encompassed four distinct and sometimes lengthy phases: Operation PROVIDE RELIEF, the humanitarian airlift out of Kenya that began in mid-1992; Operation RESTORE HOPE, the U.S.-led multinational coalition from December 1992 to May 1993 that, under UNITAF, secured the humanitarian relief effort seeking to feed and assist starving Somalis; the UN's nation-building program under UNOSOM II that followed the departure of UNITAF and included the establishment of USFORSOM; and the activities of JTF *Somalia* during the buildup and withdrawal of US forces from October 1993 through March 1994. This last phase, while occurring during UNOSOM II, is listed separately because of America's virtual repudiation of the UN's strategy in Somalia as a result of the 3-4 October 1993 battle.

Each phase of the US military involvement in Somalia, while possessing its own distinct mission, its own agenda, its own armed forces, and its own coterie of officials and officers, was inextricably linked to the other phases by logic, decisions, and events. These links can be summarized by way of a brief chronology that begins in late 1992, when most observers had concluded that UNOSOM and the US airlift of relief supplies out of Kenya into Somalia could at best alleviate a very small portion of the Somali people's suffering. Only the presence of a large, well-armed force could compel Somalia's warlords in the southern famine belt to stop using food and other humanitarian aid as a weapon in the factional struggle for political supremacy. Understanding this, President Bush placed the United States at the head of an international military coalition that began entering Somalia in December 1992 with the primary mission of providing the security necessary for humanitarian relief to reach the starving population. But the president also realized that this short-term approach could not resolve the fundamental issues that had caused the crisis in the first place. If images of starving children were not to reappear on American television sets soon after the departure of coalition forces, the United States would have to make some commitment to a long-term policy to stabilize Somalia. Bush rejected UN appeals to include countrywide disarmament and nation building in UNITAF's mandate, but he agreed to provide logistic support and a QRF to a UN-led effort to implement those programs as a follow-on to Operation RESTORE HOPE.

In the meantime, on the ground in Somalia, the UNITAF commander, Lieutenant General Robert Johnston, USMC, and key members of his staff worked closely with special envoy Robert Oakley and other diplomats in initiating several programs designed to accomplish UNITAF's mission and to "lay the groundwork" for the UN effort that would follow. Such programs included road building and repairs, other civic action measures, and the revival of a Somali police force. The command also worked with Oakley in establishing a "dialogue" with the key faction leaders, including Aideed, even while taking action in the countryside to "empower" traditional leaders, often at the expense of Aideed's supporters in the affected localities. On 4 May 1993, in something well short of a seamless transition, UNOSOM II succeeded UNITAF. President Clinton, who had followed Bush into the White House, hailed the success of Operation RESTORE HOPE and praised the troops involved for all but ending the famine and related suffering in southern Somalia.

Whether a showdown between UNOSOM II and Aideed could have been avoided is problematic, but given the far-reaching mission of UN officials, their strategy of marginalizing the warlords, the insufficient number of troops and other resources they had to accomplish their goals, and the long-standing animosity and distrust that Aideed felt toward the UN and its secretary general, the groundwork for confrontation was certainly in place. With the massacre of the Pakistani troops just one month after UNOSOM II replaced UNITAF, it was only logical for the UN to strike back at the hostile forces who had killed coalition soldiers, openly defied the peacekeeping/nation-building program, and continued to threaten what chances it had of success. The US QRF took part in the hunt for Aideed and the fighting it entailed, but fissures among the UN military contingents diluted concerted and effective coalition action against the warlord. At the insistence of retired US Admiral Jonathan Howe, the UN's top official on the scene, President Clinton dispatched TF Ranger to help hunt down Aideed and his principal lieutenants. That elite unit, after conducting several operations, found itself in the fierce street fight of 3-4 October. When the number of US casualties in that battle became public, domestic politics in the United States forced a change in the Clinton administration's policy and led to the withdrawal of all American forces in Somalia by the end of March 1994.

The preceding chapters, in elaborating this overview, have in part sought to reevaluate several points that still pass for conventional wisdom regarding the US intervention in Somalia. At no time, for example, in any phase of the undertaking, were American troops under the operational control of anyone but US commanders: Lieutenant General Johnston during UNITAF, and Major General Thomas Montgomery and Major General Carl Ernst during UNOSOM II. Furthermore, the US commitment to nation building in Somalia was made at the outset by the Bush administration; it was not "mission creep" resulting from UN pressure on a new American president inexperienced in foreign affairs. President Bush definitely sought to limit the US military's involvement in nation building but did not seek to shun it altogether—the latter being a course that would have risked undoing all that he hoped to accomplish under UNITAF. In other words, at no point was the termination of UNITAF meant to signal an end to the US military presence in Somalia. Indeed, without UNOSOM II, it made no sense to set up UNITAF, and without some US military (including combat) support, however limited, UNOSOM II stood very little chance of success.

In a similar vein, it is clear that many other activities judged to be examples of mission creep in Somalia were, in fact, the result of logical, well-considered decisions based upon a desire to accomplish—not expand—a given mission in the midst of a complex and dynamic situation. Lieutenant General Johnston's decisions to join the political dialogue with Aideed and Ali Mahdi, to allow the coalition to engage in civic action projects, to stand up the ASF, and to empower traditional local and regional leaders in southern Somalia were clearly designed to facilitate what he had been sent there to do. Likewise, it should also be clear that UNOSOM II's attempts to capture and punish Aideed stemmed not just from some emotional desire for revenge but, more important, from a logical conclusion that to leave the faction leader at large would almost certainly result in further UN casualties, the continuous disruption of UNOSOM II activities, and the ultimate failure of the peacekeeping/ nation-building mission.

Just as an examination of the US intervention in Somalia in its entirety can provide a corrective to certain misperceptions surrounding the affair, it can also remind readers of the valid military "lessons" that emerged from the experience. Many of these lessons receive coverage throughout this study. Many can also be found, often accompanied by detailed discussion, in such excellent publications as the two-volume study on Somalia by the US Army Center for Army Lessons Learned, Kenneth Allard's book on the subject, the US Forces Somalia After-Action Report (often referred to as the Montgomery Report), the book-length account, *Somalia and Operation Restore Hope*, written by Ambassador Robert Oakley and John L. Hirsch, and a series of presentations on urban operations published by the RAND Corporation. In listing and examining the military lessons of Somalia, each of these studies takes its own approach—functional, level of operation, technical, and so forth—while offering valuable insights.

The lessons of Somalia discussed in this book, in the works referred to above, and in other studies cited in the endnotes of this volume are far too numerous to be summarized in this brief concluding chapter. Instead, only six very general points will be touched upon. Presented in no order of priority, the first suggests that there needs to be a new approach to the phenomenon of mission creep, a term that came into being around the time—and perhaps as a result—of the US intervention in Somalia. Although the term lacks a precise, or even workable, definition, embedded within it is the pejorative notion of military forces engaging in activities that they had not planned to do and that they should not have been doing. Often, the phenomenon is blamed on poor military planning or poor political guidance, and to be sure, there was some of each in the Somalia experience. But even allowing for that, what passed for mission creep— the civic action projects, activities to empower the local leaders, standing up the ASF, committing some US forces to a nation-building mission, and joining the hunt for Aideed—was rarely the consequence of negligence, ignorance, stupidity, bad judgment, or hubris but more often the result of deliberate calculation arising from a need for policy makers and military commanders to adjust to a continuously changing environment over which the United States exercised degrees of influence but never complete control. This observation, if correct, calls into question the US military's approach to mission creep, namely that it is something that can and should be eliminated through thorough planning and focused judgment. A more productive approach would be to accept the inevitable gaps in information, the time constraints often imposed on military planning, the fallibility of human beings, and the complexity and dynamism of world affairs and, in the process, to recognize that almost any lengthy military operation will necessitate adjustments not anticipated in the predeployment phase by the best of policy makers, military commanders, and staff officers. In short, one should not think that "mission creep" is a phenomenon that can be banished from military operations. It would be more realistic either to anticipate the phenomenon or to do away with the term and the unrealistic expectations and distorted analyses it tends to generate.

The second point concerns a lesson that, unlike mission creep, is rarely mentioned in studies of the US experience in Somalia. In the absence of all-out combat and in the presence of a variety of "actors," both from within and outside the country, US officers at the operational and tactical levels often found themselves involved in activities that were as much or more political in nature than military. In an official interview he granted, Lieutenant General Johnston repeatedly referred to the political dimension of his day-to-day routine, as he took part in the dialogue with Aideed and Ali Mahdi, adjudicated differences and assuaged the sensibilities of foreign forces under his control, and dealt with the stream of political guidance emanating from Washington. Brigadier General Anthony Zinni, USMC, and Major General Montgomery all echoed Johnston when discussing the political nature of their respective assignments. So, too, did numerous company and field grade officers in Somalia's cities and countryside who found themselves negotiating with clan elders, keeping the news media occupied, and performing a variety of other "political" activities that they had not anticipated and for which, in many cases, they were not trained or prepared. As most officers came to realize, however, their involvement in the politics of intervention was in most cases unavoidable, not to mention essential to the accomplishment of their mission.

This political-military dimension of the Somalia intervention, when examined at the operational and tactical levels, can be loosely categorized as follows. There was, to begin with, the political guidance Johnston, Zinni, Bir, Montgomery, and others received from external sources such as the White House, Pentagon, and UN, and with which they had to contend. Often, in their opinions, the guidance betrayed an ignorance of the local situation, imposed unnecessary restrictions on officers on the scene, and amounted to unwanted interference and unwarranted micromanagement. Second, these commanders and their staffs had to deal with the politics of coalition operations, making sure that each participant was gainfully employed in a way that would not insult national honor, smoothing over national rivalries inherent among coalition partners, and dealing with the different agendas various contingents brought with them. A third type of political activity involved meeting and talking with Somalia's various and contending leaders and groups, with negotiations spanning the gamut from such critical issues as weapons control to such lesser concerns as seeking permission to repair a roof on some village edifice. To be effective in these negotiations, it was essential to know the players, their previous history together and their current interactions, their agenda, the political and social framework in which they operated, and how they might attempt to take advantage of outsiders possessing only a smattering of knowledge of Somalia and the crisis it faced. A fourth form of political activity encompassed issues internal to the US military itself: being sensitive to service sensibilities in a joint environment, ensuring cooperation and coordination among the participating headquarters and components, deciding the best courses of action to adopt, getting the resources essential to mission fulfillment, and, in the case of Montgomery and Ernst, trying to aqccomplish something productive in the face of awkward command and control arrangements.

A third point that is sometimes overlooked in the lists of lessons learned generated by the US involvement in Somalia has to do with how one regards hostile or potentially hostile forces. When hostilities occurred, as during the hunt for Aideed from June to October 1993, US commanders had to remind themselves that, even if by their standards Somalia was a backward and impoverished country, their adversary was shrewd, experienced, and could adjust and perhaps even sneak inside their decision cycle. Arguably, by 3-4 October, Aideed's forces had found the way to seize the initiative—down a US aircraft and inflict significant American casualties. But, even before and after that firefight, Aideed had shown himself capable of adapting to the military situation that confronted him. Under UNITAF, he stood no chance of prevailing militarily over the coalition forces arrayed against him, so he did not engage in major hostilities. He knew that when UNITAF left and the UN took over, the force he would face would be less formidable, and it was that force that he attacked. Following Black Hawk Down, he revised his assessment again: knowing that he could not hope to defeat the US forces under JTF *Somalia*, he simply opted to wait them out until they withdrew on or before a date that the US president had publicly announced. In short, Aideed, despite his mistakes and miscalculations, proved a credible military adversary, and each successive US commander on the ground had to learn not to underestimate him.

A fourth point concerns the "battlefield" in Somalia. Almost all US commanders, regardless of level, had to adjust to the fact that, whether in city, village, or town, their area of operations was full of civilians, many of whom welcomed and benefited from the international intervention, others who did not. The civilian presence itself did not come as a surprise to most American officers; what did was the variety of ways in which civilians could affect the operations at hand. Somalis might readily assist the coalition, as when they were hired to help with UNITAF or UN construction projects. Or they might become sources of information, helping coalition intelligence officers—when the information was accurate—build up the databases necessary for determining what was transpiring in the country. Or Somali assistance might come after no small amount of haggling, as when a local leader would promise to facilitate humanitarian relief operations in his village only after he had secured a coalition pledge to under-take some kind of civic action project. In other circumstances, groups of Somalis, driven by poverty, might mob foreign soldiers, making off with anything of value. The children were especially adept at this, which often caused troops not trained in crowd control to overreact, on occasion with negative, even tragic, results. There were also Somalis who could be open-ly hostile, taking part, when called upon, in anti-coalition demonstrations and riots, or in extreme cases, in open attacks on coalition forces. During the battle of 3-4 October, for example, Aideed's militiamen used what was for them a traditional tactic of employing women and children to shield gunmen and to identify the position of US troops. Killing these women and children did not come easily to American soldiers, but in the effort to stay alive, kill them they did, and at close range.

Whether negotiating with Somali leaders or interacting daily with the population in cities, towns, villages, and the countryside, most US and coalition troops from general officers down to enlisted personnel experi-enced some degree of culture shock. Thus, the fifth point to be made here concerns the need for cultural awareness on the part of forces entering a foreign country. Zinni, for example, admitted that he needed to know more of Somalia's culture to be effective in his talks with Aideed, Ali Mahdi, and other native leaders. Meanwhile, coalition troops throughout the southern area of operations might have benefited from just a basic cul-tural orientation prior to their arrival, thus enabling them at the outset to use their newfound knowledge to facilitate their dealings with the native population and, in the process, to avoid the unintended offenses that could alienate the very people they were there to help. The problem, as several participants and observers noted, was that few commanders, staff officers, or troops entering the country were comfortable or conversant with the cultural dimension of military operations. Thus, what these officers and enlisted personnel learned about Somali culture stemmed largely from their experience on the ground. Even then, many troops, acting from a sense of ethnocentrism, impatience, and indifference, elected to ignore the lessons. It was as if it were up to the Somalis to accommodate their beliefs and values to the foreign presence, not for the foreigners to become acquainted with Somali culture. In the extreme, the cultural barrier would be handled, not by bridging it, but by avoiding it. One of the rationales underpinning UNITAF's decision to rebuild a Somali police force was to use it as a buffer to insulate coalition troops from the people.

A sixth and final point has to do with the derivation and application of military "lessons" themselves. Too often, hard and fast lessons are drawn from an experience and then solidified as slogans, sets of criteria (as in the informal guidelines of the Weinberger/Powell "doctrine"), or even as formal military doctrine. To state categorically after the withdrawal from Somalia that US forces should not fight under foreign command, should not engage in nation building, and should avoid mission creep was to risk being unprepared for crises and threats that might not accommodate themselves to US military preferences. In a parallel example, much was said after the American withdrawal from Vietnam about US forces never again becoming embroiled in unconventional warfare. Both Afghanistan and Iraq have put that proscription to the test. Too often the military lessons that inform doctrine, officer education, training, force structure, and decision making are "one deep": they stem from the most recent military operation of significance, not from a study of a series of cases from the recent and distant past.

In this context, then, the US involvement in Somalia from 1992-1994 should be regarded as a unique experience that, even today, contains valuable lessons for the military professional, but lessons that cannot and should not be learned in isolation from those generated by the vast array of other military operations that claim space in our newspapers, after-action reports, and historical studies. In conclusion, one should be aware of what happened during the US intervention in Somalia, extract and periodically reevaluate the relevant lessons from that experience, compare those lessons with others derived from the broader military experience of the United States and other countries, and, finally, assert great care in applying what was learned in Somalia to current and future operations.

Notes

1. 29 January 2003.
2. Mark Bowden, *Black Hawk Down: A Story of Modern War* (New York: Atlantic Monthly Press, 1999). The motion picture was released in 2001.

Index

Abdi House, 116-119, 171

Aideed, Mohamed Farah, 16-17, 37, 39-42, 46, 48, 51-52, 62-66, 68, 71-74, 80-83, 88, 91, 103-110, 112-117, 119, 121-122, 126, 131-133, 139-144, 149-150, 158, 165-171, 181-183, 185-187, 190-191, 193, 196, 204-206, 208-209

Ali Mahdi Mohamed, 37, 39, 40-42, 44, 46, 48, 51, 62-65, 68, 71-74, 91, 172, 181, 187, 203, 207, 209

Amphibious Ready Group Three, 192

Arnold, Steve (Major General), 32-33, 43, 48, 63-64, 66, 76, 80, 82

Aspen, Les (Secretary of Defense), 1, 109, 116, 139, 155, 166

Atto, Osman, 103, 141, 171

Authorized Weapons Storage Sites (AWSS), 64-67, 107-108, 170

Auxiliary Security Force (ASF), 72-75, 205-206

Barre, Siad Mohammed (Major General), 13-18, 52, 74, 80-81, 83, 104, 191

Bedard, Buck (Colonel), 177

Bir, Cevik (Lieutenant General), 86-87, 101-103, 105, 110-111, 115-116, 156, 165, 168-172, 182, 191-192, 207

Boutros-Ghali, Boutros (UN Secretary General), 24-25, 35, 80, 85-88, 104, 166, 171

Buckley, John (First Sergeant), 111, 117, 125

Bush, George (President), 19, 23-25, 35-37, 46, 55, 71, 85-87, 167, 202-205

Bush, George W. (President), 202

Byrd, Robert (Senator), 166

Casper, Lawrence (Colonel), 143, 148, 150, 173-174, 189, 193

CENTCOM (US Central Command), 25-26, 28-30, 32-36, 46, 70, 76, 87-88, 94, 104-105, 111, 139-141, 157, 167, 174, 176-178, 181, 184-186.189

CENTCOM Intelligence Support Element (CISE), 104, 181

Chapter VII (UN Charter), 25, 34, 100, 172

Cheney, Richard (Secretary of Defense), 24, 36

Christopher, Warren (Secretary of State), 166-167

Civil-Military Operations Center (CMOC), 53-54, 76-77, 79, 92

Clarke, Walter (U.S. Deputy Chief of Mission), 106

Claus, Mike (Staff Sergeant), 133

Clinton, Bill (President), 1-4, 9, 36, 85-87, 89, 103, 113, 165-169, 171-172, 174, 176, 181, 191, 194, 202, 204

Combined Joint Task Force (CJTF) Somalia, 38, 40

Dallas, Mike (Colonel), 129, 143
David, Bill (Lieutenant Colonel), 126, 129-130, 148, 150-152, 155, 177
Durant, Michael (Warrant Officer), 148, 150, 154, 158

Eagleburger, Lawrence (Secretary of State), 24
XVIII Airborne Corps, 33, 178
82nd Airborne Division, 174
Ellis, Larry (Lieutenant General), 178
ENDURING FREEDOM (Operation), 202
Ernst, Carl (Major General), 157, 174-193, 205, 208
Evans, John (Captain), 110
Eyes over Mogadishu (Operation), 114, 130, 143

Farah, Mohamed Hassan, 119
Farlow, David (Captain), 114, 121-122
Ferry, Chuck (Lieutenant), 152-153
15th Marine Expeditionary Unit (MEU), 38, 43, 67
1st Battalion, 22nd Infantry Regiment, 112, 118, 124
1st Battalion, 87th Infantry Regiment, 117
1st Battalion, 5th Special Forces, 131
1st Marine Division, 30, 32, 93
I Marine Expeditionary Force (I MEF), 28-30, 33, 93
504th Military Police (MP) Company, 114
Force protection, 2-4, 46-48, 64, 69, 131, 174-175, 181-183, 192-194, 202
46th Forward Support Battalion (FSB), 122, 125
43rd Combat Engineer Battalion (Heavy), 173

Galcayo Peace Conference, 107
Garrison, William (Major General), 140, 142-143, 148-150, 155-157, 165, 180-181
Gile, Greg (Brigadier General), 148, 151
Gordon, Gary (Master Sergeant), 154
Gorski, Frank (Major), 104

Habr Gidr, 17, 37, 75, 117, 141, 145, 154, 169
Hirsch, John (UNITAF political adviser), 54, 83, 85, 90, 205
Hoar, Joseph (General), 26, 28, 34-36, 103, 105, 139, 167, 174, 176, 183-185, 190-191

Holbrooke, Richard, 2, 202
Horan, Mike (Staff Sergeant), 133, 144
Howe, Jonathan T. (Admiral), 4, 86-88, 99, 103-106, 122, 131, 139, 165, 168-170, 172, 174, 204
Humanitarian Operations Center (HOC), 54, 76-77, 92
HUMINT (Human Intelligence), 34, 49, 66, 181, 183

International Committee of the Red Cross (ICRC), 114, 119

Jess, Omar (Colonel), 16, 52, 81-82, 107
Joint Task Force (JTF) Somalia, 28-30, 32-34, 36, 38, 40, 159, 174-178, 181-194, 203, 208
Johnston, Robert B. (Lieutenant General), 29-30, 33-44, 46-54, 62-66, 70-71,73-74, 78-79, 81-91, 93, 103-104, 170, 181, 204-205, 207
Kelly, David (Captain), 114
Kissinger, Henry (Secretary of State), 168
Klimp, Jack (Colonel), 67
Klingaman, James (Captain), 144

Lesnowicz, Jr., Ed (Lieutenant Colonel), 67-68

Magruder, Lawson (Brigadier General), 44, 52
Manifesto Group, 16
McCree, Chad (Captain), 121
McKnight, Danny (Lieutenant Colonel), 150
Mass distribution Site (MDS), 75
Meade, David (Major General), 177-178
Meriam, Mengistu Haile (Lieutenant Colonel), 14-15
Meyerowich, Drew (Captain), 150-155
Mission creep, 70, 77, 91-92, 201, 203, 205-206, 210
Montgomery, Thomas (Major General), 86-88, 102-107, 111, 116-117, 119, 122, 129, 140-144, 148, 150, 155-157, 166, 169-172, 179, 182-187, 189-194, 205, 207-208
MORE CARE (Operation), 191
Morgan, Said Hersi, 52, 81-82

National Reconciliation Conference, 84
National Security Council Deputies Committee, 23
National Security Service (NSS), 13-14
Nelson, Shawn (Specialist), 147
NATO, 4, 107

215

Newbold, Gregory (Colonel), 38, 43, 64, 75-76
96th Civil Affairs Brigade, 76
977th Military Police (MP) Company, 121-122

Oakley, Robert (special representative), 36, 40-42, 48-49, 54, 62-65, 69-73, 79-80, 82-83, 85, 87, 89-91, 103-104, 107, 167-171, 181, 183, 187-188, 190-191, 204-205

Pace, Peter (Brigadier General), 174, 177
Pakistani peacekeepers, 18, 23, 100, 104-105, 107-114, 116, 120, 123, 132, 150-154, 170
Peace enforcement, 25, 30, 172
Perino, Larry (Lieutenant), 145, 147, 149, 153-154
Powell, Colin (General), 3, 24, 26, 139, 202, 210
Project Hand Clasp, 75
PROVIDE COMFORT (Operation), 29
PROVIDE RELIEF (Operation), 19, 23, 25-26, 34, 88, 203
Psychological Operations (PSYOP), 47, 49, 52, 64-65, 94, 110, 119, 126, 131, 185

Quick Reaction Force (QRF), 105-106, 109, 115, 118-119, 123-124, 126, 129-132, 140, 143-145, 147-148, 150, 152-153, 155-157, 173-174, 176, 179, 181, 185-188, 192, 203-204

Radio Mogadishu, 107, 110
RENAISSANCE (Operation), 76
RESTORE HOPE (Operation), 9, 23, 25, 28, 30, 32-38, 40, 43, 45-47, 50-55, 61-62, 66-67, 70, 73, 76-77, 79, 81, 85-94, 201-205, 208
Reynolds, John (Lieutenant), 127-128
Rules of Engagement (ROE), 34-35, 45, 47, 118, 123, 125, 130-131, 133, 175
School of Advanced Military Studies (SAMS), Fort Leavenworth, Kansas, 178

Scowcroft, Brent (National Security Adviser), 24
2d Battalion, 14th Infantry Regiment, 123-124, 131, 152, 154
2d Battalion, 22nd Infantry Regiment, 173
2d Battalion, 87th Infantry Regiment, 43, 117
Security Council Resolution 767, 19
Security Council Resolution 814, 99
Security Council Resolution 837, 109

Security Council Resolution 885, 171
Selassie, Haile (Emperor of Ethiopia), 14
7th Transportation Group, 45
Shinn, David (State Department), 116, 131
SHOW CARE (Operation), 185-186
Shughart, Randy (Sergeant First Class), 154
Somali National Alliance (SNA), 107-109, 112-119, 121-123, 125-127, 133, 139-140, 142, 144-145, 148, 165, 167, 169, 171-173, 176, 179, 181, 185, 190
Somali National Front (SNF), 17
Somali National Islamic Front (NIF), 42
Somali National Movement (SNM), 15, 17
Somali Patriotic Movement (SPM), 16-17
Somali police, 69-70, 73, 75, 83, 91-92, 100, 120, 141, 204, 209
Somali Revolutionary Socialist Party (SRSP), 13
Somali Salvation Democratic Front (SSDF), 15-16
Soviet military aid, 12
Spataro, Stephen (Lieutenant Colonel), 71-73
Special Operations Command and Control Element (SOCCE), 111
Steele, Mike (Captain), 146, 153
Struecker, Jeff (Sergeant), 145-146
Suich, Mark (Captain), 124, 126-127, 129
Sullivan, Gordon (Chief of Staff, US Army), 176
Supreme Revolutionary Council (SRC), 13

Task Force (TF) Falcon, 123
Task Force (TF) Hope, 51, 64
Task Force (TF) Kismayo, 51-52
Task Force (TF) Mogadishu, 67-68
Task Force (TF) Mountain Warrior, 143
Task Force (TF) Ranger, 110, 131, 139-146, 148-149, 153, 155-157, 167, 180, 194, 204
Task force (TF) Raven, 123, 131, 152, 156
Task Force (TF) Safari, 118, 121, 156
10th Aviation Brigade, 129, 173
10th Mountain Division, 3, 5, 30, 32-33, 43, 45, 63, 82, 87, 93, 102, 105, 109, 111, 124, 133, 144-145, 148, 151, 155, 173, 177, 179, 194
Third Army (US), 172
3rd Battalion, 9th Marines, 67
3rd Battalion, 11th Marines, 66-67
3rd Battalion, 75th Ranger Regiment, 141, 143

13th Corps Support Command, 46
300th Military Police (MP) Company, 114, 121-122
362d Engineer Company, 123
24th Infantry Division, 172
22nd Marine Expeditionary Unit (MEU), 190

United Nations, 3-6, 9, 17-19, 23-28, 30, 34-37, 40-42, 54, 61-62, 70, 72,
    80-81, 83, 85-89, 99-107, 109-111, 113-122, 124, 131-133, 139-141,
    148, 155, 157-158, 165-172-174, 176, 179-184, 187, 190, 201, 203-
    205, 207-208
United Nations Department of Peacekeeping Operations, 132
United Nations Logistics Support Command, 178, 182-183
United Somali Congress (USC), 16-17, 107, 109, 113-119, 121, 123, 142,
    148, 165, 169, 173
UNITAF (United Task Force), 6, 30-31, 36, 38-42, 44-48, 50-55, 61-94,
    99-100, 103-107, 109, 114, 167-171, 176-177, 179, 181, 193, 203-
    205, 208-209
UNOSOM I (UN Operation in Somalia), 6, 18-20, 54, 74, 81, 107, 113,
    115-117, 120, 122-123, 128, 130
UNOSOM II, 61, 70, 72, 74, 85-88, 94, 99-117, 119-124, 130-133, 140-
    141, 145, 150, 155-159, 165-173, 175, 179, 182-185, 190-191, 203-
    205
United States Information Service (USIS), 74
USS *Abraham Lincoln*, 173

Victory Pioneers, 14
Vlasak, Marian (Captain), 125

Walls, Chuck (Captain), 110
Western Somali Liberation Front (WSLF), 14
Whetstone, Mike (Captain), 148, 154-155
Wilhelm, Charles (Major General), 32, 42, 45, 50, 65, 67-68, 76, 83
World Food Program, 72

Zinni, Anthony (Brigadier General), 5, 29, 48-50, 61-63, 66, 69, 71-72,
    79-81, 83, 88, 90-91, 160, 168-170, 181, 183, 207, 209

About the Authors

Robert F. Bauman has taught at CGSC since 1984. He received a B.A. in Russian from Dartmouth College (1974) and a Ph.D. from Yale University (1982). From 1979-1980 he was a graduate exchange student at Moscow University with grant support from the Fulbright-Hayes Program and the International Research and Exchanges Board. Dr. Baumann is the author of *Russian-Soviet Unconventional War in the Caucasus, Central Asia, and Afghanistan* (Combat Studies Institute [CSI], 1993) and coauthor of *Invasion, Intervention, Intervasion: A Concise History of the U.S. Army in Operation Uphold Demo*cracy (CSI, 1998). A recent recipient of a grant from the U.S. Institute of Peace, Dr. Baumann is coauthor of a forthcoming book and writer-producer of a documentary film on the US and multinational peacekeeping mission in Bosnia. He has also written extensively on the history of the Bashkirs and served as a visiting professor of history briefly at the Bashkir State University in Ufa in fall 1992. Dr. Baumann is the acting director, Directorate of Graduate Degree Programs, US Army Command and General Staff College (CGSC).

Lawrence A. Yates is a teacher and researcher on the Research and Publication Team, CSI. He received a B.A. and an M.A. in history from the University of Missouri, Kansas City, and a Ph.D. in history from the University of Kansas. He is the author of several articles on US contingency operations since World War II, has written a monograph on the US intervention in the Dominican Republic in 1965, is coeditor and a contibutor to *Block by Block: The Challenges of Urban Operations,* and is completing a book-length study of US military operations in the Panama crisis, 1987-1990. He also teaches courses on unconventional warfare, interventions, and stability operations.

Lieutenant Colonel Versalle F. Washington taught at CGSC from 2001-2003 and was the 2003 CGSC Military Instructor of the Year. He received a B.S. from the United States Military Academy (1985) and an M.A. (1994) and Ph.D. (1995) from Ohio State University. He is an engineer and has served with engineer units in Germany and commanded an engineer company in the Persian Gulf War. LTC Washington is the author of *Eagles on Their Buttons: A Black Infantry Regiment in the Civil War (*University of Missouri Press, 1999). He is the Professor of Military Science at the University of Dayton.